AF726615
JAN 21 1974
Library
DAR-ES-SALAAM
HAUT COMMISSARIAT DU CANADA

STRENGTHENING THE WORLD BANK

STRENGTHENING THE WORLD BANK

by Escott Reid

published by
The Adlai Stevenson Institute
CHICAGO, ILLINOIS

THE ADLAI STEVENSON INSTITUTE OF INTERNATIONAL AFFAIRS

OFFICERS & DIRECTORS

Mr. James F. Hoge, Jr.
Chairman

Mr. William R. Polk
President

Mr. John F. Cotton
Vice President

Mr. Peter Diamandopoulos
Director of Studies

Mrs. Edison Dick
Vice Chairman

Mr. Daggett Harvey
Vice Chairman

Mr. Stanford Goldblatt
Treasurer

Mr. Newton N. Minow
Secretary

The Honorable George W. Ball
Mrs. Charles W. Benton
The Honorable William McCormick Blair, Jr.
The Honorable Edmund G. Brown
Mr. Goodwin Chase
William R. Clarke, M.D.
Mr. Donald Duster
Mr. J. Wayne Fredericks
Mr. Angelo Geocaris
Mrs. Samuel A. Hartwell
Rev. Theodore Hesburgh
The Honorable Paul G. Hoffman
Mrs. Marshall Holleb
Mrs. Philip Hummer
Lady Jackson (Barbara Ward)
The Honorable Philip M. Klutznick
Mr. Martin Koldyke
The Honorable Charles H. Percy
Mr. Lawrence B. Perkins
The Honorable Francis T. P. Plimpton
Mrs. Mildred Robbins
Mr. Herbert Salzman
Mr. Farwell D. Smith
Mr. Hermon D. Smith
Mr. Gardner H. Stern, Jr.
The Honorable Adlai Stevenson III
Mr. Maurice F. Strong
Mr. William Swartz
Mr. Robert W. Tullis
Mr. Maynard P. Venema
Mrs. Elizabeth Weymouth
The Honorable Franklin H. Williams
The Honorable W. Willard Wirtz
Mrs. Arthur Young

Library of Congress Catalog Card Number: 73-87437

The Adlai Stevenson Institute of International Affairs, Chicago, Illinois 60637

© 1973 by Escott Reid, All rights reserved
Published 1973. First impression
Printed in the United States of America

The Adlai Stevenson Institute of International Affairs takes no stand, either of approval or disapproval, regarding statements made by authors in its publications.

THE ADLAI STEVENSON INSTITUTE OF INTERNATIONAL AFFAIRS has for over six years served as a center for efforts to bring fresh insights to bear on major policy problems.

The chief sources of these insights are the Institute's Fellows, a group of men and women whose active experience in government, teaching, or private undertakings has brought them face to face with the important issues of today's complex world. During their terms as Fellows, they build upon this experience through independent study and research on projects of their own design. Frequent meetings among them to discuss one another's work encourage the exchange and cross-fertilization of ideas. In the carrying out of projects, the Institute emphasizes not only the generation of new solutions, but their application for maximum benefit to society.

FELLOWS 1973–1974

David N. Berkhausen
Olumbe Bassir
Lord Caradon
Iva Carruthers
John Cotton
Peter Diamandopoulos
Frank Ervin
Hassan Fathy
Saul Friedlander
Mohamed Hakki
David Halberstam
Kenneth Hansen
Fuad Jabber
Murray Kempton
Ibrahim Abu Lughod
William J. Mares
Liberty Mhlanga
Rodrigo Botero Montaya
Norval Morris
Patrick T. Murphy
Enrique Peñalosa
Judd Polk
Yevgeni M. Primakov
Clyde Ross
Sabi H. Shabtai
Neil Sheehan
Anthony Storr
U Thant
Sanford J. Ungar

EXECUTIVE ADVISORY COMMITTEE

John Cotton
Peter Diamandopoulos, *ex officio*
Frank Ervin
Kenneth Hansen
Murray Kempton
William J. Mares
Enrique Peñalosa
William R. Polk

For L. B. Pearson

PRIME MINISTER

Mr. Escott Reid has dealt with a subject larger than the title of his book suggests. He has not attempted merely an evaluation of the World Bank. His plea for greater imagination and sympathetic understanding of the nature and urges of different societies should be heard by all those who influence international economic arrangements.

(Indira Gandhi)

New Delhi,
July 20, 1973.

Contents

Introduction

This is a pioneer work. It is, so far as I know, the only book which takes one of the half-dozen principal international institutions and puts forward specific proposals for making it more effective.

It draws heavily on detailed studies of the Bank which Escott Reid carried out as consultant to the Canadian International Development Agency, initiated during the period when I was President of that Agency. It thus benefits immensely from the extensive consultation he was able to have with officials of the Bank, which was good enough to cooperate in this study project.

The access this gave him both to records and to the thinking of Bank officials and others closely associated with its work make the book more than usually authoritative. But, its greater value is that it is interesting and readable, comprehensive and specific. It deals with the volume of lending by the Bank Group, the terms of lending, and the sources of its funds; with the quality of lending and, in particular, the necessity of the Bank Group's doing more to help its developing member countries raise the standards of living of the poorest two-fifths or so of their people; with the administration of the Bank Group and the work of the executive directors who represent the member governments; and with the relations between the Bank Group and other international organizations. It proposes amendments to the international agreements establishing the Bank Group.

This book is an attempt to look at the Bank Group as a whole. It does not let the trees get in the way of seeing the forest.

This is the kind of book which could have been written only by someone who knows from the inside how governments operate, how difficult it is for them to choose between alternative policies, and who has participated in the making of big decisions on government policy. It could have been written only by someone who has worked in a senior position in the Bank Group, and who has many friends among the management and staff.

Escott Reid has always been an innovator. He was an innovator when he directed the Canadian Institute of International Affairs in the thirties. He was an innovator in discussions on the formation of the International Civil Aviation Organization, the United Nations, and the North Atlantic Treaty. He was an innovator in the second half of the sixties, as the founding principal of a small bilingual college in Toronto which placed special emphasis on public affairs.

His talents for innovative thinking are clearly reflected in the ideas put forward in this book concerning the future role of the World Bank Group. And, as the hallmark of a true innovator is that he can recognize and embrace good new ideas whatever their origin, it in no way detracts from the value of those ideas to suggest that many of them have come from within the Bank itself. Indeed, this book and the studies which preceded it were undertaken at a time when the Bank, under the dynamic and enlightened leadership of Robert McNamara, was already deeply involved in a process of reorientation and change. This process has already moved the Bank in very much the direction Escott Reid advocates.

But, there can be no "instant" change in an institution the size and complexity of the World Bank. Change is a dynamic and continuing process, and Robert McNamara is not one who only thinks and talks change —he makes it! But, it inevitably takes time for the sweeping changes in the scale, quality, and orientation of the Bank Group's activities McNamara has initiated so vigorously during his presidency to be fully and effectively reflected in its operations. Even the best of machines can be pushed only so fast without overheating. And no one knows better than McNamara the manager of men that the changes initiated by McNamara the leader of thought will be most significant when they are translated into reality by the Bank itself.

Escott Reid underlines the importance of the argument McNamara has been putting forward, that if the poorest countries are to meet the minimum needs of their people not in a generation from now but in ten or fifteen years, as they should, they must make fundamental changes in their economic and social policies, and the task of the Bank Group is to help them make these changes.

His plea is that the World Bank Group should concentrate its efforts on helping those of its member countries which most need help and which most deserve help. The countries which, in his opinion, most need help are the poorest ones, the countries where average income a head is not more than about $300; they have a total population of 1,350 million. The countries which, in his opinion, most deserve help are those of the poorest countries which are determined to provide every one of their people with a minimum bundle of essential goods and services—food, clothing, and shelter—within ten or at the most fifteen years. At present, in most of the poorest countries the conditions of life of the poorest two-fifths or so of the people are not getting much better; in many, they have got worse in the last ten years. These people need more food to fill their empty bellies, clothing to replace their rags, better shelter from heat and cold wind and rain.

One of the valuable by-products of the work Escott Reid contributed in writing his book is the sharpening of some of the tools with which we probe into the mysteries of development.

He found that there is no generally accepted definition of what is a developing country, and that most writers lump together all the countries they consider to be developing. They speak, for example, of rates of growth of gross national product in the "developing countries," disregarding the profound differences between countries like Upper Volta and countries like Argentina, one with a gross national product per capita of $60 and the other with $1,160. Thus, he has divided the countries of the world into four categories: the rich countries, which contain a quarter of the population of the world; the very poor countries, which contain half; and, in between, the middle-income and the poor countries.

When he applied these definitions to the estimates of population and of gross national product contained in the latest World Bank *Atlas*, that for 1972, he pointed up the following important facts. In the sixties the very poor member countries of the World Bank had a rate of growth in GNP of only 3.7 per cent a year, while the better-off developing countries (the middle-income and the poor) had a rate of growth of 6.2 per cent. If these rates of growth continue, it will take the very poor twenty years to double their gross national products, whereas the better-off will double theirs in twelve.

Working on projections of population and of gross national product, he found that in the year 2000 it is likely that the rich countries of the world (non-Communist and Communist) will have an average income per person of between $9,000 and $10,000 (with the purchasing power of the 1970 U.S. dollar), compared with $2,800 in 1970; a very poor country such as India, which stands in the middle ranks of very poor countries, an average income of $225 to $460, compared with $110 in 1970. And this upper figure of $460 could be reached only in the unlikely event that India is able to increase its production by 7 per cent a year, twice the rate achieved in the sixties, and to so reduce its annual rate of growth in population that, by 2000, its population would be only 950 million.

On the most optimistic assumptions about India's progress, the gap between average income in India and that in the rich countries will have increased in terms of 1970 dollars from $2,600 in 1970 to about $9,000 in the year 2000.

Escott Reid says: "The situation of India is not unique. The income of the average person in virtually all the other poor countries of the world at the end of the century is not likely to be much better than that of the average person in India. It may be worse. And the total population at the end of the century of the countries which are now very poor is likely to be about 3,600 million, almost three-fifths of the population of the world. The Bank Group is likely to have enough to do not just for decades but for generations."

I have learned a great deal from Escott Reid. Indeed, my own career in international development owes much to the inspiration, guidance, and support I have received from him. And I have benefited greatly by reading this book—though there are some things in it with which I do not agree. But one need not fully agree with either Escott Reid's diagnosis or the specific measures he proposes to acknowledge the value, the importance, and the timeliness of this formidable work.

It should be read by all who have a serious interest in the issues that will determine the future of the majority of people on this planet and in the institution that more than any other is helping to shape that future.

Maurice F. Strong

Foreword

It was in October 1970 that I began the investigation which led to my writing this book. I had been arguing for years that the time had come for governments to take a new look at the principal international economic and social institutions which had been set up, some after the First World War, most during or immediately after the Second World War. These institutions had been created at a time when the world was not so conscious as it became later of the importance of helping the governments of the developing nations in their efforts to improve the conditions of life of their poorer citizens, and of the difficulties involved in this endeavor. They had been established when most of the states now members of them had not yet gained their independence. I hoped that the Canadian government might take a lead in initiating a re-examination of these institutions, a re-examination which would indicate the kinds of changes in their policies, administrations, and constitutions which would make them more effective instruments of the international community in combating world poverty.

Maurice Strong, who was then head of the Canadian International Development Agency, agreed with me and arranged that I be given a contract by the Agency to prepare memoranda for it on this subject, beginning with the World Bank Group. This was not because we believed that the World Bank Group stood most in need of reform, but because it was the institution I knew most about. I found the task I had set myself more difficult than I had expected, with the result that I did not complete the memoranda until March 1972. I then decided not to try to cover any of the other international economic and social institutions, but instead to use the material I had got together on the World Bank Group as the starting point for writing a book on the subject. The Agency released me from my contract, and I have spent my time since then preparing this book. Since I began my investigation, the Bank Group has changed, and my views about it have changed.

I completed writing the book in the spring of 1973, when Robert McNamara had completed the first five years of his ten-year term as

President of the Bank Group, and when it seemed probable that the next two years would be a period of consolidation after five years of rapid expansion in its activities, and of important changes in the nature of those activities and in the administration of the Bank Group.

This book is based on personal experience, on publications of the Bank Group (including a number of restricted and confidential documents), and on talks and correspondence with officers of the Bank Group. I have also had talks and correspondence with present and former executive directors of the Bank Group, with officers of other international agencies, and with officers concerned with aid in national governments, both aid-giving and aid-receiving.

This book has the advantages and disadvantages of having been written by an outsider who was from 1962 to 1965 an insider. Because I was director of the South Asia and Middle East Department of the Bank in those years, I have first-hand knowledge of the Bank. Because many years have elapsed since I was a member of the staff, I may not realize the extent of the changes which have taken place since I left.

I lived in India as an ambassador from 1952 to 1957. From 1962 to 1965, I traveled on behalf of the World Bank to South Asia and the Middle East. But, apart from holidays in Greece, Spain, Mexico, Central America, the Caribbean, and Ceylon, and membership thirty years ago in a government trade mission to South America, I have no direct knowledge of the other middle-income and low-income countries which borrow from the Bank Group. My prescriptions for reforms in the Bank Group may well be unduly influenced by my experiences in the underdeveloped countries I know best—India, Pakistan, and Bangladesh—and by my respect and affection for the peoples of those countries. But I believe that the strong nationalist feeling in those countries, which is the basis of their antipathy to attempts by outsiders to intervene in their domestic affairs, is likely before long to show itself in most of the other developing countries where it does not now appear evident.

Some officers of the Bank Group who have seen drafts of parts of this book have said that the Bank Group is already doing many of the things I advocate. The essential point is, of course, the extent to which it is already doing them and how much more it is doing them now than three or four years ago. For this reason I have tried wherever possible to find statistical indicators of how far precept is reflected in practice in such matters as: the increase since 1968 in the number of senior officers who come from countries which are not rich; the number of officers exchanged with the Food and Agriculture Organization and with the UN Educational, Scientific, and Cultural Organization; the proportion of loans devoted to local costs; and the number of Bank missions which are helping member countries to work out projects for submission to the Bank Group which will create more employment without slowing down the rate of increase in the production of essential goods and services. I have not always been successful in finding these statistical indicators.

Other officers have said that I am asking too much of the Bank

Group, that I am suggesting it play too prominent a role in the international aid effort. My answer is threefold. First, I am describing a program for strengthening the three World Bank institutions (the Bank proper, the International Development Association, and the International Finance Corporation) to be carried out, not in a few years, but over a period of ten years or so. Second, institutions such as the Bank Group often have a greater capacity to respond effectively to challenge and to forceful and imaginative leadership and to grow with increasing responsibility than those who toil in them realize. Third, the needs of the poorer countries are so great that any conceivable expansion of the Bank Group's activities would leave plenty of room for expansion of the activities of the other international and national aid agencies.

Another comment from officers of the Bank Group is that I am too hopeful about the possibilities of substantial reforms being made in the international aid system, that I am unduly influenced by my participation twenty-five or thirty years ago in the creation of the UN, the International Civil Aviation Organization, and the North Atlantic Treaty, when, under the pressure of hot war and cold war, it was possible to remold the world a little closer to the heart's desire. In particular, they believe that it is folly to recommend that the rich countries should agree to a diminution of their voting strength in the governing bodies of the Bank Group. They say that, even if other rich countries were prepared to go along with this, the United States would not; that the opposition in the House of Representatives would be too strong. They also suggest that it is most improbable that the rich countries would agree to the kind of increase in the resources of the International Development Association which I recommend.

My answer is that I, of course, agree that the possibilities of making substantial changes in the international system are not as great as in the 1940's; nevertheless, it seems to me that, so far as the World Bank Group of institutions is concerned, a number of recent developments have on balance increased not only the necessity but also the possibility of making changes in the policy and administration of the Bank Group, and in the balance of power within it. International relations and men's thinking about international relations are becoming more fluid, with changes in the relationships between Western Europe and Eastern Europe, between the United States, the Soviet Union, and China, and with the increasing economic strength of Japan and of the European Economic Community. What was impossible in the late sixties is becoming probable in the second half of the seventies; thus, in the late sixties the House of Representatives of the United States would have voted by an overwhelming majority against the exchange of embassies with Peking; before the mid-seventies it will probably have voted by an overwhelming majority in favor of this exchange. This development came as a result of strong leadership and a gradual awakening to reality. Strong leadership and a gradual awakening to reality might similarly result in a recognition that as the poorer countries become increasingly unwilling to accept advice on their development from outsiders, the Bank Group must become a less unequal partnership between the rich and the poorer nations, so that its advice would not be considered by the poorer countries to be advice from outsiders. The increasing support in the United States and in a number of other rich member countries for proposals to direct a greater proportion of their economic assistance through multilateral, rather than bilateral, channels increases the likelihood that the International Development Association will receive larger gifts from these governments so that it may make more interest-free loans to very poor countries. The need to make substantial structural changes in the international monetary system in the seventies increases the likelihood that international agreement will be reached to provide cost-free resources to the International Development Association through the special drawing rights of the International Monetary Fund and to insure a greatly increased volume of borrowings for the Bank from the central banks of its members on a long-term contractual basis. These changes would reduce the Bank Group's dependence on gifts from the governments of rich countries and on the sales of its bonds on their capital markets; and this would make it easier to reduce their power in the governing bodies and in the administration of the Bank Group. The increasing realization that development means not only increased production of essential goods and services, but also more employment and a more equitable distribution of income, increases public support in the member countries of the Bank Group for the necessary changes in its policy and administration.

What may be even more important in the longer run is the constantly increasing political power in the rich countries of people born since the mid-thirties. It seems likely that a majority of the political leaders and the molders of public opinion who have already emerged from this generation, or who will emerge in the next ten years or so, will be more likely than their counterparts in previous generations to support the kind of fundamental changes I advocate.

But, while these factors are encouraging, they provide a basis not for optimism but for hope. The proposals set forth in this book can become effective only if the governments which are members of the Bank Group make changes in the policies on international development which they pursue directly and through the international organizations of which they are members, notably the World Bank Group, the regional banks, the UN Economic and Social Council, together with the institutions grouped around this Council or intimately associated with it, such as the UN Development Program. The ultimate responsibility for making the necessary changes in the Bank Group and the other international organizations rests on national governments, since these international organizations are the creatures and instrumentalities of national governments.

The changes required in the policies of the governments of the rich countries are profound. Appropriations for aid must be greatly increased. Tariff and non-tariff barriers to the entry of the goods of low-income countries must be abolished. The governments and the nationals of low-income countries must be given more influence in the international aid agencies. Governments must be prepared to support large expenditures in developing countries on experimental labor-intensive projects where risks of failure are great, since it is only as a result of many experiments in many countries on many different kinds of labor-intensive projects that the governments of developing countries will learn in time how to reconcile the need to increase production of essential goods and services for the mass of the people with the need to divert a greater share of the national income to the poorest two-fifths.

The governments, the legislatures, the voters of rich countries will not make these changes in their policies until they become convinced, as few are today, of the importance of rich countries helping developing countries to create during the next ten or at most fifteen years societies which provide every man, woman and child with at least the bare essentials of food, clothing and shelter. The pace at which they move toward this conviction will depend in large part on how rapidly the governments of developing countries, and the better off, politically powerful groups in those countries, likewise become convinced, as few are today, of the importance of this goal.

The fact that the World Bank Group and the other international institutions concerned with the struggle against world poverty are creations and instrumentalities of national governments does not mean that these institutions should not have freedom of initiative and action within the broad lines of policy laid down by those governments: indeed, they *must* have it. They also have the right and duty to attempt to influence the policies of national governments toward them. A senior civil servant in a national bureaucracy does not do his duty if he does not exercise freedom of initiative and action within the broad lines of policy established by his government, and if he does not use his creative intelligence, specialized knowledge, and diplomatic skills to influence the policies of his government on matters relating to his department of government. The same is true of senior international civil servants. The policies of international institutions directed by far-sighted secretaries-general, presidents, and directors-general supported by strong bureaucracies have often been well in advance of the policies of the member governments. These senior civil servants have played the role great presidents and prime ministers, such as Roosevelt, Churchill, and Nehru, have played. These captains of mankind push and prod and pull and lead; they persuade, coax, cajole, shame, flatter; they bully political parties, legislatures, and electorates into doing what they want. Great secretaries-general, presidents, and directors-general of international organizations have used similar tactics to secure the acquiescence of governments in proposals they would otherwise have ignored or rejected.

The World Bank Group has done much for the poor countries of the world in the quarter century of its operations. It could have done more had it been subjected to more constructive criticism from outsiders and had it been more willing to listen to outside critics. Might not this, for example, have moved the Bank Group to give up many years before 1968 its ideological objections to lending to government-owned industry and government-owned development banks? And what of the failure to lend anything for small-scale rural development works; the allocation to small-scale industry up to 1971 of only 3 per cent of total lending to industry; the failure of the Bank and the International Development Association up to 1971 to lend directly for tourism; the failure up to 1968 to devote more than a small proportion of lending to the local costs of projects; the failure to reduce the overwhelming preponderance of citizens of rich countries in the senior ranks of its management and staff?

My hope is that this book will do something to make it less probable that the Bank Group will make comparable mistakes in the future. My hope also is that the faults as well as the merits of this book will stimulate others to write much better books about what could be done to strengthen the World Bank Group and the other agencies, both international and national, which are concerned with the economic and social development of the poorer countries.

I dedicate this book to L. B. Pearson, prime minister, colleague, friend, under whom I had the privilege of working for many years in the Department of External Affairs of Canada. He tried hard to persuade the governments of the rich nations of the world to do more, through the World Bank Group and in other ways, to help in the struggle against world poverty. I hope this book will serve to carry on his work.

Escott Reid
June, 1973.

CHAPTER ONE

The Role of the Bank Group

The role of the World Bank Group of institutions and of international aid in general is limited. Much the greater part of the burden of efforts to improve the standards of living of the poorer peoples of the world has been borne and will continue to be borne by the poorer peoples themselves. "In the 1960's, domestic savings [in the poorer countries] financed 85 per cent of total investment."[1] In India, "more than 90% of the resources devoted to development come from India itself."[2] Even if official development assistance were to reach the Pearson Commission's target of seven-tenths of one per cent of the total gross national product of the rich countries, it seems clear that the poorer countries would still have to finance about the same proportion of the investment required to support a reasonable pace of economic and social advance.

But, it is not only or even chiefly a question of the share of investment the people of the poorer nations must meet from their meager incomes. It is much more that the pace of economic and social advance in the poorer countries depends on governments, business, and individuals in those countries adopting attitudes, policies, priorities, and programs conducive to this advance. These new attitudes, policies, priorities and programs will, to a greater or lesser degree, depending on the country, be in conflict with existing ones, which will be supported in most of the poorer countries by special interest groups, such as the larger landowners, who exercise immense political power.

Thus the attainment of a sustained fast pace of economic and social advance (by which is meant economic growth plus jobs plus social justice) requires in most if not virtually all of the poorer countries a lessening of the economic, social, and political power of the wealthiest 10 per cent or so of the population. It always requires greater social mobility so that many more of the ablest people can rise to the top and displace those who have acquired positions of authority because of caste, creed, color, social origin, birth, influence, wealth, or corruption. It requires a willingness to accept good advice, even from foreigners, and an ability to distinguish between good and bad advice. There must be a willingness to forego prestige projects, such as impressive airports, universities, hospitals and new capital cities, big dams, steel plants, nuclear power stations, super-highways, or an international airline, when the economic and social return on these is less than on other possible projects, such as better primary education, more outpatient clinics and mobile health units, small and medium-size irrigation projects, conventional power stations, small industry, secondary roads (and mud roads from these to the villages), grain storage facilities in the villages, rural development works and the provision of good seeds, fertilizer, insecticides, credit, and knowledge of improved farming practices to small and medium-size farmers, as well as the larger landowners.[3] A sustained fast pace of economic and social advance demands the utmost possible effort to live in peace with neighboring countries and to spend little on defense. In almost all the poorer countries, it means a determination to press ahead with massive birth control programs. Above all, the peoples of the poorer countries must be willing to sacrifice some of today's goods for tomorrow's hopes.

Aid from the World Bank Group and from other aid agencies to a poorer country has the greatest potential for good when it makes it easier for the government of the country to adopt sensible attitudes and to implement sensible policies relating to development. Aid from the World Bank Group and from other aid agencies has the greatest potential for harm when it makes it easier for the government of a poorer country to adopt attitudes and to implement policies which are not sensible. Aid may strengthen politically powerful local interest groups which have or believe they have vested interests in resisting changes conducive to economic and social advance. Gifts of food to countries with unwise agricultural policies have in the past served to relieve the pressure on them to adopt more sensible agricultural policies.[4] Advisers provided by aid agencies have recommended techniques of production and technologies appropriate to rich countries but not to countries suffering from severe shortages of capital and dangerously large surpluses of labor. Almost all the poorer two-thirds of mankind live in such countries. The provision of foreign capital at low-interest rates to pay for imports of duty-free machinery for capital-intensive industry in the poorer countries has supported unwise domestic policies leading to an underpricing of capital and an overpricing of labor, which result, not only in less employment and less social justice, but also in a slower rate of economic growth.

Aid of the right kind, if given in adequate volume and guaranteed over a suitably long period of time, and if not offset by the raising of tariffs and other barriers against the exports of the poorer countries, can have a decisive influence for good on the economic and social development of a poorer country. It can make it possible for that country to import more goods and services. This will enable the government to step up its level of investment in development programs and projects of a kind which will result in a substantial increase, not only in the production of goods and services needed by the mass of the population, but also in employment. Increased employment will lead to a more equitable distribution of income. Aid of the right kind can help a country to build up local management ability, entrepreneurial energy, administrative resources, skilled labor, and debt-servicing capacity. All this could well mean that the real rate of growth in income per head would be double what it would have been without the injection of outside aid, and that unemployment and underemployment would be half what they would have been. In terms of capital formation, of social progress and social justice, of lessened misery, and of the release of latent energies of mind, body, and spirit, the consequences can be vast.

"There is no doubt that with all the aid-weariness and the desire to get rid of aid as quickly as possible, and despite all the hankering after revolutionary panaceas, the developing countries can benefit immensely from a net inflow of external resources on concessional terms for many decades to come."[5] This was the considered conclusion in 1970 of I. G. Patel, then the senior official in the Indian department of economic affairs, who has long been concerned with aid matters and is one of the foremost critics of the past policies and attitudes of aid agencies. His conclusion is supported by two other eminent economists, one from a Communist country, Hungary, and one from the United States. The Hungarian said in 1969: "The future of economic development in developing countries depends mainly on the future of the flow of assistance."[6] The United States economist said in 1965: "For most underdeveloped countries, foreign assistance is already a critical source of development finance and one of the main hopes for accelerated growth in the future."[7]

Because aid of the right kind can be crucial, because of the central position of the World Bank Group of institutions in the international aid community, it is essential that whatever changes are required in the three World Bank Group institutions to enable them to make the greatest possible positive contribution to the international aid effort should be made promptly. The governments of the rich countries of the world which are members of the Bank Group and which, because they provide almost all its financial resources, are largely instrumental in forming its policies, should make whatever changes are required in their own policies in the Bank Group and should press for the necessary changes in the Bank Group. They should provide the Bank Group with greatly increased resources. All the rich countries of the world, whether or not they are members of the Bank Group, should increase greatly the aid they are now providing bilaterally or through international agencies other than the Bank Group.

The capacity of the rich countries, both non-Communist and Communist, to step up greatly the volume of real resources transferred by them to the poorer countries is likely to increase rapidly. An authoritative study by the Organization for Economic Cooperation and Development published in 1970 estimated that the real income (in terms of stable dollars) of the average person in the OECD countries will go up by about 50 per cent in the seventies. The report went on to say:

The standards of affluence which these [rates of growth] imply are in dramatic contrast to the continuing problem of poverty, malnutrition and disease in most of the rest of the world. A faster rate of development will require policy action by the developing countries themselves. But an increase in the effort and resources devoted to development assistance, in all its forms, and the improvement in the effectiveness of such assistance, has become an urgent world commitment for the advanced industrial countries of OECD.[8]

In 1970 the total GNP of the rich member countries of the Bank was $2,000 billion. By 1985 it will probably be twice that much in real terms—in terms of 1970 dollars. In 1970 the net transfer of official development assistance from these rich countries to the developing countries was about $6 billion.[9] If in 1985 it were $24 billion, four times as much as in 1970, this would mean that these countries would be devoting to development assistance only $18 billion out of the $2,000 billion increase in their annual GNP's. This is less than 1 per cent of the increase; the remaining 99 per cent would be available for providing for the increases in their population, raising their standards of living, poverty campaigns at home, defense, anti-pollution measures, space research, and other purposes. The increase in population in this fifteen-year period will probably be from 630 million in 1970 to about 720 million in 1985; the per capita GNP will likely go up from about $3,200 to about $5,600. (This is a more conservative forecast of per capita GNP than that cited above from the OECD study, according to which the increase would be 50 per cent in the ten years from 1970 to 1980.) The proportion of the total GNP of the rich member countries which would be transferred as official development assistance in 1985 would be six-tenths of 1 per cent.

The total GNP of the rich non-member countries was about $550 billion in 1970 and will probably be about $1,225 billion by 1985. If they, too, were to devote a little less than 1 per cent of the increase to official development assistance, this would mean that they would increase their official development assistance by about $6 billion a year. The increase in their population will probably be from 290 million in 1970 to 330 million in 1985. Their per capita GNP would likely go up during this period from about $1,900 to $3,700.*

There is general agreement that the purpose of aid from the World Bank Group and other agencies is to make it easier for the governments of developing countries to pursue sensible development policies. The disagreement is over who is to be the arbiter of what are and what are not sensible development policies. There are two extreme theoretical positions. One is that the government of the poorer country should be

*See Annex 5, pages 250 to 253.

the sole arbiter; that it alone can be considered by an international agency or by another government as the interpreter of the country's system of values and development priorities, its social goals, and the aspirations of its people; that aid agencies must not question that government's decisions but must assist it to carry them out expeditiously and efficiently. The other extreme position is that the aid agencies know what is best.

The adoption of one extreme view could mean that aid agencies would finance whatever the most brutal, corrupt, inefficient, reactionary dictatorship, such as that which governed Haiti for many years, declared were sensible programs of development, even though it was common knowledge that those who ran the regime were interested not in development but in accumulating more power and wealth for themselves, and that they would use outside aid to increase their power and the size of their bank accounts in Switzerland. The adoption of the other extreme view could mean that aid agencies would require borrowing countries, as a condition of aid, to accept the values and priorities of the white wealthy countries which, because they provide the funds, control the aid agencies.

Neither of these two positions will come within the scope of practical politics in the foreseeable future. Both of them are nonstarters. Until aid on concessional terms can be financed largely from sources other than taxes imposed by the governments of rich countries on their citizens, these governments will be compelled by the realities of the domestic political process to adopt policies on aid which will enable them to convince the taxpayers that they are making reasonable efforts to insure that the aid financed out of their taxes is being well used. This applies to their own bilateral aid programs and to the multilateral agencies they contribute to, such as the World Bank Group, the regional banks, and the UN Development Program. As for the other extreme position, sentiment in the poorer countries limits both the willingness and the ability of their governments to accept intervention by aid agencies in their affairs. They are compelled by the realities of their domestic political processes to adopt policies which enable them to assure their citizens that they are not sacrificing the independence of their country in return for aid.

Proponents of all the schools of thought on international aid are compelled to accept, however reluctantly, the need to apply some system of rationing to the flow of aid money, since this money is scarce, and the softer it is the scarcer it is. Because it is scarce the more that goes to one aid-receiving country the less there is for other countries. Thus an aid-receiving country will naturally favor a system of rationing which will result in the greatest flow of real resources to it on the easiest terms. There is no common front among aid-receiving countries. Very poor countries favor a system which provides more aid to them than to the less poor. Countries with large populations favor a system which emphasizes the level of aid per head of population. Countries which believe they make better use of aid than other countries favor a rationing system which rewards merit as they define it.

What is at issue is not the need to establish a rationing system but the nature of the rationing system and, in particular, the extent of intervention in the affairs of aid-receiving countries which it entails. Those, both in the poorer countries and in the rich countries, who favor a relatively high level of intervention say that intervention of the right kind serves the interests of the people of the developing countries. They believe, however, that aid agencies should limit their intervention to broad and central aspects of development policy, and express opinions on these only after penetrating investigation. Aid agencies, in striving to come to agreement with the poorer country, should make all reasonable concessions to reach agreement. If a reasonable compromise cannot be reached, the agencies should, in the interest of the poorer country, substantially reduce the flow of aid. Those who favor intervention ask whether it is to the advantage of the people of an aid-receiving country that aid agencies accept the development priorities of the government even when it is obvious that the government is assigning high priority to prestige projects which promise less economic and social return than other, less ostentatious, projects. They ask whether India would not be better off today if the aid-India consortium had from its beginning in 1958 insisted, as a condition of increased aid, that India allocate a greater proportion of its development resources to agriculture; whether Pakistan would not be better off today if the aid-Pakistan consortium had from its beginning in 1960 insisted that Pakistan allocate a greater proportion of its development resources to East Pakistan and to the poorer people in both East and West Pakistan; whether Mexico and Brazil would not be better off today if the Bank Group and other aid-givers had urged for the past fifteen years or so that their governments should do much more to insure that the mass of their people benefited from their country's increasing per capita GNP.

Many who would most vehemently deny that they are interventionists believe that, since international efforts to help developing countries will be of no avail unless those countries make major changes in their political, social, and economic policies and institutions, aid should depend on the extent to which a country meets such performance criteria as equitable income distribution, land and tax reforms, effective trade and exchange rate policies, limitation of military expenditures, and the promotion of social justice. This policy was advocated by the signatories of the "Columbia Declaration," which was signed by a very large majority of those who were present at the final sessions of the 1970 Columbia Conference on International Economic Development. The signatories included spokesmen for what the editors of the proceedings called the radical minority at the conference.[10]

Radicals who attack the World Bank Group for using the "leverage" its control of funds gives it to secure changes in the policies of borrowing governments are normally opposed to any aid to governments which pursue policies abhorrent to them. In this they are supported by most liberals. The list of governments which, in their opinion, should be or should have been blacklisted might include the governments of Haiti under the elder Duvalier, Pakistan under Yahya, Indonesia under Sukarno, Ghana under Nkrumah, Greece under the Colonels, and Portugal and South Africa under any of their governments for the past twenty years or so. They believe that the *quid pro quo* for aid to countries with governments like these is not a mere change in government policies, priorities, or programs relating to development but a change in the regime. This attitude could be described accurately as an extreme form of intervention in the domestic affairs of a sovereign state. "In a world in which the right to seek aid is widely assumed, even the withholding of aid is an infringement of sovereignty."[11]

The discussion at the annual conference of the Society for International Development in 1971 demonstrated that among liberal westerners interested in international development there is a growing demand that international development assistance be directed toward more jobs and greater social justice, not simply to more rapid economic growth.[12] Robert McNamara, the president of the World Bank, is a leading exponent of this view. But, the more the World Bank Group accepts this doctrine, the more it becomes involved in efforts to influence the general development plans and policies of its borrowers on issues much more politically delicate, much more traditionally domestic, than issues related to growth in the gross national product on which the World Bank Group has in the past attempted to exert leverage or influence.

Some of those who urge that aid agencies renounce efforts to obtain changes in general development policy as the price of obtaining aid contend that the development within western countries of aid policy toward their own poor citizens provides an analogy for international aid from the richer countries to the poorer. They point out that western countries have in the last hundred years moved away from a "poor law" concept, under which aid went from the state only to the "deserving" poor, and the use of the aid by the deserving poor was closely scrutinized, to a welfare state concept, under which aid goes from the state to the poor as part of a redistribution of income appropriate to a just society, and the poor are entitled to use the aid as they wish.

The weakness of this analogy is that, under existing interstate relations, aid goes from the agencies not directly to poor people but to or through the governments of the poorer countries. It is one thing to give money to poor people, whether or not they are "deserving," to use as they wish; it is an entirely different thing to give money to the governments of poor countries, whether or not they are "deserving," to use as they wish. To give money to governments which are not deserving, in the sense that they are not seriously interested in social and economic development, may well mean giving money which ends its journey not in the hands of poor people but in the bank accounts of the rich.

An analogy from domestic policies likely to be more relevant is with a welfare state, not in a wealthy unitary country such as Britain, but in a wealthy federal country such as the United States or Canada. The governments of these federations are enmeshed in serious difficulties and dilemmas when they try, in partnership with the governments of the constituent states or provinces, to work out agreed programs for helping the constituent units to improve the conditions of their poorer citizens and poorer regions. They have experimented with conditional grants and loans, unconditional grants and loans, equalization payments, and payments made directly to the poor. Of these practices, the only one which seems applicable to international aid at the present stage of international relations is the conditional loan or grant in those wealthy federal welfare states where shared-cost programs, subsidized by the central government, are not imposed on the constituent states or provinces but stem from negotiations with them. In these federal countries the results of the negotiations are embodied in formal agreements, which set forth the nature of the program to be subsidized (for example, hospital and medical insurance schemes or post-secondary education), the standards of performance to be met, and the other conditions which must be fulfilled in order to qualify for the subsidy. One condition may be matching contributions or the provision of certain facilities. The fulfillment of the conditions set forth in the agreement automatically results in the payment of a subsidy of a certain amount. The agreements are not on a year-to-year basis but extend over a period of years.

If Bank Group lending were to follow this pattern, the Bank Group would work out with groups of borrowing member countries the programs to be financed by conditional Bank and IDA loans, and the conditions to be attached to the loans for each program. The results of these negotiations would be embodied in agreements between the Bank Group and individual member countries. The agreements would be for a specified period of years. The agreements would be submitted to the executive directors of the Bank Group for approval. Fulfillment of the conditions set forth in the agreement would automatically result in a Bank or IDA loan of a specified amount without further reference to the executive directors. This system embodying agreed conditions, automatic application and continuity would differ markedly from present systems.

Informed opinion in some of the major poorer countries appears to be moving toward advocacy of an international system of this kind. Thus I. G. Patel suggested at a conference in 1970 that "every developing country [should] share in available aid for some easily acceptable and identifiable objectives such as raising the level of education or health facilities or urban housing or irrigation use or electricity available."[13]

Two years later Mahbub ul Haq, who had for thirteen years been associated with Pakistan's economic planning, proposed that each developing country should define for itself "minimum (or threshold) consumption standards," which should be available to every person in the country "in a manageable period of time, say a decade." These would be expressed "in terms of a minimum bundle of goods and services that must be provided to the common man to eliminate the worst manifestations of poverty: minimum nutritional, educational, health and housing standards, for instance." This would be the basis for the development plan of the country.[14]

J. K. Galbraith had said very much the same thing six years before. He called his development criterion for the poorer countries the popular consumption criterion. Economic development would be anchored to the consumption requirements of the poorer 80 per cent or so of the people. This he said:

> *Obviously means a major emphasis on food, clothing, shelter and education . . .* [*and*] *operates equally against automobiles, any but the most inexpensive housing, luxury consumer goods and conspicuous public goods. . . .* [*This*] *fixes objectives and establishes the priorities in the distribution of investment. . . . This is not a decision for agriculture or for industry or for light industry as opposed to heavy industry. It is a choice for the industrial structure which supplies the typical or modal citizen. That person wants perhaps first of all, an abundant supply of inexpensive food. But back of an improved agriculture lie fertilizer plants and a chemical industry and well-designed agricultural implements and an efficient transportation system and hence a source of steel.*[15]

The difficulties of operating a system of conditional grants in wealthy federal states so that the system does, in fact, provide every citizen with the minimum necessities of life, regardless of which constituent unit of the federation he lives in, are so great that they are leading, not so much to demands that the grants from the federal government to the governments of the constituent units become unconditional, as to demands for unconditional cash payments direct from the federal government to all citizens in the poorest fifth or so of the population so as to bring their incomes up to a national minimum. The difficulties of operating an efficient system of conditional loans within the international community will be even greater than within a national community, since the differences between the constituent units of the international community are much greater than those between the constituent units of a federal state, and the sense of belonging to the same community is more remote. Perhaps in time these difficulties may likewise result in the international community making unconditional cash payments direct to the poorest people in the world to bring their incomes up to an agreed international minimum. But that is a long way off. It may well be, however, a more probable development than the establishment of a system of loans and grants from the international community to the governments of the poorer countries to be used as those governments see fit. A system of unconditional grants could not long continue to operate in a federal welfare state if one or more of the constituent states or provinces were under the control of a brutal, corrupt and reactionary government. The taxpayers in the other constituent states or provinces who were footing the bill for these grants would soon insist that the system be terminated. The same thing would happen even sooner in an international aid community. It seems therefore inevitable that transfers of resources from richer countries to poorer countries cannot in the foreseeable future be unconditional.

This book proposes changes in the policies, programs, administration, and constitutions of the World Bank Group which might become effective in the next ten years or so. These changes would not only be useful in themselves but would also promote the evolution of the World Bank Group into an agency whose primary task would be to grant conditional loans to the governments of developing countries in order to assist them to provide essential goods and services to every man, woman, and child in the country within ten or fifteen years.

Poverty, population and race are the three main problems of our time. The World Bank Group can help its members deal with the problems of poverty and population. To give the most help it should do two things. It should accept as its working definition of development that today development means creating during the next ten or at most fifteen years societies which provide every man, woman and child with at least the bare essentials of food, clothing and shelter. First things must come first. Secondly, it should recognize that its ability to help its member countries deal with the problems of poverty and population is limited by the excessive preponderance of rich white countries and their citizens in its governing bodies and in the senior ranks of its management and staff.

CHAPTER TWO

The Structure and Operations of the World Bank Group

The World Bank Group is in law three separate international financial institutions created and owned by governments. In fact it is one institution. When it lends money at more or less conventional rates of interest on loans guaranteed by the government concerned, it calls itself the International Bank for Reconstruction and Development, or the World Bank, and lends from its World Bank account; when it lends interest-free money on loans guaranteed by the government, it calls itself the International Development Association and lends from its IDA account; when it invests money in private enterprises without government guarantee, it calls itself the International Finance Corporation and invests from its IFC account. The first two accounts are much more important than the third. Lending from the World Bank account is running at a rate of about $2,000 million a year; from the IDA account, at about $1,000 million a year; from the IFC account, at only a little over $100 million a year. Over four-fifths of the loans from the World Bank account go to the better-off developing countries. Exactly four-fifths of the loans from the IDA account go to the other developing countries—the very poor. The total volume of lending by the Bank Group to developing countries is twice what all the other multilateral aid agencies combined are providing.*

The Bank has a board of governors, as do IDA and IFC. There is in fact, however, not three but one board of governors. The same is true of the board of executive directors, the president, the management and staff, and the policy on loans.

One disadvantage of the present situation is that it is easy for people to come to the erroneous conclusion that the three institutions are not equally concerned with directing their activities toward the economic and social betterment of the borrowing country. They may

*All statistics in this chapter are for January 1, 1973, unless otherwise noted. The principal statistics for June 30, 1973, are given in Table 1, pages 223 to 226.

believe that the Bank is concerned with financing bankable projects, IFC with financing profitable private investments, and only IDA with financing programs and projects for economic and social betterment. This would not, indeed, be surprising, since views smacking of this heresy were at one time held by some senior members of the staff of the Bank Group.

I remember that when I joined the staff of the Bank in 1962, Eugene Black, then president of the Bank, told me that it would be six weeks or so before I took over the direction of the South Asia and Middle East department and that I should spend the interval in getting to know as much as I could about how the Bank Group operated. Believing from my experience in diplomacy that there are two occasions when you know something about a foreign country, once after about a month in the country and once after about four years, I wrote a memorandum after my first month there. One of the senior officers—one of the least hidebound—said that where I was off the track was that I was proposing criteria for the conduct of operations which were appropriate to IDA but not to the Bank. Within about a year of this discussion, it was conventional wisdom that the Bank and IDA should use the same criteria in judging the worth of a project submitted to them for financing. The belief, however, persisted, both within and outside the Bank Group, that just because the enterprises IFC financed had to show good chances of making a reasonable profit, IFC should not be so concerned as the Bank and IDA with the extent to which its investments would also benefit the country as a whole. Only when Robert McNamara took over the presidency of the Bank Group in 1968 was this belief declared a heresy, one that might well never have arisen if the three components or aspects of the Bank Group had in law as in fact formed part of one institution.

It might also have been a good thing if the International Bank for Reconstruction and Development had never dubbed itself the "World Bank," since the use of the word *World* made it easier for those concerned to forget that it was not a universal institution but one embracing within its membership only two-thirds of the population of the world (attributing to the member state China only the population of Taiwan, since China has been represented in the Bank Group by persons appointed by the government in Taiwan, not in Peking). Almost all the non-Communist countries of the world are members; the only Communist members are Romania and Yugoslavia. But, even the word *Bank* is inaccurate: it is not a bank but a development fund. (Perhaps when Peking has taken over the representation of China in the Bank Group, and the Soviet Union and the eastern European states have become members the present misleading situation will be tidied up by substituting for the three existing international agreements establishing the Bank, IFC, and IDA, one comprehensive international agreement establishing one agency. The most appropriate name for this agency would be World Development Fund.)

The sources of funds of the World Bank, IDA, and IFC differ. The

Bank has about $12,000 million invested in loans to its member governments and in liquid assets, over three-fifths of which was raised by selling its bonds. On these bonds, the Bank is now paying about 7 per cent interest, which is just about the rate it charges its borrowers. It could charge less than 7 per cent and still be able to pay the interest on its borrowings and the costs of administration because it does not pay interest or dividends on about a third of the $12,000 million it has invested. This rent-free money, as Eugene Black used to call it, is made up of the usable paid-in portion of the subscriptions member governments have made to the shares of the Bank ($2,200 million), and of reserves built up out of earnings ($1,700 million). The Bank has been able, not only to build up reserves of $1,700 million out of earnings, but also to transfer $700 million from these reserves to IDA because the member governments have not asked for dividends on their shares but have treated their paid-in subscriptions as if they were interest-free loans.

The Bank thus has an endowment of almost $4,000 million, which, if it charges about the same interest rate on its loans as it pays on its bonds, enables it to earn a surplus of about $200 million a year. (Usually about half the surplus is transferred to reserves and the rest to IDA.)

The Bank is dependent on its six principal rich member countries for over 70 per cent of its finances. These countries—Britain, Canada, France, Germany, Japan, and the United States—provide two-thirds of its usable paid-in capital. By foregoing dividends on this capital, they are also responsible for two-thirds of the reserves. Their citizens hold 80 per cent of the outstanding bonds the Bank has sold on the capital markets of the world, and their central banks, 70 per cent of those sold to central banks. Almost all the rest of the finances of the Bank come from the other rich member countries.

Unlike the Bank, IDA has been financed entirely by gifts from governments made either directly or by foregoing dividends on their shares in the Bank. By the middle of 1974, IDA will probably have received about $5,600 million directly from governments, and about $900 million from Bank profits. Four-fifths of this money will have come from the governments of the six principal rich member countries.

IFC is financed in much the same way as the Bank except that it does not itself sell its bonds on capital markets or to central banks, but borrows from the Bank money the Bank has raised by selling bonds. The Bank has lent IFC $260 million. IFC has raised another $180 million by sales of its shares to its member governments ($107 million) and by building up reserves ($73 million). Two-thirds of IFC's money comes from the governments of the six principal rich members of the Bank.

These six principal rich members of the Bank Group provide in one way or another three-quarters of the financial resources of the Bank Group.[1] Almost all of the remaining quarter is provided by the other rich member countries.

This dependence of the Bank Group on its rich member countries is reflected in the distribution of votes in its governing bodies. The population of the six principal rich countries is 500 million, little more than one-fifth of the total population of the Bank Group, but they possess about half the votes. On the other hand, the six most populous of the poorer members—Bangladesh, Brazil, India, Indonesia, Nigeria, and Pakistan—with a total population of 930 million, possess less than one-sixth of the number of votes held by the six principal rich members. The entire group of rich countries in the Bank Group has one quarter of the population of the Bank Group but possesses almost two-thirds of the votes. In the Bank Group, he who pays the piper can call the tune.

This imbalance stems from provisions in the international agreements establishing the three institutions: the number of votes each member state has in the governing bodies depends on the number of shares it owns, which in turn depends on its relative economic strength, as reflected in its national income, imports, exports, and central bank reserves. Thus the United States casts 63,750 votes in the Bank and Nepal 362. The only concession the agreements make to the doctrine that all sovereign states are equal is that each member state, because it is a state, regardless of the number of shares it owns, is given 250 votes. But this is a token concession: these votes add up to less than 10 per cent of the total votes.

Each member state appoints a governor and an alternate governor of the Bank Group. All the governors from the eleven principal rich member countries are either ministers of finance or governors of central banks. Of the eleven alternate governors, six are governors or deputy governors of central banks and one is a deputy minister of finance. Only three of the other four are responsible for the operation of their national aid agencies. Thus ministers of finance and central bankers from rich countries, not the cabinet ministers responsible for the operation of the national aid agencies or the executive heads of those agencies, have the power to control the policies of the Bank Group.

The board of governors of the Bank Group has delegated most of its authority to the executive directors, of whom there are twenty. Each has an alternate. All but three of the present executive directors have full-time appointments; the three not on full time serve also as executive directors of the Bank Group's sister institution, the International Monetary Fund. All the alternate directors serve full time. The directors and their alternates are paid by the Bank Group, not by the governments which appoint or elect them, each director receiving $37,000 a year free of income tax, and each alternate $29,000. The total cost to the Bank Group of the board of executive directors is about $3 million a year; of the board of governors, about $1 million.

Each of the five largest shareholders (Britain, France, Germany, Japan, and the United States) appoints one executive director, while the other fifteen are elected by a group of countries. Countries do not elect a country to represent them but a person. One director represents Canada, Guyana, Ireland, and Jamaica; another, eighteen African countries. Each appointed director casts the number of votes to which the country which appointed him is entitled; each elected director casts the total of the votes of the countries he represents. He must cast these votes as a unit. The five largest shareholders appoint alternate directors. In law, each of the elected directors appoints his alternate. In fact, however, neither he nor his government but one of the governments which helped to elect him appoints the alternate.

One of the most important powers possessed by the board of executive directors is to interpret the international agreements, subject to appeal to the board of governors: their decisions are final. Thus the constitution of the World Bank Group is what the board of governors of the Bank Group says it is. This makes the constitution flexible. It also gives the final word in interpreting it to the rich member countries, since they possess almost two-thirds of the votes.

The president of the Bank is, *ex officio*, also president of IDA and IFC, and is appointed by the board of directors of the Bank. Hitherto the board has appointed a person nominated by the president of the United States. The normal period of appointment is for five years, but this can be extended: Eugene Black served for thirteen, and McNamara has had his appointment extended to ten. The president of the Bank Group is also chairman of the board of directors, and in that capacity submits for their consideration policy issues and proposals for loans, borrowings, and administrative budgets. The board can reject his recommendation that a loan be granted (though it has never done so), but it cannot itself propose a loan. The president is chief of the operating staff of the Bank Group and, subject to the general direction of the board of directors on questions of policy, is responsible for its organization, appointment, and dismissal.

The Bank Group has a large, well-paid staff—1,700 professional officers and 1,800 non-professional—and a highly centralized system of administration. Of the professional officers, almost 30 per cent receive more than $22,500 a year free of income tax. Ninety-five per cent of the professional officers work at the Bank Group's headquarters in Washington, which occupies an entire square block of buildings two blocks from the White House and less than a mile from the State Department. Their location symbolizes the dominant position the United States government has had in the Bank Group and still has, though to a steadily diminishing degree. Because the staff is large, well paid, and must do a great deal of traveling, the administrative expenses of the Bank Group are high—$100 million in 1972. In terms of the volume of operations, however, this may not be an unreasonable figure. It amounts to about 3⅓ per cent of the volume of lending that year, or a little over ½ of 1 per cent of the volume of loans outstanding that year ($18,000 million). Included in these expenses are expenditures on the staff, the governing bodies, consultants, travel, offices, and communications.

The Bank and IDA share the same staff, and certain departments of the Bank-IDA staff also serve IFC. At the top of the staff is a group of sixteen senior officers called the president's council or the management.

The operational work of the Bank and IDA is carried out by five regional offices located at the headquarters. One covers East Africa, one West Africa, and one Asia. The fourth covers Latin America and the Caribbean, and the fifth, Europe, the Middle East, and North Africa. Each has its own experts on projects in four sectors: agriculture, education, transportation, and public utilities. The regional offices other than those for Africa also have their own experts on development finance companies. There is a central projects staff, consisting of experts on all these five sectors plus four sectors where the total staff is not yet large enough to be split up among the regional offices: population, tourism, urbanization, and industry. This staff guides and assists the regional offices and tries to insure uniform policies in each one with respect to each sector. Both the regional office and the central projects staff employ a number of economists. In addition to a large central economics staff, there are financial, legal, and administrative departments and a department of information.

The principal task of the staff of the Bank Group is to help those of its developing member countries which wish to borrow from it to identify and prepare suitable projects for Bank Group loans. The amount of work required depends, in the main, on whether or not the borrowing country is experienced in dealing with the Bank Group and has sophisticated economic planners and administrators with whom the Bank Group has established relations of mutual confidence. It also depends on the nature of the project. If it is a loan for improving the railway system of a country where the Bank Group has already made loans for railways, relatively little work will be required for each million dollars lent. If, on the other hand, it is a loan for publicly financed small-scale rural development works, a great deal of work will be required, for the Bank Group has had no experience (up to the spring of 1973) of this kind.

When a project has been provisionally identified as of high priority and suitable for Bank Group financing, the Bank Group may, at the request of the UN Development Program, make a pre-investment or feasibility study of it; or, it may in other ways help the borrower advance the project to the point at which it is attractive enough to warrant full investigation by a Bank Group appraisal mission. The appraisal of a project usually embraces six aspects: economic, technical, organizational, managerial, operational, and financial. Members of the appraisal mission will attempt, in informal and formal discussions, to elicit from the local experts proposals for improvement in all six. They will, for example, call the attention of these experts to techniques likely to improve the design of the project and reduce its costs, as well as pass on information the Bank Group has acquired about lessons to be learned from the history of similar projects in other developing countries.

The mission submits its report to the Bank Group headquarters, and if the management and staff decide that the project is appropriate for financing, subject perhaps to certain modifications, formal negotiations take place in Washington between the borrower and the Bank Group. If these negotiations result in agreement, the president of the Bank Group submits a report on the project to the executive directors and recommends to them that a loan of a certain amount be granted for the project, subject to the conditions set forth in the proposed loan agreement. Approval by the directors is followed by the signature of the loan agreement.

The final stage in the course of the life cycle of a Bank Group project is supervision by the Bank Group staff during the period of construction and operation. The borrower is required to submit regular reports on the project to the Bank Group. Supervisory missions are sent out from Washington to examine the work which is being done, to scrutinize the accounts of the borrower, to examine the way in which the goods and equipment purchased out of the loan are used and maintained, and to satisfy themselves that the management and administration of the project are effective. The purpose of the supervision is to insure that the project is executed as planned or, if necessary, modified because of changed circumstances.

The Bank and IDA do not tie the expenditures financed by their loans to specified sources of supply. Borrowers are free to use the loans to make purchases in any member country of the Bank and in Switzerland. The borrowers are normally required to purchase through international competitive bidding, and this may result in important savings to the borrower. Thus the Bank has estimated that international competitive bidding on telecommunication equipment "has led to considerable reductions in costs—about 30% on average and much more in some cases."[2]

This complicated process is very time-consuming, both for the Bank Group and for the borrower. It usually takes from two to three years from the time a project is provisionally identified as probably of high priority and suitable for Bank Group financing until the project is approved by the executive directors. The politicians and administrators of a borrowing country who are drawn into a dialogue with the staff of the Bank Group on a project will often conclude that the Bank Group is unduly conservative, rigid, cautious, bureaucratic, and slow. There is always tension in Bank Group operations, stemming from the determination of the staff to insure that the money of the Bank Group will be well spent, and from the desire of the borrowers to get ahead with their development projects quickly with ttle interference from outsiders.

CHAPTER THREE

The Evolution of the Bank Group[1]

The International Bank for Reconstruction and Development was three years old when Eugene Black became president in July 1949. Its two affiliates, the International Development Association and the International Finance Corporation, had not yet been created. Its professional staff numbered only 140. In the first three years of its existence it had lent a total of only $650 million, almost all of this for the reconstruction of Western European countries, not for the development of its poorer member countries. For the first ten years or so of Black's presidency, the Bank had to move with very great caution to secure and maintain the confidence of Wall Street, since without that confidence it would not be able to raise funds in sufficient volume at reasonable rates. It had to overcome suspicions in United States financial circles of an international organization. It had to demonstrate that it was a hard-headed business operation which lent only to credit-worthy countries for projects which careful Bank investigation had shown were well conceived and well designed, which would be well constructed and well managed and yield a high rate of return. In its lending to middle-income and low-income countries, the Bank concentrated first on railways, roads, ports, telecommunications, and steel. Gradually, with increasing sophistication, the Bank came to realize that there was little use in insisting that its loans go only to high-quality, high-priority projects if the borrowing country was wasting the foreign exchange received from other sources or if it was failing to mobilize its own domestic resources for development and to use them sensibly, whether they were derived from taxes, savings, or the profits of publicly owned companies. The Bank's studies of the credit-worthiness of a borrower gradually became studies of the whole economy of the borrowing country, with particular reference to its economic, financial, and developmental policies, programs, and performance.

Black's task was to make "international development financing respectable."[2] He succeeded. By the end of the fifties, the Bank was lending at a rate of $700 million a year, almost all of this to its developing member countries. It had firmly established its credit rating on Wall Street. It was strong enough to run the risk of creating in 1960 a soft loan affiliate, the International Development Association, to enable it to provide interest-free loans to its poorest and neediest members, many of whom had exhausted or were close to exhausting whatever credit-worthiness for World Bank loans they had once possessed.

Until IDA was founded, the Bank did not have to beg for money from governments, as most international institutions have to. Before it could sell a bond issue in a country, it had to get permission from the government, but this did not imply the degree of dependence on governments which results from the need to get grants from them. The Bank had been endowed by governments, and in consequence was relatively independent of governments. This is the great advantage of endowments: they foster autonomy and independence. But, when IDA was founded, the Bank Group had to join the long line of agencies and institutions soliciting national governments for grants. This has made the Bank Group dependent, as it had not been before, on the good will of the governments which are the major contributors to IDA, especially the six largest contributors, who are responsible for four-fifths of IDA's resources—the United States, Britain, Germany, France, Canada, and Japan.

At the beginning of the sixties, the Bank was permeated by a United States atmosphere and flavor, and its thinking was dominated by United States predelictions and prejudices. During the sixties, this atmosphere became progressively diluted, though it was still strong at the beginning of the seventies. During the sixties, United States predelictions and prejudices about economic and social development in low-income countries changed. The predelictions and prejudices of the World Bank Group changed even more.

The World Bank's image of itself in the early sixties as a conservative, project-lending investment bank was reflected in the specialized vocabulary of private investment banking, which senior members of the staff constantly employed at the weekly meetings of department heads. When they were recommending loans to relatively high-income countries, they were "sweetening the Bank's portfolio." They talked of "rolling paper over." George Woods had great difficulty in 1963 and 1964 in persuading some of the senior officers of the Bank that there was not something improper or even indecent in his proposals that the Bank should charge a higher rate of interest to its more credit-worthy customers than to its less credit-worthy, and that it should help its poorer customers to draw up projects which it would then consider for financing.

The Bank in the early sixties was project-minded, paying little attention to the importance of combining economic growth with greater social justice. The majority opinion in the Bank was that the task of the Bank was confined to deciding whether a project submitted to it by a potential borrower was first-rate in terms of a cost-benefit economic analysis, or could be made first-rate in terms of such an analysis. Some consideration was given to whether the project was a first-rate project within a first-rate program for the development of the sector of the economy in which it was located, less to whether it was a first-rate project within a sensible program for the social as well as the economic development of the country as a whole. Increasing attention was given to the need for economic planning in developing countries, but social considerations were decidedly secondary.

The Bank in the early sixties kept its distance from other UN specialized agencies, from UN organs such as the Economic and Social Council, and from UN development programs. The Bank and the International Monetary Fund occupied the same building in Washington, but they kept each other at arm's length. The Bank's opinion of FAO and Unesco was so low that when in the early sixties it decided to increase its lending for agriculture and education, it might well have established within its structure its own FAO and its own Unesco had George Woods not insisted that it should experiment with setting up cooperative programs with FAO and Unesco under formal agreements between the Bank and these two institutions.

In 1961 and 1962, the last two full years of Black's presidency and the first two years of IDA's operations, average annual lending by the Bank was $746 million, by IDA $118 million, and by IFC $14 million, a total of $877 million. During the last three years of George Woods' presidency (1966, 1967, and 1968), average annual lending went up to $821 million, $248 million, and $45 million, a total of $1,114 million. This was not a very substantial increase. It amounted to less than 20 per cent in real terms. The change in the Bank Group during Woods' presidency was not in the volume but in the nature of its operations. Under his presidency the Bank Group laid increased emphasis on the importance of the objective his successor, Robert McNamara, defined in 1969 as a search, not "for good investments in sick economies," but for ways "to understand what makes economies sick in the first place and to take those remedial steps that will encourage recuperation and health." "We want," said McNamara, in language Woods would have approved, "to seek out those projects, those procedures, those policies that will assist economies as a whole to get into the mainstream of self-generating growth and progress."[3]

There were further changes under Wood's presidency. The Bank Group increased greatly the proportion of its lending to agriculture and education. It embarked on program-lending to India and Pakistan. It financed more local costs and it gave a higher preference to local suppliers in low-income countries. It made the terms of Bank lending more flexible by extending grace periods and maturities. It gave more help to its very poor member countries in preparing projects for its consideration. It broke away from the confinements of an ideological hostility to public ownership of national development banks and of manufacturing industry. It became more and more forthright about the importance of reducing the rate of population growth in low-income countries, and of scientific research on the problems of low-income countries, including research on contraception. It established more aid coordination groups. It progressively improved its relations with the UN Development Program and with those UN specialized agencies which were changing the emphasis of their activities from conferences and research to development. The Bank Group became more aware of its responsibilities to do its best to assist in coordinating the development activities of national aid agencies and of international institutions. Woods took over an agency which was still pretty much a conservative project-lending investment bank, which kept itself aloof from all the other international agencies concerned with the economic and social development of low-income countries, which considered itself superior to all these agencies except its Bretton Woods twin, the International Monetary Fund (IMF), and which also treated some of the other agencies rather contemptuously. Five years later the Bank Group was well on its way to becoming an international development agency concerned with both the social and the economic development of the poorer two-thirds of mankind, an agency no longer isolationist but regarding itself as a member of a community or galaxy of UN aid agencies.[4]

By the time McNamara had reached the mid-point of his ten-year term of office, it seemed likely that by the end of his term he would have trebled the volume of lending (in real terms) of the World Bank Group and that he would thus have achieved his quantitative objective for Bank Group lending. It was not clear how successful he was going to be in realizing his other main objective, which might be called qualitative, to change fundamentally the emphasis, the nature, and the direction of Bank Group lending, so that it would give developing countries the greatest possible help in their efforts to reconcile the pursuit of growth in the production of essential goods and services with more employment and more social justice.

The task Eugene Black set himself was to make international lending for development respectable. The task Robert McNamara has set himself is to make international lending to help the poorest two-fifths or so of the peoples of the developing countries respectable.

There is one aspect of the future development of the Bank Group on which McNamara has so far said little in public. This is the belief recently expressed by a number of developing countries, especially by India, that the Bank Group will not be able to do for development what it could and should do unless there is some shift of power and responsibility in the management of the Bank Group from the rich to the poorer countries. In a speech in December 1971, the finance minister of India said:

There is a feeling among millions of people in the developing world that the kind of partnership we have so far secured through our international economic institutions is a grossly unequal one. . . . The international institutions we created in the wake of the Second World War, such as the World Bank and the International Monetary Fund, reflected a philosophy which appears totally out of date today to most countries which had very little say in the shaping of those institutions. The developing world today was the colonial world then and had little say in deciding how our international economic institutions should function. The big powers who won the war but not without the suffering and sacrifices of the people of the then colonial world reserved for themselves a predominant position in the governing bodies of the international institutions. Even those institutions which came into being at a later date and on a regional scale are run by and large on the principle that those who pay the piper must be allowed to call the tune. I am not one of those romantics who feel that power whether economic, political, or military will not speak in some way or the other no matter what the form of organisations we seek to create. But the time has come when we can no longer take for granted the present distribution of power and responsibility in the management of our international institutions. If there is to be a genuine World Partnership, it has to be reflected first and foremost in a greater willingness to share in the process of making decisions regarding how this partnership is to be actually brought about in practice.[5]

Maynard Keynes firmly believed that the twin institutions of the World Bank and the International Monetary Fund had both been misnamed. "I shall always," he said at the inaugural meeting of the two institutions, "hold to the view that the christening [of the twins] has been badly done and that the names of the twins should be reversed."[6] The Bank should, in his opinion, have been called an international fund for reconstruction and development; the Fund, an international bank. Keynes was surely right. The principal disadvantage in calling it a bank has been that this encouraged those in charge of its lending program in its early years to apply criteria for its loans appropriate to private investment banking, thus retarding the metamorphosis of the Bank from a conservative investment bank into a development assistance agency. The principal advantage in calling it a bank was that this made it easier for it to establish its credit rating on Wall Street in its early years. Perhaps if it had not been called a bank, its articles of agreement would not have provided that "each member shall deal with the Bank only through its Treasury, central bank, stabilization fund or other similar fiscal agency, and the Bank shall deal with members only by or through the same agencies,"[7] but would have given each member government freedom to designate whatever channel of communication between it and the Bank it considered appropriate and to change the channel from time to time in accordance with changing conditions. Donor governments might have begun by designating their departments of finance or central banks as their channel of communication; but later, as they established their own national aid agencies, have designated these agencies as the channel. The designation of departments of finance or of central banks as channels of communication resulted until about 1970 in the executive directors of the Bank reflecting the views of those departments, rather than the views of those in the national government charged with responsibility for national policy on international development. Departments of finance and central banks tend to be more conservative on development policies than national aid agencies.

The result was that for twenty years or so after Black became president, the initiative for most of the changes which took place in the Bank came not from the executive directors representing donor countries but from the three presidents of the Bank, from modernizing members of the staff of the Bank Group, from the principal aid-receiving countries, such as India, and from the representatives of donor governments not to the Bank but to such bodies as the Development Assistance Committee (DAC) of the Organization for Economic Cooperation and Development (OECD) and Bank consortia and consultative groups. In Washington, the United States Agency for International Development (USAID) exerted a constructive influence on Bank policy, but, for the most part, it did not exert this influence through the United States executive director of the Bank.

From 1949 to about 1970, a few executive directors supported with great enthusiasm most of the changes made in the policy of the Bank Group, particularly the expansion of IDA and the emphasis on population control and agricultural research; most executive directors, however, acquiesced in most of the changes, rather than pressed for them. Some governments and executive directors actively resisted such changes as program lending, local cost financing, increases in preference for procurement in low-income countries, and extension of assistance by the Bank Group to research into agricultural, population, and other problems of low-income countries. As guardians of the covenant under which the Bank was founded, the executive directors exercised in general up to about 1970 a conservative influence in stopping the Bank Group from going beyond what they considered to be the limits established by the covenant. Until about 1970 they did very little to alter the Bank Group in any positive way. From about 1970 on, executive directors representing donor countries have been reflecting much more the views of their national aid agencies, and they have been playing an increasingly liberal and positive role.

The history of the past twenty-five years indicates that the World Bank Group is a vigorous organism capable of healthy growth and of adaptation to change.

CHAPTER FOUR

The Incidence of World Poverty

The principal international agencies concerned with problems of world poverty have not been able to reach agreement on the meaning of many of the terms they use to describe countries such as "less-developed (or underdeveloped or developing)"; "poor"; "rich"; "low-income"; "developed"; "industrialized." The result is that the statistics prepared by these agencies are not comparable. There has been no agreement on how to divide the category of developing countries into distinct subcategories, such as least developed (Chad, Dahomey, Upper Volta), more developed (Iran, Iraq), and most developed (Argentina, Singapore), as suggested by the UN Committee for Development Planning.[1]

An analysis of the lending by the Bank and IDA demonstrates the importance of such a division. To say that the Bank and IDA in the four years ending in mid-1972 lent their developing member countries an average of $1.28 a year for every one of their inhabitants hides the fact that the very poor countries received only 72 cents a head while the other developing countries, the better-off ones, received three times that amount ($2.10).[2] Knowledge of this skewed distribution provides a clue to understanding many of the Bank Group's problems. Yet, the tables in the Group's annual reports show distribution of loans by geographical region, not by categories of relative poverty.

Just as the figure $1.28 hides about as much as it reveals, so too does the statement that in the 1960's gross national product in the developing countries (non-members of the Group, as well as members) rose by 5¼ per cent a year. In the very poor countries (which have a total population of 2 billion) the growth rate was only 4 per cent a year. In the better-off countries (which have a total population of 850 million) it was 6.3 per cent. The difference between a 4 per cent and a 6.3 per cent growth rate is the difference between doubling the gross national product in eighteen years and doubling it in twelve years.

(Things, however, are now moving in the right direction. Thus the UN Committee on Development Planning has not only suggested that the countries of the world be divided into developed, intermediate, the more developed of the developing and the least developed of the developing, but it has also drawn up a list of the least developed of the developing and this list has been approved by the General Assembly of the UN.[3] The Committee has not yet, however, been able to reach agreement on what countries belong to each of the other three categories.)

The following are examples of conflicting criteria now used by the main international agencies: the United Nations and its various organs, especially the UN Conference on Trade and Development (UNCTAD); the Development Assistance Committee (DAC) of the Organization for Economic Cooperation and Development; and the World Bank. Table 2 pages 227 to 236 lists the countries of the world in descending order of gross national product per capita in 1970. On this scale Kuwait's GNP per capita is over four times the average for the whole world. Moreover, Kuwait is an exporter of capital on a large scale. Yet the UN, UNCTAD, and DAC consider it a developing country. Again, according to UNCTAD, Argentina, Hong Kong, and Singapore are developing countries, Turkey is not, and yet their GNP's per capita on the World Bank scale are more than three times that of Turkey. To cite a third example, DAC lists Cyprus, Greece, and Spain as developing countries and not Portugal, yet their GNP's per capita are nearly 50 per cent higher than Portugal's.

Since the principal international agencies concerned have reached agreement on only one category, the least developed, and since the definitions used by each contain inconsistencies and anomalies, for purposes of clarification, I have divided the countries of the world into four groups based on the World Bank's estimate of GNP per capita in 1970: rich countries, middle-income countries, poor countries, and very poor countries.[4] "Developing" countries are defined as meaning the middle-income countries, the poor countries, and the very poor countries; these are the three worlds of development.

In using estimates of GNP per capita it is important to keep constantly in mind the limitations of these estimates. Estimates of population in about two-thirds of the world, for instance, have a margin of error of plus or minus about 5 per cent, so that when the *World Bank Atlas* states that Indonesia's population in 1970 was 116 million, one should read somewhere between 110 million and 122 million. Estimates of GNP expressed in local currency lump together the production of luxuries for th rich and the production of essential goods and services for the mass of the population. They measure the production *only* of goods and services, not of social justice, violence, social mobility, infant mortality, the sense of belonging to a community, the possibility of dignity and serenity. Estimates of GNP per capita conceal the profound differences which exist in virtually every country between the rich and the poor and between the better-off regions of the country and the poorer regions. To these limitations must be added the distortions which result from converting local currency into a common unit, the U.S. dollar, in order to get a basis for international comparison. The method used in making this conversion tends to exaggerate the real differences of income between the richer countries and the poorer countries.

Thus, a table listing countries in order of their GNP per capita does not measure accurately degrees of wealth or poverty, and it measures even less accurately degrees of development or underdevelopment. Nevertheless, as the chairman of the Development Assistance Committee of OECD said in his annual report for 1970, "Per capita GNP has been adopted as a shorthand device for expressing a country's relative poverty. Despite its crudeness, this is probably the most important single indicator of a country's strength."[5] This conclusion is borne out by Table 2, which lists the countries of the world in descending order of their GNP per capita; the order in which countries are listed coincides generally with commonsense conclusions about their comparative economic strength. And, in our efforts to make a sensible division of the countries of the world into four categories—rich, middle-income, poor, and very poor—it is the order of countries in such a table that we are concerned with.

The problem of precisely where to draw the boundary lines between these categories is not susceptible of any entirely satisfactory solution. All we can hope to find is the least unsatisfactory of many unsatisfactory formulas.*

There would be a manifest advantage if the formulas used accorded with popular usage. A common statement about problems of economic development is that two-thirds of the world is poor. Another common statement refers to the poor half of mankind. The definitions of the categories of poor and very poor countries used in this book are based on this common usage. The very poor countries are those at the bottom of a scale listing countries in descending order of GNP per capita whose populations add up to about half the population of the world. The low-income countries (sometimes here referred to as the poorer countries), consisting of poor and very poor countries, have populations adding up to about two-thirds of the population of the world. The very poor countries had GNP's per capita in 1970 of less than $160, the poor countries, $160 to $430.

There is no generally accepted definition of rich countries in common usage. Robert McNamara stated in 1972 that the "wealthy nations of the world" possess 25 per cent of its people.[6] Rich countries as defined in this book are those at the top of a scale listing countries in descending order of GNP per capita whose populations add up to a quarter of the population of the world. This has the advantage of

*Annex Four, pages 248 to 249, is a supplementary note on the incidence of world poverty. It discusses the problem of where to draw the boundary lines between the four categories and the principal differences between the categories used in this book and those used by international agencies.

bringing the Soviet Union within this category, which accords with common sense. About a twelfth of the population of the world, then, is within the remaining category, middle-income countries. The rich countries had GNP's per capita in 1970 of $1,600 to $4,760, the middle-income countries, $440 to $1,400.

In using the terms rich, middle-income, poor, and very poor countries, it is essential to keep in mind the distinction between the very poor countries and the poorer half of mankind, the rich countries and the richest quarter of mankind, and so on. The very poor countries whose populations add up to about half the population of the world do not contain the poorer half of mankind. Some of the poorer half of mankind live in poor countries or even in middle-income countries. Almost all the poor in rich countries would be considered moderately well off in very poor countries. The wealthiest 10 per cent of the people of a very poor country, like India, include families with incomes a head of only $360 a year. The average income of everyone in poor countries is only $300 a year. The problem of extreme poverty in the world is the problem of the very poor countries and of the very poor people within other countries, just as the problem of poverty within a country like the United States is the problem of poor regions and of the poor within other regions. And just as within the United States poverty programs have to deal both with poor regions and with the poor in other regions, so within the international community, poverty programs have to deal both with low-income countries and with the poor within other countries.

The following two tables summarize the results of applying the above definitions to the estimates in the 1972 World Bank Atlas of

POPULATION

Countries	*Members of World Bank* (million)	*Non-Members of World Bank* (million)	*Total* (million)	*Total* (per cent)	*Annual Growth rate* (per cent)
Rich	629	291	920	25.0	1.1
Middle-income	256	53	309	8.4	2.0
Poor	502	14	516	14.0	2.8
Very poor					
India	538		538		
Other Bank members	538		538		
China		836	836		
N. Vietnam		21	21		
Total	1,076	857	1,933	52.6	2.2
Total	2,463	1,215	3,678	100.0	2.0

population and GNP's for all countries. The estimates of population are for mid-1970, those of GNP for 1970, and growth rates for 1960-70.*

GROSS NATIONAL PRODUCT [7]

Countries	*Members of World Bank* ($ billion)	*Non-Members of World Bank* ($ billion)	*Total* ($ billion)	*Total* *Annual Growth rate* (per cent)
Rich	2,019	547	2,567	5.5
Middle-income	209	59	268	6.5
Poor	150	5	155	6.0
Very poor	108	124	232	4.0
Total	2,486	735	3,222	6.1

Because these estimates of GNP exaggerate the real differences between the rich countries and the poorer countries, we might arbitrarily reduce the estimates of the GNP of rich countries by 40 per cent and increase the estimates of the poor countries by 20 per cent and of the very poor countries by 40 per cent. This would mean reducing the average per capita GNP of rich countries from $2,790 to $1,675, increasing the figure for poor countries from $300 to $360, and of very poor countries from $120 to $170. The estimate for middle-income countries would remain unchanged at $870. The result is:

Countries	*Adjusted GNP* ($ billion)	*Adjusted GNP* (per cent)	*Population* (per cent)
Rich	1,540	66	25
Middle-income	268	12	8
Poor	186	8	14
Very poor	325	14	53
Total	2,319	100	100

*For the purpose of these tables, Taiwan is considered to be a member of the Bank and mainland China a non-member, though in fact it is "China" which is a member. Romania, which became a member in 1970, is included as a member. In Tables 2 and 3, pages 227 to 237, it is listed among the non-members. Romania had in 1970 a population of 20 million and a GNP of $18,850 million.

Even when the crude figures of GNP are adjusted in this way, the figures indicate that the richest quarter of the world consumes two-thirds of the goods and services produced every year in the world and that the poorest two-thirds of the world consumes less than one-quarter (22 per cent).

The incidence of poverty in the world

Seven out of ten of the people of the developing countries live in the very poor countries, countries with a GNP per capita of not more than $150. In general, the poorer a country, the more intractable are its problems of development. Therefore, well over seven-tenths of the problems of development relate to the very poor countries. And nine-tenths of the peoples of the very poor countries live in one region of the world, the mainland of Asia south of the Soviet Union and east of Iran plus neighboring Indonesia. This region is an almost unbroken mass of deep poverty. Out of its total population of over 1,800 million,* only 115 million live in countries which are not very poor (Mongolia, the two Koreas, Malaysia, Singapore, South Vietnam, and Thailand). The other almost solid block of deep poverty is in that part of black Africa which lies north of Angola, Zambia, and Mozambique and south of the Arab states. There are 220 million people in this region and all but 30 million of them live in very poor countries. (Those which are not very poor are Cameroon, Ghana, the Ivory Coast, Liberia, Sierra Leone, and Senegal.) Apart from these two blocks, there are only four countries in the world which are very poor—the Sudan, the two Yemens, and Haiti—and they have a total population of only 30 million. The problem of deep poverty in the world is the problem of China, south and southeast Asia, Indonesia, and black Africa. On a world scale of poverty, there is virtually no deep poverty in the Americas, Europe, or Oceania.

Six countries alone contain 90 per cent of the people of the very poor countries. They are, in order of population: China, India, Indonesia, Bangladesh, Pakistan, and Nigeria. The core of the problem of deep poverty in the world is the deep poverty of these six very populous, very poor countries.

Almost nine out of ten of the people of the developing countries live in low-income countries—the very poor countries plus the poor countries. Nine out of ten of the people of the low-income countries live in Asia, Indonesia, and Africa. The Americas, even when the United States and Canada are excluded, are much less poor than Asia (excluding Japan and the U.S.S.R.) and Africa. This is demonstrated by the following table:

*To avoid a misleading impression of accuracy, population figures are rounded off to the nearest five million. Countries are mentioned by name only if they have populations of a million or more.

POPULATION

	Total (million)	*Rich and middle-income countries* (million)	*Low-income countries* (million)	*Percentage in low-income countries*
Asia (excluding the U.S.S.R. and Japan)	1,842	23	1,819	99
Africa	349	25	324	93
Americas (excluding the U.S.A. and Canada)	281	129	152	54

There is clearly a close relationship between heat and poverty. In general, the closer a country is to the equator, the poorer it is likely to be. Rabindranath Tagore's description of India's climatic handicaps applies to much of the poorer two-thirds of the world: "We live under the tyranny of the tropics, paying heavy toll every moment for the barest right of existence. The heat, the damp, the unspeakable fecundity of minute life feeding upon big life, the perpetual sources of irritation, visible and invisible, leave little margin of capital for extravagant experiments."

* * *

Of the 920 million people who live in rich countries, 508 million live in the United States, Canada, and Western Europe, 285 million in the Soviet Union, Czechoslovakia, East Germany, and Hungary, and 105 million in Japan.* More than six out of seven of the people who live in rich countries live in white countries in the northern hemisphere. The only rich countries with populations of a million or more which are not in the northern hemisphere are Australia and New Zealand. The only rich country which is colored is Japan. The only rich white country with a large colored population is the United States. Thus, probably about 775 million of the inhabitants of the rich northern hemishere countries are white. Of these, perhaps 75 million do not belong to the richest quarter of mankind. This leaves us with about 700 million rich whites living in rich white northern hemisphere countries, less than one-fifth of the population of the world.

There are 2,450 million people in the poor and the very poor countries. Virtually all of them live to the south of these 700 million rich northern whites. Possibly about 2,250 million are colored. Perhaps 150 million of these do not belong to the poorer two-thirds of mankind. This leaves us with about 2,100 million poor colored people living in low-income southern countries, almost 60 per cent of the population of the world, and three times the number of the rich northern whites.

The 700 million rich whites in rich white northern countries are separated from the 2,100 million poor colored people in low-income southern countries not just by color and poverty and geography and by the things that usually go with national poverty—hunger, illiteracy, ignorance, disease, social inequality; but also by culture, tradition, religion, ways of life. The rich whites derive their culture from Palestine, Greece, and Rome; relatively few of the colored poor do. The rich whites are increasingly non-religious; the religious minority of the rich are Christian. A high proportion of the colored poor are religious and their main religions are Hinduism, Buddhism, Islam, and Animism. Only one in ten of the rich whites are farmers or agricultural laborers, whereas two out of three of the colored poor are. Very few of the rich whites work under the tyranny of the tropics; the majority of the colored poor do, and the pitiless tropical sun induces lassitude even in healthy people, much more so in people who are ill-fed and weakened by many endemic diseases. The greatest gulf which divides mankind is not between east and west or between communism and capitalism; it is between the rich northern whites and the colored southern poor.[8]

*The remaining 22 million live in Australia, New Zealand, Israel, Libya, and Kuwait.

CHAPTER FOUR

RICH COUNTRIES

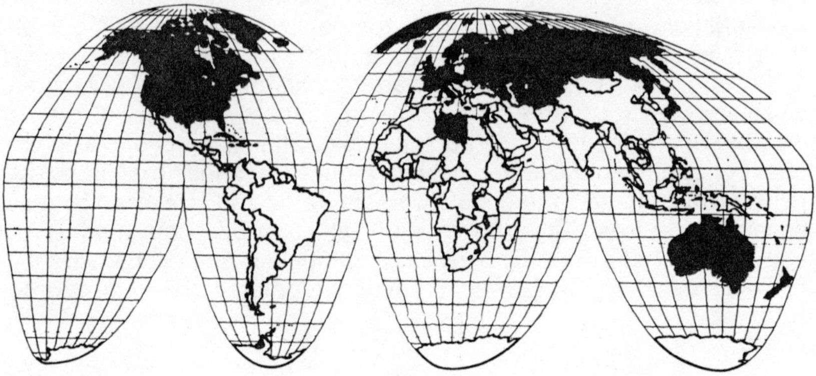

MIDDLE-INCOME COUNTRIES

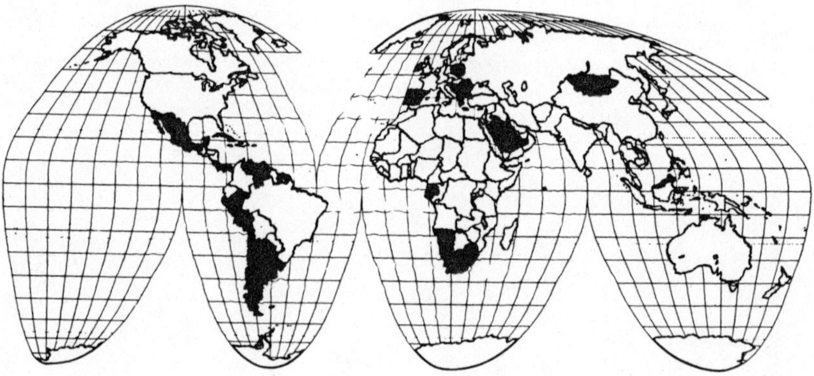

THE INCIDENCE OF WORLD POVERTY

POOR COUNTRIES

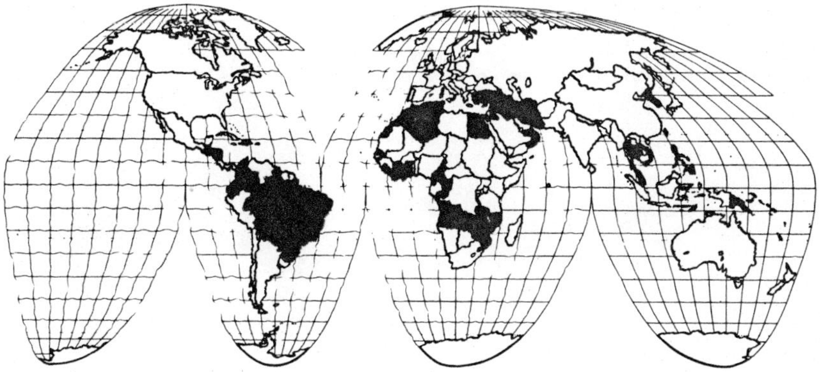

VERY POOR COUNTRIES

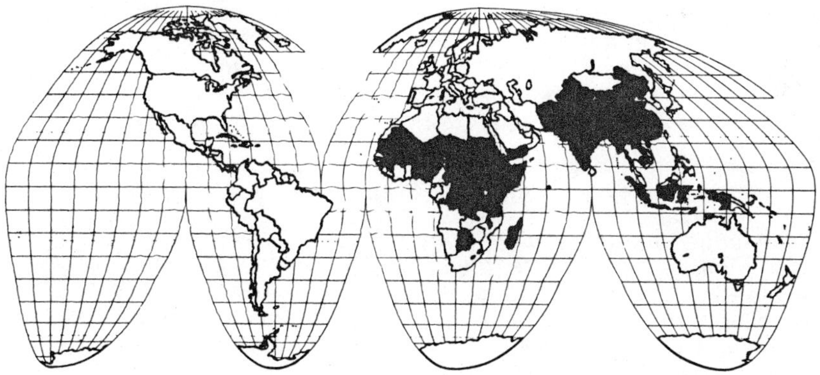

CHAPTER FIVE

Robert McNamara's Qualitative Goals

Robert McNamara had been in office for only six months when he announced to the board of governors of the Bank Group in the autumn of 1968 his quantitative goal for Bank Group lending during his first five years of office. This goal was that during those five years the Bank Group should lend twice as much as during the preceding five years; this, he said, would mean lending as much as in the preceding twenty-two years of the Bank Group's existence.[1] At the next meeting of the board, one year later, he began to outline in public his beliefs about what the qualitative goals of the Bank Group should be. He said:

> [W]*hat we need—and what we must fashion—is a more effective over-all development strategy. . . . Progress in the solution of the problems of* [population planning, educational advance, and agricultural growth] *is fundamental to such a strategy. But . . . no such strategy will be complete unless it provides for an attack on the interrelated problems of unemployment, urbanization, and industrialization.*[2]

Since then he has in a series of public speeches been elaborating his ideas. Thus he has emphasized his belief that:

> *In the longer run, the most important issue is population planning. Its goal must be to stabilize the planet's population several decades earlier—and several billions lower—than would otherwise occur. Since reducing birth rates to replacement levels will necessarily require decades, we must reshape development programs now in order to take account of what is certain to be a continuing rapid growth of population to levels heretofore considered unlikely* [a minimum of 11 to 16 billion people compared with 4 billion in 1974].[3]

In his opinion, the continuing rapid growth of population, which is concentrated in the developing countries, will lead to even greater unemployment in those countries than the present level of 20 to 25 per cent unless certain measures are taken. The provision of an increased number of productive jobs at proper pay is essential, not only to reduce these tragic and dangerous levels of unemployment, but also to insure a more equitable distribution of income in low-income countries, since in these countries employment is the most efficacious way of securing a more equitable distribution of income.

[E]conomic growth is a necessary condition of development in any poor country—but it is far from being a sufficient condition. . . . [E]conomic growth in a poor country, in its early stages, is likely to penalize the poorer segment of the society relative to the more affluent sectors unless specific action is taken to prevent such an effect. . . . [T]here must be more equitable and comprehensive tax measures; land reform laws; tenancy security policies; and, above all, concrete programs to increase the productivity of small farmers. . . . What are required are feasible fiscal, agrarian, and educational reform measures that can be fully and fairly enforced. What is needed most of all is a determination to move against the inequities of income distribution. . . . [Unless developing countries] relate the goals of national growth to realistic targets of more equitable income distribution . . . no amount of external assistance, whether in the form of aid or trade, will do much to improve the welfare of the lower 40% of their populations which are living in conditions of the most abject poverty.[4]

The low-income countries must adopt development programs which would include: "rural and urban public works; the building of market roads; construction of low-cost simple housing; reforestation programs; expansion of irrigation and drainage facilities; and similar low-skill, labor-intensive, and economically useful projects"; the creation of effective institutions to help small farmers; the use of labor-intensive methods of construction in the countryside; and the development of more labor-intensive technologies in manufacturing industry. But more than this is required:

[I]nstitutional reforms to redistribute economic power are critically required in many developing countries: land reform, corporate reform, tax reform, credit and banking reform, and many others.. . .[S]hifts in the patterns of public expenditure represent one of the most effective techniques a government possesses to improve the conditions of the poor. Too often these expenditures—on health, on transport, on water supply, on education—end by benefiting the already privileged far more than the mass of the disadvantaged.[5]

The task, then, for the governments of the developing countries is to reorient their development policies in order to attack directly the personal poverty of the most deprived 40% of their populations. This the governments can do without abandoning their goals of vigorous over-all economic growth. But they must be prepared to give greater priority to establishing growth targets in terms of essential human needs: in terms of nutrition, housing, health, literacy, and employment—even if it be at the cost of some reduction in the pace of advance in certain narrow and highly privileged sectors whose benefits accrue to the few.[6]

One of McNamara's principal advisers on development policy is Mahbub ul Haq. In a speech in 1971, Mahbub ul Haq dotted the *i's* and crossed the *t's* of what McNamara had been saying:

In Pakistan, which experienced a healthy growth rate during the 1960's, unemployment increased, real wages in the industrial sector declined by one-third, per capita income disparity between East and West Pakistan nearly doubled, and concentrations of industrial wealth became an explosive economic and political issue. And in 1968, while the international world was still applauding Pakistan as a model of development the system exploded—not only for political reasons but for economic unrest. Brazil has recently achieved a growth rate close to 7% but continuing maldistribution of income continues to threaten the very fabric of its society.[7]

It was no doubt this kind of judgment which led McNamara in his speech to the annual meeting of the Bank in 1972 to say: "When the highly privileged are few and the desperately poor are many—and when the gap between them is worsening rather than improving—it is only a question of time before a decisive choice must be made between the political costs of reform and the political risks of rebellion."[8]

These are eloquent statements by McNamara of what the qualitative goals of development should be, as contrasted with the quantitative goal of rapid increase in the GNP. They have been accompanied by similar statements on the qualitative goals of Bank Group operations:

[I]f the developing countries do adopt policies to insure that the benefits of growth will be more equitably distributed among their own peoples, then these countries both need and deserve the assistance necessary to insure that a reasonable rate of over-all growth can be achieved.[9] . . . *The Bank Group's role in all this is clear. Our mandate is to assist. That assistance must be both in the form of the policy advice leading to sound social and economic development programs . . . and an augmented capacity to provide financial support for those programs.*[10]

McNamara has not, of course, been alone in emphasizing the qualitative aspects of development. Thus, David Hopper, president of the International Development Research Centre, in his opening statement to the inaugural meeting of the board of governors in Ottawa on October 26, 1970, said:

The justifications for emphasizing allocation measures in the search for development priority have roots deep in the traditions of economic science, but there is about them an air of peculiar neglect of the genuineness of human vitality and the urgent authenticity of human poverty. The indignation provoked by this neglect demands now that allocative efficiencies be sought within a framework of distributive justice; that the quest for the levers of growth be tempered by an equally assiduous search for the fulcra of welfare; and that progress be measured as the means of satisfying real human need, not as an end product of an heroic accounting exercise. While the obligation for resolving successfully these often contradictory demands rests with foremost weight on those who lead each nation, the substance and the conditions from which they spring cannot be disregarded by any who aspire to be instrumental in giving added vigor to the accomplishments of development.[11]

In 1970, Dudley Seers headed a mission organized by the International Labour Organization (ILO) on the problem of obtaining full employment in Colombia. In his report, he said:

The first need is that there should be an official commitment to the goal of full employment, a commitment clear and firm enough to convince both the public service and the private sector that henceforward a concern for the employment implications will permeate every policy. . . . The commitment should be made in the full knowledge that it implies a change in the direction of development, broadly towards more concern with the social implications, and less with economic growth for its own sake. Like any major shift, it requires uncomfortable rethinking of many economic and social issues. It means completely changing people's attitudes to agriculture, to manual work, to modernisation. It means inducing all decision-makers, by regulation or incentives, to think very hard before they bring in labour-saving machinery. It cannot but hurt some people, and therefore requires overcoming opposition that may, on some points, be stubborn. [12]

In 1971 the discussion at the annual conference of the Society for International Development was on jobs and justice as the development targets for the seventies.[13]

These are indications of the widespread support which now exists for the thesis about the qualitative goals of development and of Bank Group operations which McNamara has been advocating. The central problem now confronting McNamara is how the Bank Group can best help the governments of its middle-income and low-income borrowers to work out and finance policies, projects, and programs which will lead to these goals. What are the operational implications for the Bank Group of the pledge which McNamara has given to help those countries which are determined to advance to these goals?

Gradually since 1969 the nature of the operations of the Bank Group has been changing. During the first two years the change was slight. In the summer of 1971 one officer of the Bank Group wrote to me in a private letter:

The Bank has an image of an institution predominantly concerned with financing capital goods. Changing this image may, in practice, be much harder than it sounds. Thus far most of the Bank's official pronouncements emphasizing such aspects as employment, income distribution and nutrition have been more in the nature of general exhortations and have often been only loosely related to operational reality.

Since then change has become more rapid. The proportion of those on the staff who are experts on health, population control, the environment, labor intensive technologies, and programs designed to help the rural poor is increasing. The Bank Group is giving its developing member countries more help in their efforts to reduce their birth rates and to reconcile economic growth with the protection of their environment. The importance of the new qualitative goals is being reflected in the country program papers, which set forth the proposed lending program to a particular country over the next five years, in the reports of the periodic country economic missions and sector missions, in the nature of the projects and programs submitted to the Bank Group for its consideration, in the nature of the appraisals of projects and programs, and even more gradually in the nature of the loans submitted to the executive directors for their approval. The Bank Group is giving more support to research on technological adaptation and innovation. Recent agricultural projects benefit greater numbers of farmers and at a much lower capital cost per farmer than the capital-intensive irrigation schemes on which the Bank Group used to concentrate. Loans for labor-intensive small-scale industry have increased. Local cost financing, the key to large Bank Group involvement in development schemes to help the rural poor, has greatly increased. By doubling the volume of lending, McNamara has probably doubled the potential influence of the Bank Group on the development policies of its borrowers. These are triumphs for McNamara.

But, during the last fiscal year of the World Bank Group for which statistics are available, the year ending in mid-1972, the World Bank lent Brazil $437 million. It lent Mexico, Iran, and Turkey a total of $539 million. The loans to these four countries constituted one half of the total lending by the Bank that year. These countries are not noted for their devotion to McNamara's new gospel of development. The explanation of this gap between precept and practice is that it takes from two to three years for the Bank Group to process a loan, so that, a change in lending policy is not likely to take effect for this period. If this explanation were the whole story, the change which McNamara began to press for at the beginning of the fiscal year 1970 should have a marked effect on lending in the fiscal years 1973, 1974, and 1975. At present, however, it seems unlikely that much of the nine to ten billion dollars which McNamara expects the Bank Group to lend in these three years will do much to reduce the number of unemployed in the developing countries or to increase the share of the national income going to the poorest two-fifths of the people.

If one were to ask the officers of the Bank Group who are directly engaged in the process of making loans to explain this, most of them would reply that it is McNamara's insistence that the volume of lending by the Bank Group be maintained at its present level, or even be increased. Perhaps McNamara does not insist on this; but this is what they believe. These officers contend that there would be a much faster advance toward the qualitative goals of Bank Group lending if McNamara were to tell them that he considers these goals to be so important that he is prepared to accept at least a temporary reduction in the volume of lending by the World Bank itself, if this is needed to speed an advance toward the qualitative goals.

The connection between volume and quality is important for two reasons. The first is that the Bank Group's ability to persuade the governments of borrowing countries to adopt new policies will be greater if the Bank Group uses its loans as carrots and sticks. The Bank Group must be able to make clear to these governments that if they adopt policies leading to more production, more jobs, and a more equitable distribution of income, and propose to the Bank Group the kinds of projects which will help them to implement these policies, they will receive a large volume of loans; if not, they will receive little. Thus, a country which had been borrowing $200 million a year from the Bank Group might be told that lending to it could go up to $300 million a year, or drop to $50 million. This attempt to use leverage could be successful only if the Bank Group was, in fact, prepared to reduce drastically its lending to countries which had not accepted the new qualitative goals of development.

The second reason is that projects designed to yield high returns (in terms not only of production but also of jobs and a better distribution of national income) require a much greater investment of time by the professional staff of the Bank Group for each million dollars lent than do large loans for railways, ports, highways, power, telecommunications, steel plants, and so on, which in the past have made up the great bulk of Bank Group lending. If the professional staff of the Bank Group is under pressure to maintain or increase the present volume of lending, it will be reluctant to assume the heavy burden of helping the borrowing countries to identify and work out complex time-consuming projects. Instead, the staff will concentrate on putting through the traditional kinds of projects. This certainly happened during the first five years of McNamara's presidency. When he subjected the officers of the Bank Group to great pressure to double the volume of lending, the officers found themselves compelled to abandon or put aside a substantial proportion of the proposals or suggestions that came before them to help borrowers work out projects designed to increase employment without in the long run slowing down the rate of increase in the production of essentials.

It is therefore important that the officers of the Bank Group responsible for its operational activities should now be brought to feel that their contributions to the Bank Group and their worthiness for promotion are no longer to be judged by the volume of loans they process, but rather by how far the loans they process—*and* their reluctance to recommend loans to countries not sufficiently concerned with the qualitative goals of development—contribute to speedy progress toward the qualitative goals of Bank Group lending. This would convince the developing member countries that the Bank Group is sincere when it says that it would welcome requests from them for help in working out and financing policies, programs, and projects which will lead to these goals.

The task of the Bank Group is to make it easier for the governments of the poor and the very poor countries to reconcile the need for greatly increased production of essential goods and services with the need to provide more food and clothing and better shelter for their poorest people. I remember in my time in the Bank a project which put starkly the choice between increased production of food and more social justice. It was an irrigation project. Preliminary analysis indicated that if the water from the irrigation project was made available to all the farmers in the area, the production of food grains would probably go up by about 50 per cent; but if the water was used only on the more fertile half of the arable land in the area, the production of food grains would probably double or even treble. The difficulty was that most of the better land was owned by the richer farmers and most of the poorer land was owned by the poorer farmers, so that if the water was used in the most productive way, the poorer farmers would benefit very little. The country needed much greater production of food grains, since most of its people did not have nearly enough to eat. It also needed to reduce the appalling poverty of the poorer farmers, the underemployed artisans, and the landless laborers.

It is clear that a Bank Group mission sent at the request of the borrowing government to appraise such a project should assist the government to work out proposals which would increase to the utmost extent possible the indirect benefits which the poorer farmers and the landless laborers would derive from the project, even if only purely economic considerations were to govern the distribution of the water from the project. Thus the farmers who got the water should be charged the highest possible price consistent with preserving the incentives to them to use the water so as to obtain the greatest possible increases in the production of food grains. The cost to them of farm machinery and of agricultural credit should be set at the highest possible level so as to encourage them to use labor-intensive and not capital-intensive methods of farming. This would mean more work for the poorer farmers and the landless laborers on the farms of the richer farmers. There should be increased taxation of the incomes of the richer farmers. The increased revenues of the government resulting from these measures should be used to pay for a large publicly financed program of development works in the villages in the area to conserve water and soil and to provide productive jobs at reasonable rates of pay for the poorer farmers, the underemployed artisans, and the landless laborers. The government should help the poorer farmers in every possible way to increase production without using water from the irrigation project.

The Bank Group on its side would provide the government with the results of comprehensive programs of research, which it had helped to finance, into the problems of poorer farmers in low-income countries, most of whom farm unirrigated land, which has irregular and scanty rainfall. The research would include the development of new strains of grain, new implements, including small mechanized cultivators, new methods of cultivation, and new ways of providing credit.

When all these possibilities were exhausted, the government of the borrowing country might say that, in spite of the urgent need to increase the production of food grains, some of the water from the irrigation project must go to the poorer farmers who cultivated the poorer lands. The mission sent by the Bank Group to appraise the project would then, in cooperation with the local experts, work out for the consideration of the government its estimate of what this would cost in tems of reducing the increase in production which would otherwise have resulted, so that the government would be aware of the real cost of this effort to reconcile the competing demands of increased food production in a half-starved country and increased social justice in an unjust rural society.

CHAPTER SIX

More Employment: Obstacles in the Way

The obstacles in the way of the Bank Group's accelerating the help it gives its developing member countries to work out policies, projects, and programs designed to increase employment without slowing the rate of economic growth are serious. Robert McNamara has emphasized the lack of knowledge as the first of these obstacles. Thus in his speech to the board of governors in 1971 he said:

We have to admit that in this whole area [*of helping small farmers and of an integrated approach to rural development*] *we are still feeling our way. None of us in the Bank or in the development community at large can yet presume that we are experts at designing the most effective institutions for helping small farmers, or that we know enough about the use of labor-intensive methods of construction, or how best to launch large-scale rural works programs. All these matters manifestly need further study and experimentation.*

Later in the same speech, referring to manufacturing industry in developing countries, he said:

Admittedly, the empirical knowledge in all these matters is incomplete. That is why the Bank is at present exploring whether there are ways in which it might encourage the development of more labor-intensive technologies. And it is why our research program is examining the possibilities of labor/capital substitution, in order to provide both ourselves and our member countries with a more complete picture of how these issues work out in practice.[1]

The Bank Group in its research program has been investigating such matters as the changes in design or bid requirements which could have been made in earlier projects which would have increased their labor content without in the long run diminishing their real net economic benefits. It completed early in 1973 what one of its officers called "an operationally oriented study of experience with African rural development projects." The new central projects department for agriculture will experiment with various new approaches. The Bank Group is trying to draw lessons from the successes or failures of earlier projects designed to emphasize employment. It is investigating the possibilities of extending the use of shadow prices for labor, capital, and foreign exchange from the evaluation of projects to the design of projects and of drafting specifications for bids on these projects.*

When McNamara, in his speech to the board in 1971, coupled the needs for experimentation and study, he stressed that the kind of desk research already being conducted by the Bank Group should be accompanied by research in the field, where, as the chairman of the Development Assistance Committee of OECD has put it, various ideas are tested "in practice on an extensive basis." (He might well have said, "on an extensive and expensive basis.")

The chairman of DAC included this argument in his 1970 annual report, in which he stressed the importance of looking "in all economic sectors for methods of production which will use more manpower and less capital and still keep over-all costs competitive." "Here," he said, "is another role for imaginative research finding new applications for our vast body of scientific and technical knowledge." He pointed out that while it is not possible to offer any easy or clear-cut solutions for the problem of creating gainful employment in low-income countries, we do know enough to move in the right directions and we know that delay could be disastrous. He went on to say: "A whole package of new initiatives will be required . . . It will undoubtedly be necessary to test various ideas in practice on an extensive basis before firm conclusions can be reached. But the stakes are so high that it is essential to press ahead with all these steps and even to accept the risks of some failures. They can be instructive too."[2]

In his 1971 annual report, the chairman of DAC returned to the charge, saying:

The modification of production practices, throughout the economy, but especially in agriculture and construction, to find new ways to replace costly and scarce capital with cheap and plentiful labor without loss of true cost efficiency—not present capital-subsidized cost efficiency—will require not only new policies to give prices to labor and capital that reflect their true scarcity or abundance, and hence, cost to the society, but also an enormous amount of localized technical and economic research of a very practical sort. (Underlining added)[3]

If the Bank Group is to make rapid progress toward its goal of more jobs and greater social justice, it must intensify the desk research it is now doing on how best to substitute labor for capital in developing countries where labor is overplentiful and capital is scarce, and that probably means in 90 per cent of the developing world. It must complement this research by granting loans for experimental projects of many different kinds in many countries under many varying conditions, accepting the risks of some failures. At the same time, it should coordi-

*Shadow prices are defined in Annex Nine, page 261.

nate its efforts closely with those of the International Labour Organization, the United Nations Development Program (UNDP), and the regional banks and agencies, such as the International Development Research Centre (IDRC) in Ottawa.

Well before the Bank Group and DAC had come to recognize the central importance of combatting underemployment and unemployment in developing countries, the director-general of the ILO had launched a world employment program at the 1967 session of the International Labour Conference. As part of its world employment program, "pilot country missions were envisaged, to study, with the help of other agencies, the causes of unemployment in particular types of country, and to bring out what needed to be done internationally as well as nationally."[4] The first pilot mission was sent to Colombia and produced, under the direction of Dudley Seers, the chief of the mission, a report, *Towards Full Employment*, unprecedented in its scope and penetration.

The Bank Group should conclude with the ILO an agreement similar to those with FAO, Unesco, and WHO. This agreement would provide for cooperation between the Bank Group and the ILO in identifying and preparing projects designed to yield high returns in terms of employment as well as production and suitable for financing by the Bank Group.

Since, as the chairman of DAC has pointed out, some experimental labor-intensive projects are likely to be failures, the low-income member countries of the Bank Group with their limited resources will properly be reluctant to propose them to the Bank Group (or to carry them out with their own resources) if they must bear the costs of the failures, particularly since the benefits of the experiments, whether successes or failures, will also accrue to countries other than those in which the projects are undertaken. Their reluctance would be lessened if the Bank Group were to decide that if an experimental labor-intensive project financed by an IDA loan turns out to be a failure, the Bank would assume the responsibility of meeting all the future payments on the loan. This would convert the IDA loan into a grant. Since IDA loans are interest-free and run for fifty years, the cost to the Bank of taking over all amortization payments on IDA loans totaling $100 million would be one payment of only $13 million (discounting future payments at 7 per cent, the cost of money to the Bank). This payment could be made out of a special research fund financed from Bank profits.

The president of the Bank should request the executive directors to approve the establishment of such a special joint international research fund on employment creation in low-income developing countries, analogous to the research fund established on agriculture. The Bank would ask the other agencies especially concerned with employment creation, notably the ILO, UNDP, the regional banks, and the International Development Research Centre in Ottawa, to cooperate in establishing, financing, and operating this fund, from which they also would draw. The Bank Group might offer to transfer to this fund up to

$100 million of IDA funds a year for five years or so, beginning with the year 1975, the first year of the fourth replenishment of IDA.

The chairman of DAC, in his report for 1971, said: "Bank expenditures on research relevant to the success of its lending operations in promoting development remain at a level no industrial corporation or government department would tolerate."[5] An IDA contribution of $500 million to an international research fund on employment creation disbursed over ten years plus other Bank Group expenditures on research, notably in agriculture and in contraception, might mean that by the end of the seventies the Bank Group would be spending up to $150 million a year on research (in 1972 dollars), and that this might increase to $250 million a year (in 1972 dollars) by the mid-eighties. An expenditure of $150 million a year by the end of the seventies would probably amount to between 3 and 4 per cent of the Bank Group's lending operations. This would go far to meet the chairman's valid criticism.

The more labor-intensive a project is, the less foreign exchange it uses. The higher the proportion of the local cost of labor-intensive projects the Bank Group is prepared to finance, the greater the encouragement it will give. The financing by the Bank Group of local costs puts foreign exchange at the disposal of the borrowing governments; virtually all the developing countries, other than the oil-rich countries, suffer from severe shortages of foreign exchange. These countries can use the foreign exchange resulting from Bank Group loans for local costs to finance high-priority purposes in economic and social development, including essential imports and the payment of interest and amortization on new loans for high-priority development projects. It would be helpful, therefore, if the Bank Group were to decide that it would finance all the direct and indirect foreign exchange costs and at least two-thirds of the local costs of experimental labor-intensive projects. (This would apply to financing by the Bank proper, as well as by IDA.)

The international agreements establishing the Bank and IDA, if strictly interpreted, would make it very difficult for them to go in for the necessary expansion of local cost financing. The agreement on the Bank is particularly restrictive. It is only "in exceptional circumstances" that the Bank can finance even the indirect foreign exchange costs of a project. As for local costs, these can be financed only "in exceptional circumstances when local currency required for the purposes of the loan cannot be raised by the borrower on reasonable terms." The agreement on IDA is less restrictive. It states that IDA, "in special cases, may make foreign exchange available for local expenditures."

Under McNamara's presidency, these provisions have been broadly interpreted to mean that the Bank and IDA may provide loans for local expenditure if three conditions are met. First, that the borrowing country has a suitable development program and fiscal policies, and is making an adequate development effort. Second, that the development program requires funds in excess of the savings that can be raised locally and of the capital, public and private, obtainable from other external sources. Third, that the Bank and IDA cannot provide adequate amounts of the required funds by financing only foreign exchange expenditures on development projects because there are insufficient investment opportunities of this kind or because, even where these may be sufficient, the Bank and IDA could better advance the country's development if they directed their financing toward other projects of key importance requiring some financing of local expenditures.

These interpretations have enabled the Bank Group to increase greatly its financing of the local costs of projects.[6] In 1968, 10 per cent of IDA credits went for local costs; in 1971, 23 per cent; in 1972, 17 per cent. The increase in local cost financing under Bank loans was slight, from 5 per cent in 1968 to 7 per cent in 1971 and to 6 per cent in 1972. Taking Bank and IDA loans together, local cost financing went up from $49 million in 1968 to $264 million in 1971 and to $297 million in 1972. The percentage increase in Bank-IDA lending for local costs was from 5 per cent of total lending in 1968 to an average of 10 per cent in the years 1971 and 1972. Local cost financing as a proportion of total Bank-IDA financing doubled. Some loans granted in 1972 were almost entirely for local costs. Thus the IDA loan of June 1972 to India in support of its family planning program covered, in addition to the total foreign exchange costs of $2 million, $19 million of the local costs. (All the remaining local costs, apart from land and the operating costs of the projects, were borne by the Swedish development agency.) IDA loans to some very poor countries have financed 90 per cent of the local costs.

A number of important rich member countries have in the past been opposed to extensive local cost financing. They argued that what they needed to rally the support of powerful export interests in their countries behind the World Bank Group was a simple, clear proof that their country got back in export orders all or more than all the money it made available to the Bank Group by permitting the Bank to sell its bonds on their capital markets or to their central banks, or by gifts from the government to IDA. Their objection to increased local cost financing was that it would result in a falling off of their exports which could be identified as directly attributable to Bank Group loans.

In general it has been the governments of France, Germany, and Japan which have tried in the past to put a brake on the expansion of the financing of local costs by the Bank Group; their exports to developing countries are more likely to be finished capital goods, rather than the goods the developing countries would probably purchase with free foreign exchange. It is possible that these and other governments inclined to favor a go-slow policy on local cost financing are now prepared to acquiesce in a further substantial increase in local cost financing, perhaps from the 10 per cent level of 1971 and 1972 to 20 per cent by 1976 or so and possibly 30 per cent by the end of the seventies, provided that extensive local cost financing is restricted to projects where the arguments for it are particularly strong, as in rural development, small industries, and population control. It will certainly be easier for these governments to acquiesce if the total volume of Bank

Group lending increases at such a rate that the volume of contracts awarded their nationals under Bank Group loans does not fall off, even though the proportion of local cost financing is mounting.

If, however, an important group of member governments is not prepared to acquiesce in a substantial further increase in local cost financing, and cites in support of its opposition the provisions in the international agreements, it may well be necessary for McNamara to propose amendments to the agreements and to make special visits to the capitals of the reluctant governments to put the case for the amendments to the cabinet ministers principally concerned and, if necessary, to the heads of government. The amendments might provide that the Bank and IDA may make foreign exchange available for local expenditures on a project or program, if in their opinion this would better advance the development of the borrowing country than the provision of foreign exchange for other projects or programs. McNamara would have on his side the fact that informed and influential public opinion in western countries increasingly realizes that the usual kind of aid in the form of capital goods is not enough, and that an increasing proportion of outside aid must be in a form making it easier for the governments of the poorer countries to tackle their frightening unemployment and underemployment problems. If informed and influential public opinion has reached this point, it should be possible to carry it the necessary one step further: to an understanding that an increasing proportion of aid must go to finance the local costs of labor-intensive projects. Governments know that if they fail to heed the president's arguments advanced in private conversations, he will have to turn to public argument in an effort to shame them into supporting him. He has a world-wide forum for his arguments in his speeches, especially his speeches to the annual meetings of the board of governors.

Approval by the member governments of these two proposals, on local cost financing and on a special research fund on employment creation, would stimulate developing countries to submit to the Bank Group labor-intensive projects and projects with labor-intensive technologies, or to ask the Bank Group to help them work out such projects. The Bank Group may at present be in danger of putting the cart before the horse by trying to work out this sort of project on its own without first trying to remove the principal obstacles to its borrowers' ability and willingness to participate with it in this sort of project. The task of the Bank Group is rather to remove the obstacles preventing its borrowers from submitting innovative projects to it and, at their request, help them work out these projects so that they will be suitable for Bank Group financing. This will not mean a minor role for the Bank Group; it will mean a major role, and a role demanding fundamental changes in the attitudes of the staff of the Bank Group and in the administration of the Bank Group.

The expertise of most of the officers responsible for the operational activities of the Bank Group is relevant to the old standard type of Bank Group projects, not to the new, experimental, labor-intensive, socially-conscious type. Many of the agricultural experts, for example, are so production-minded that they have been reluctant to turn down proposals for loans to increase coffee production in developing countries which would be better served by loans enabling them to substitute something else for their present production of coffee. They have also been reluctant, in their negotiations with borrowing countries on agricultural loans, to press hard the arguments for including in the conditions of the loans provisions which would insure a more equitable distribution of the expected benefits between the richer farmers and the poorer farmers and the landless laborers, provisions such as higher charges for irrigation water, higher taxes on imported labor-saving machinery, higher charges for credit and other inputs, higher taxes on the richer farmers. The same is true of many of the engineers on the staff. Many of them adhere to engineering standards which are not necessarily economically desirable and which are certainly not compatible with labor-intensive techniques. They are reluctant to suggest that a developing country would be better off with lower quality roads constructed by labor-intensive methods than with higher quality roads constructed by capital-intensive methods; or that it is more important to build mud roads from the villages to feeder roads and improve these than to improve the main roads.

It is essential, therefore, that sociologists, anthropologists, political scientists, geographers, and other social scientists be infiltrated into the staff at all levels. Their influence and that of the younger, more socially-conscious economists, agricultural experts, and engineers will tend to correct the predilections of the older generation of economists, agriculturalists, and engineers on the staff.

In addition to bringing new and younger blood into the senior ranks of the professional staff, it is also essential to establish three innovative centers within the administration of the Bank Group. The rural development unit established in the spring of 1973 can become one of these centers though it might be better if it were confined to dealing with rural development works. Another center would be a new unit to deal with small-scale industry. These two new projects departments should be put in charge of creative, intelligent, ambitious empire-builders. Such officers will spur the Bank Group into moving quickly into these two new fields, fields into which the Bank Group must move on a massive scale if it is to help its member countries to work out high-priority projects to increase employment. The Bank Group at present knows very little about rural development works and small industry. But this is not a reason for the Bank Group not lending for projects of this kind. It is rather a positive reason for lending, since the Bank Group learns by doing. It learns on the job. To make the learning rapid and productive, the early projects must be especially well prepared. Aggressive empire-builders in charge of departments on rural development works and small industry will see to it that the intellectual and financial resources of the Bank Group directed to these projects are sufficient to insure their being well prepared. These two new directors of department will be energetic in encouraging and assisting borrowing countries to formulate policies on large-scale programs of rural development works and large-scale development of small industry, and to build up the appropriate intermediary institutions through which the Bank Group would make its loans. They would nurture and direct these two groups of national development institutions, just as the director of the development finance companies department of the Bank so successfully over many years nurtured and directed national development finance companies.

The policy planning division established by McNamara in October 1972 under Mahbub ul Haq can become the third innovative center in the administration of the Bank Group. When this unit was created, McNamara announced that it would "analyze the Bank's development policy structure to identify gaps, weaknesses and innovative opportunities, and conduct development policy studies." The most important task of this new unit would be in the area, not of policy planning, but of policy implementation. It would keep under constant review the progress of the operational staff in translating the president's directives on the Bank group's qualitative goals into specific programs and projects suitable for financing. The five regional offices of the Bank, IDA, and IFC would make periodic reports to this monitoring unit. The members of the unit would also keep a skeptical eye on country programming, feasibility studies, project appraisals, and loan documents, so as to test whether claims that qualitative goals were receiving high priority were in fact translated into practice. For this purpose, it would not be necessary that they examine every feasibility study, project appraisal, or loan document. They could make random spot checks. They could examine projects claiming to be labor-intensive to determine how far they could have been made more labor-intensive without reducing their economic return in the long run. This unit would be a sort of devil's advocate; it would question whether the assertion of an operational unit of the Bank Group that it was moving with all dispatch to the qualitative goals was justified. Occasionally it would be the task of this unit to exclaim that the emperor had no clothes. It would report directly to the president.

Finally, to hasten achievement of these goals, it might be wise for the president to set specific quantitative targets at which the operational staff would aim. One such target might be that by 1978 a third of the projects coming before the executive directors for approval would be specifically directed to reducing unemployment and underemployment without in the long run slowing down the rate of increase in the production of essential goods and services; and these projects would add up to one-third of the money lent.

There is no substantial difference of opinion among the professional staff on the importance of the Bank Group's trying to help its developing member countries to reconcile economic growth with the attainment of more jobs and more social justice. Where there are differences is on the proportion of the Bank Group's limited resources of skilled manpower and of IDA funds which should be devoted to these tasks. Thus, while everyone in the Bank Group concerned with the problem emphasizes the great difficulties resulting from lack of knowledge of the subject, and the great amount of research and experiment required in order to make a break-through, some officers contend that the Bank Group should not be expected to play the major role. That major role, they contend, should be played by the developing countries and by donor governments. But, to this it is enough to reply that because the problems are so complex and ignorance about possible solutions so profound, the Bank Group is uniquely fitted by the magnitude of its intellectual and financial resources to undertake the tasks set forth in this chapter. In a sense, these are not the major tasks, these must be assumed by the developing countries. The argument in this chapter, however, is that the developing countries need the help of the Bank Group if they are to undertake these tasks; they need loans from the Bank Group to cover a large proportion of the local costs, as well as all the direct and indirect foreign exchange costs of labor-intensive projects; they need an assurance that the Bank Group will pay the costs of the projects which fail; they need technical advice and assistance from the Bank Group.

This is not to say that national aid agencies do not also have important contributions to make; they do particularly in aid-receiving countries where their country has some kind of special interest—historical, cultural, sentimental, economic, political—which would elicit support from the government and the taxpayers for the thesis that the national aid agency finance risky, but well-thought-out, experimental labor-intensive projects. Indeed, one of the most fruitful areas for closer cooperation between the Bank Group and national aid agencies (a subject discussed in Chapter Eighteen) should be in identifying, appraising, and supervising these experimental projects. Some of these might be undertaken jointly by the Bank Group and a national aid agency. Others, including many of the more speculative, might be undertaken by a national aid agency with the Bank acting for it as executive agent in appraising the project and, it might be, in supervising it. For other projects, after appraisal by a mission including officers from both the Bank Group and a national aid agency, the national agency might assume full responsibility, requesting the Bank Group, however, to associate one or two of its officers with the project so that the Bank Group also could profit fully from the experiment.

CHAPTER SEVEN

Productive Jobs at Proper Pay

The massive unemployment and underemployment existing in middle-income and low-income countries not only waste resources, they are also sources of serious social dangers because they perpetuate an inequitable division of the national income between the better-off members of the community and the very poor. Rich countries can afford to use children's allowances, old age pensions, generous payments to the unemployed, guaranteed income supplements, to transfer income from their better-off to their very poor citizens. Low-income countries cannot afford these kinds of social services. About the only effective means they have for transferring income to the very poor is to give them work at reasonable wages.

In low-income countries, this must be the kind of work which will increase the production of essential goods and services, because the production of essential goods and services is now so low that if it were divided among all the inhabitants in equal shares, everybody would suffer from too little food, too little clothing, and from shelter inadequate to protect them from heat and cold, wind and rain. The task of the Bank Group is to help low-income countries identify and work out labor-intensive projects which yield a high real rate of economic return. This task is very difficult. It is very urgent. It is very expensive in terms of scarce skilled manpower and of money.

It seems probable that in many, if not almost all, middle-income and low-income countries, a rigorous comprehensive analysis by the Bank Group's periodic country economic missions, based on earlier sectoral studies, on appraisal reports on projects, on experimental projects and other kinds of research, will show that there need be little or no conflict between the objective of increasing employment and that of increasing the production of essential goods and services. Although there is need for much more hard economic analysis and empirical research to establish the point, an increasing number of economists believe that economic theory during the 1950's and 1960's tended on balance to exaggerate the conflict between these two objectives.

In any event, whatever the strength of the argument that measures to increase employment at a much more rapid rate than at present will slow down the rate of economic growth, there is almost unanimous agreement among economists that some measures can undoubtedly be taken by developing countries to increase employment without slowing down the rate of economic growth. The usual lists of measures include a whole range of proposals to eliminate those incentives which now, as a result of mistaken government policies, exist in almost all developing countries to use capital-intensive, rather than labor-intensive, methods of production, even though the net economic benefit to the community through using labor-intensive methods would be greater.* The incentives leading to the use of capital-intensive methods, when labor-intensive methods would cost the economy less, are low charges on loans and credits, which do not reflect the real cost of capital; overvalued exchange rates, resulting in low prices for imported agricultural or industrial machinery, prices which do not reflect the real costs of the imports to the economy; high levels of protection to capital-intensive domestic industries; inequitably low effective rates of taxation on the larger landowners, which increase their profits and enable them to enlarge their farms; a preference to the larger farmers over the smaller farmers in the availability and in the costs of irrigation water, fertilizers, seeds, credit, and technical assistance; a preference to the larger industrialists over the smaller industrialists in the allocation and the costs of credit and of scarce materials.

Ernest Stern has given the following list of the special preferences which governments of developing countries have given for both imported and domestic capital:

Tariffs on capital goods are often the lowest in the tariff schedules; credit is much more easily obtained for large-scale units or for capital goods imports; rapid depreciation allowances, tax holidays and other benefits further reduce the cost of capital. As a result, foreign exchange allocations are skewed toward capital goods imports.[1]

Two striking examples of "prices and costs working against the fuller use of human resources" in the countryside are cited by de Vries:

Calculated in terms of wheat, the cost of a tractor in Pakistan is only half of one in Iowa. In Ivory Coast a loan to finance farm equipment is made at half what it costs in Germany.[2]

Governments of developing countries can speed up the rate of increase in employment without slowing down the rate of economic growth if they make the changes in their policies on foreign exchange, credit, taxation, and tariffs required for the market prices of the factors of production to coincide with true economic costs. There is disagreement among economists, however, about the degree of importance to be attached to this reform. Mahbub ul Haq asks: "How large a segment

*A definition of net economic benefit is given in Annex Nine, page 261.

of the economy does the price adjustment affect, when there is a large subsistence sector in these countries and the modern industrial sector generally contributes less than 10% of total output?" He goes on to say, "No one will dare suggest that price corrections will not move these economies in the right direction. But are they decisive? Or do they make only a marginal impression on the unemployment problem?"[3]

The three areas of activity in which it seems likely that the Bank Group should concentrate its efforts to help its developing member countries identify and work out labor-intensive productive projects are construction, small-scale industry, and rural development works. A large diversion of the Bank Group's intellectual and financial resources to these three fields of activity would increase greatly the contribution its loans make to bettering the conditions of the mass of the people in the borrowing countries. This is especially true of the poorer two-thirds of the farmers, the landless laborers, and the underemployed artisans, who constitute almost half the total population of the middle-income and low-income member countries of the Bank, probably about 700 million people out of 1,600 million. The Bank Group has hitherto done little for these 700 million people, the people described by Rabindranath Tagore as "eternal tenants in an extortionate world, having nothing of their own." McNamara's greatest single contribution to the thinking of the Bank Group is his insistence that it is high time the Bank Group did more for these "eternal tenants."

Construction

The DAC chairman's Report for 1970 makes the following statement about construction projects in low-income countries financed under foreign aid:

> *Construction has . . . the special characteristic that much of it is done by foreign firms who have been awarded contracts, often after international competitive bidding. Since most of these firms grew to international stature in industrial countries, their methods are those most economic where labour is expensive per hour. Would it not be worthwhile to explore the feasibility of putting minimum local employment requirements in the bid documents or giving some advantages in the bidding to the contractor guaranteeing productive employment to the most local labour? There might even be a chance that in terms of social costs it would pay to have a limited trade-off between employment and price, based, of course, on modified work procedures.*[4]

Under McNamara's leadership, the Bank Group has been paying increasing attention to these considerations. It has been consulting with its borrowing member countries on the steps to be taken to change specifications and work procedures on infrastructure projects, both those financed by the countries and those financed by the Bank Group. It has been considering various incentives to contractors to use more labor and less capital. One possible financial incentive would be for the contractor to pay from his own pocket only the shadow price of unskilled labor, which would otherwise be unemployed, and for the government to pay the difference between the shadow price and the wage in fact paid. This might mean that the government would meet one-third to one-half the cost of the wages of unskilled labor used on construction projects.

The Bank Group should press ahead with its efforts to help its borrowers work out projects for road-building which would test under varying conditions the comparative real advantages and disadvantages (using shadow prices) of labor-intensive projects with lower standards, lower initial costs, and higher maintenance costs against the kinds of projects it has normally financed in the past. Experimental projects should not, of course, be confined to road building. They should be extended rapidly to other kinds of construction, such as the building of dams, irrigation works, and schools. Labor-intensive construction projects of this kind would have the advantage that they could suitably be undertaken by local, rather than foreign, contractors. The foreign exchange cost of work undertaken by local contractors is likely to be lower than if the work is undertaken by foreign contractors, and the use of local contractors will help build up technological and managerial skills in the borrowing country.

These suggestions have to do with the actual construction projects. But there are also possibilities of using the expenditures of the work force to stimulate development. When a construction project employs many thousands of workers for many years, these expenditures are substantial. If local agriculture is organized to take advantage of this temporary but certain market, and if it is given a reasonable preference, agriculture in the area may become efficient enough to sustain itself at a higher level after the construction work is finished. This would increase employment, stimulate agriculture in the project area, and save foreign exchange. It is interesting to speculate how much further ahead Pakistan would be today, economically and socially, if these possibilities had been taken fully into account by the Bank Group and Pakistan in setting conditions for the awards of contracts for the Indus Basin works and the Tarbela dam. The value of the contracts for the Indus Basin works in Pakistan and for Tarbela was $1,700 million. In bid documents for large construction projects certain to employ many thousands of people over many years, the Bank Group should therefore require that the contractors insure that local agriculture is given a reasonable preference in providing food for the working force on the project, both foreign and locally recruited. The Bank Group should assist the local government to provide planning, technical assistance, and credits to promote the establishment of efficient agriculture in the project area. (Similar measures should be undertaken to encourage the establishment of small-scale industry in the project area to take on work for the contractors and sub-contractors.)

Small-Scale Industry

Most small-scale industry[5] has a much greater labor content than most middle-size or large industry. For this reason, and because it is hard to see how balanced economic growth can proceed in most middle-income and low-income countries without much more development of small-scale industry than is now taking place, the Bank Group should divert substantial intellectual resources to help its borrowers work out projects to stimulate efficient, economic small-scale industry, particularly in the smaller towns and in the villages. It should grant a substantial volume of loans for small-scale industry.

The Bank Group stated in 1972 that it had "not provided much assistance, directly or indirectly [through national development finance companies], to small-scale industry, particularly firms employing less than 20 workers. . . . A few operations have been carried out for the direct benefit of the small-scale industrial sector (industrial estates, etc.), but most have benefitted medium and large-scale firms. . . . The Bank Group has so far provided direct support for small-scale industry only in Pakistan." The total lending of the Bank Group to manufacturing operations in the five years ending in mid-1971 was $1,356 million. Of this, only $37 million went to enterprises with fewer than 20 employees and only $202 million to enterprises with fewer than 100 employees.[6] The developing member countries of the Bank Group would be much better off today if, instead of devoting 3 per cent of its lending for manufacturing operations to enterprises with fewer than 20 employees, the Bank Group had devoted 30 per cent to first-rate programs for helping these enterprises.

In the long run, the most profound effect of an increase in the number, vitality, and efficiency of small-scale industries will be the building up of a new group of qualified entrepreneurs and managers. The very limited numbers of these people constitute one of the greatest obstacles to speedy economic development in most middle-income and low-income countries. These countries, if they are to advance more rapidly, need many more people able to organize production, prepared to take risks to make profits or gain prestige, who have pride of workmanship, who are initiators of new ideas, who are innovators. Efficient small-scale industry can be a nursery for such men.

At present, in most middle-income and low-income countries, many men with the intelligence, imagination, and drive to raise themselves from small-scale industry to middle-size industry and eventually from middle-size to big industry are held back by difficulties they could overcome with a little outside help. They frequently have great difficulties in obtaining credit, or must pay exorbitant rates of interest to local moneylenders. They probably have to operate with inadequate working capital. They cannot finance the new equipment they urgently need. They do not have the time or the administrative skills to deal with the complicated licensing and other quantitative controls existing in most of the developing countries. They cannot get the scarce raw materials they need or they must pay exorbitant prices on the black market. They normally do not have marketing networks. They have no easy access to technical assistance on how to improve their management, their methods of production and marketing. Most important of all, in many countries they cannot get foreign exchange to pay for the imported equipment they need. The World Bank report in 1970 on the East Pakistan small industries project said that limited access to foreign exchange was the principal reason for the slow growth of small-scale industry there.

There are a number of provisions in the loan granted by IDA in 1970 for small industrial firms in Bangladesh which could usefully be included in other loan agreements for small-scale industries.* First, the loan is intended primarily for new small-scale manufacturing units, including agricultural support industries, which offer opportunities for foreign exchange earnings or savings and require a minimum of protection. Second, the loan is not restricted to industries on industrial estates. Thus the choice of location becomes a business decision, the validity of which can be tested in the appraisal of the project. Industrial estates are forced to compete on equal terms with other possible locations. This will help curb tendencies to incur excessive costs in building and operating industrial estates. (In order to avoid conflicts of interest, the appraisal agency must not be responsible for the industrial estates program.) Third, in appraising a project, due account will be taken of the willingness of the enterprise to take advantage of the technical assistance offered by the Bangladesh Small Industries Corporation in working out the details of the project and in improving methods of production and of operation. Fourth, projects will be appraised and supervised by the Corporation, which will also prepare investment briefs providing technical and marketing data for new projects. The Corporation has been built up with outside expert technical assistance and will continue to have this assistance. Finally, the commercial banks, which through their branches know the credit-standing of applicants for loans from their commercial dealings with them, are given a financial stake in the success or failure of projects.

One reason for the Bank Group's slowness in helping its member countries to develop efficient small-scale industry is that until 1968 it refused to lend to any national development finance company owned by the government, although these companies would be likely to be more interested in lending to small-scale industry than would the development finance companies which the Bank Group supported, since control of almost all those companies was in the hands of big industrialists.

Bank Group loans for small-scale industries would not, of course, be made direct to small-scale industries. Loans would be made to specialized intermediary national institutions, which would pass them on to small-scale industries. The national institutions would supplement the funds received from the Bank Group with funds provided by the local government and by local commercial banks. They would "as-

* The loan granted in 1970 was, of course, to Pakistan. This loan was replaced in January 1973 by a loan to Bangladesh for an identical project. (World Bank press release, January 11, 1973.)

sist small-scale industries in matters of finance, technology, management, and accounting." They would "identify potential entrepreneurs, select suitable activities in which small-scale production can be viable, prepare feasibility studies, provide technical and managerial guidance, and secure access to finance on appropriate terms." Because "the requirements [of small-scale industry] are very different from those of large-scale industrial projects," the president of the Bank should, as suggested in the book *World Bank Operations*, establish a new unit of the Bank Group to concern itself solely with the problem of the development of small-scale industry.[7] This unit would assist borrowing countries to formulate policies for the development of small-scale industries and to build up appropriate national institutions to which the Bank Group loans would be made. It would provide these institutions with technical assistance linked with the loan projects.

The Bank Group should, in association with UNDP, the UN Industrial Development Organization (UNIDO), the ILO, and the regional bank concerned, make sector studies of small-scale industry in all middle-income and low-income member countries of the Bank Group having a capacity during the next decade for substantial development of small-scale industry and desiring the Bank Group to help them develop this capacity. This program might have to be spread over five years, and require the addition of about a hundred experts to the professional staff on five-year contracts. The reports of the sector missions would provide a basis for measuring the true economic return, based on shadow prices, likely to result from investments in small-scale industries in each country. This return can be high if adequate weight is given to the relatively low amount of foreign exchange required, the high labor content, and the stimulus to the emergence of entrepreneurs and managers. A high real return to the economy would justify appropriate government subsidies to cover losses incurred by the small industries corporations. Since a small industries corporation cannot do its job unless it takes very considerable risks, these losses would probably be substantial, even though the corporation were to charge, as it should, (in order to encourage the use of labor-intensive, capital-saving technologies), a realistic interest rate of, say, 10 per cent plus the annual rate of inflation in the country. When a loan for small-scale industries is financed by IDA, the money should be passed by the government to the small industries corporation on IDA terms.

Rural Development Works

Small-scale rural development works provide a good indication of the scale of operations required to make an impact on unemployment and income distribution in the low-income countries, the kinds of benefits likely to flow from well-planned and well-administered programs, and the kinds of difficulties likely to confront a government determined to combat the poverty of the poorest of its fellow citizens.

Dudley Seers recommended in 1971 in the study of Ceylon (now Sri Lanka) which he made for the International Labour Organization that

Ceylon should in the next few years have a program of small-scale rural development works which would employ 100,000 workers,[8] this in a country of only 13 million people. The corresponding figure for India would be 4 million workers full-time or 8 million half-time. For this the wage bill for the laborers might be about $500 million a year.

The programs would not be massive programs of rural relief. They would be integrated programs of small-scale, labor-intensive development works likely to yield high real rates of economic return in both the short and the long run, either by increasing agricultural production or by reducing the farmer's costs and by improving his ability to market his crops. The projects for increasing agricultural production would include measures to improve the quality of land and to conserve water and soil by leveling land, by contouring embankments, damming rivulets and streams, constructing ponds for holding rain water and irrigation and drainage channels, by digging surface wells, desilting existing canals and small reservoirs, and by planting trees. The other projects would consist mainly of improving the roads from the farms to the markets, thus reducing the costs to the farmer of improved seeds and fertilizer and the cost of bringing his crops to market. Labor otherwise unemployed would create valuable capital goods.

If a program of rural development works is restricted to projects yielding a high real rate of economic return, and in most developing countries there is no lack of such potential projects, the program will increase the production of food and put money in the hands of the poorer peasants, the underemployed artisans, and the landless laborers. They will spend this money on the bare essentials of life, which they now lack. They will buy more food to fill their empty bellies, thus providing a market for the increased production of food resulting from the projects on which they have been employed. They will buy more clothing to replace their rags; in most developing countries, simple clothing material can be produced locally. Their employment on productive work at reasonable rates of pay will thus create more production and more employment; it will increase the share of the poor in the national income and, in most of the developing world, it will lead to almost no increase in the demand for imports. It will therefore not be a drain on scarce foreign exchange.

The power structure in many rural areas in many of the low-income countries, notably in India, Pakistan, and Bangladesh, is a serious obstacle to the success of large programs of rural development works. The rural elite, composed of the larger landowners and the moneylenders, will try to get control of any development works program to abort or twist it to serve their own purposes. The larger landowners will try to evade paying the real value to them of improvements made on their farms as a result of the works projects. The moneylenders will try to seize part of the wages of the laborers to pay off debts incurred at exorbitant rates of interest. Corrupt officials will try to charge the government for work which has not been done, or for wages which have not been paid. Governments determined to help the rural poor, and it is only to these governments that the Bank Group should make loans for rural works projects, will, therefore, have to work out measures providing reasonable assurance to the Bank Group that the projects will be so organized and monitored that they will in fact help the rural poor. In the long run, as Arun Shourie has suggested,[9] this means that in many very poor countries the governments will have to help the poorer farmers, the underemployed artisans, and the landless laborers to organize themselves against those who hold power in the villages.

Some waste is inevitable on all development projects; on rural development works the waste may be above the norm. On these, as on other Bank Group projects, waste must be kept to a minimum. But, as one senior official of the Bank Group said to me at the beginning of 1973 when we were discussing rural development projects, "At least, when we waste money on projects to employ the poorest farmers and the landless laborers, we will be wasting money on the right people."

In a speech in 1969, Mitchell Sharp, the foreign minister of Canada, said:

Successful revolt, like successful government, calls for effective infrastructure, the kind of thing aid programs are designed to provide. There are countries where one can only hope that in due time the assistance they receive from us will give to the people the sinews they need to rise up and cast aside the cruel weight of unjust and unprincipled government.[10]

The people who control unjust and unprincipled governments are not likely to use foreign aid to provide their poorer fellow citizens with the sinews for successful revolt. But governments which are determined to strengthen the economic, social and political power of their poorer fellow citizens will use foreign aid for these purposes, including loans from the World Bank Group for rural development and for other programs designed to yield high returns in terms of production, jobs, and a more equitable distribution of income.

CHAPTER EIGHT

Better Credit-worthiness

An estimate of the credit-worthiness of a borrowing country is an estimate of the risks of lending to it. For the Bank Group, the risks are that the borrowing country may default on its debts, or make such drastic adjustments in its economy to pay its debts as to impede seriously its economic growth or require its creditors to come to its assistance by additional loans over and above their expectations.

The most important single indicator of the credit-worthiness of a country is the relationship of the cost of its debt service (interest and amortization) to its actual and potential earnings of foreign exchange plus the foreign exchange likely to result from foreign investments and aid. Foreign exchange earnings are likely to be high in a country which has, in relation to its population and income, a high level of high-priced exportable natural resources, such as oil, iron ore, bauxite, and tourism, or a demonstrated aptitude for producing manufactured exports. Geographical proximity to, or contiguity with, one or more highly developed countries stimulates economic development and provides possibilities of large foreign exchange earnings.

Another important factor affecting the credit-worthiness of a country is its potential for domestic savings and the capacity of its government to translate a considerable proportion of these savings into foreign exchange, provided that this foreign exchange is not wasted but is available for high priority purposes, such as the servicing of past debts and of new debts incurred for development and the purchase of essential imports. Foreign exchange used to purchase gold to be smuggled into the country for private hoarding, or to build up private bank accounts in Switzerland or to purchase luxury imports does not increase a country's credit-worthiness.

In general, the higher a country's GNP per capita, the greater is the potential for domestic savings and the greater "its capacity to raise funds for the service of its foreign debt."[1] A country will increase its domestic savings if it increases its taxation, especially of the middle class, and if it develops a well-organized local financial system designed to attract savings. A country will increase its ability to translate these savings into foreign exchange if it provides adequate incentives for exports. A low-income country may find it necessary to conserve its foreign exchange for high priority development purposes by restraining tourist expenditures abroad and the export of capital to rich countries, and by getting gold out of private hoards into the reserves of its central bank.

A country whose GNP is increasing in real terms at well above the average rate is likely to be a better credit risk than one whose GNP is barely keeping pace with its growth in population. A rising GNP per capita increases a country's potential for domestic savings. If maintained over a period of five years or so, it usually indicates that economic advance has acquired momentum. The indices now available of growth rate in GNP per capita are, however, subject to wide margins of error.

Moreover, indices of growth in GNP per capita, even if accurate, provide no more than a rough indication of the rate of economic growth and, as emphasized above in Chapter Five, a period of rapid economic growth accompanied by great unemployment, an increase in the disparities between regions and classes, and a continued growth of urban slums may well create such political and social tensions that the period of rapid growth will be followed by a period of no growth or even of retrogression. Therefore, an important factor affecting credit-worthiness is the extent to which the country is succeeding in providing all its people with at least the bare necessities of life—food, clothing, and shelter. In the poorer countries of the world, there must be social advance if there is to be economic growth; and there must be economic growth if there is to be social advance. The credit-worthiness of a country depends both on the pace of social advance and on the rate of economic growth.

The willingness of a government to adopt the measures necessary to promote economic growth by mobilizing domestic resources for development, by using efficiently these resources and those made available from abroad, by translating domestic resources into foreign exchange, and by conserving these resources, depends in large part on the importance the government attaches to economic development. The capacity of a government to carry out such measures depends on the strength and the competence of its administration. Thus the attitude of a government to economic development and the strength and the competence of its administration are factors affecting its credit-worthiness.

The credit-worthiness of a country is also affected by the reputation its government has acquired for taking seriously the obligations it has assumed to service its debts.

A country's capacity to service its debts can be affected positively or negatively by international political factors, since these affect the flow of foreign aid to it on soft terms. South Korea, Taiwan, and Thailand received relatively large amounts of aid from the United States on soft terms in the sixties and early seventies because of their close political ties with the United States, and a large flow of soft aid, if wisely used, will improve a country's credit-worthiness for aid on harder terms. The same was true to a lesser degree, in the sixties and early seventies, of Ethiopia, Finland, Greece, Indonesia, Iran, Panama, Portugal, Spain, and Turkey. The United States has in the past tended to give priority to these countries and to most of the Latin American countries in allocating its soft international development assistance funds, thus increasing their credit-worthiness for World Bank loans. Those countries of black Africa which were formerly parts of the French empire have received relatively large amounts of soft aid from France. Because of their place in the international political spectrum, some countries such as Afghanistan, Algeria, Burma, Egypt, and Zaire have received little or no soft aid from western governments. Egypt has received a good deal of soft aid from the Soviet Union, and Cuba a great deal. Tanzania and Zambia received an interest-free loan of $400 million from China in 1970.

IDA is important not only to the poorer countries but to the foreign lenders to those countries; the more money IDA is able to lend to the poorer members of the Bank Group for high quality, high priority development projects, the safer are the loans of foreign governments, the investments of private foreign capital, the loans of the Bank, and the investments of IFC. The reason is that a flow of interest-free IDA loans for first-class projects of economic development—a sort of equity investment—strengthens a country's economy without adding greatly to its burden of foreign debt. It thus increases the ability of the borrowing country to service its foreign debts.

Credit-worthiness is in a constant state of flux. It changes with changes in all these factors. Foreign exchange earnings may increase as the result of the discovery or development of internationally demanded natural resources, of export-oriented manufacturing, of tourism, or of a rapid growth in demand in industrialized countries. As a result of changes in regime or in policy in a borrowing country, there will be changes in the level of domestic savings, in the nature and level of effective taxation, in the priority the government attaches to economic development, in the strength and competence of government administration, and in the country's place in the political spectrum. As a result of changes in regime or in policy in rich countries, there will be changes in the importance their governments accord to a borrowing country's place in the international political spectrum, and in the level of the soft aid with which they provide it. A borrowing country improves its credit-worthiness if it increases domestic savings and translates them into foreign exchange by giving high priority to the development of export-oriented industry and of tourism. Rich countries improve the credit-worthiness of borrowing countries if they open their markets to their goods and help them exploit those markets, if they cooperate with them in implementing schemes under which they will secure higher prices for the principal commodities they export (especially tea, coffee, and cocoa), and if they do more to promote private investment in the borrowing countries for high priority development projects on appropriate terms and conditions.

The World Bank Group is already doing much to improve the credit-worthiness of its borrowers, especially of its low-income borrowers; it can do more for both its middle-income and low-income borrowers. Thus, in selecting projects for financing, it should give greater weight than in the past to potential foreign exchange earnings or savings. (Foreign exchange is earned by increasing exports; foreign exchange is saved by replacing imports.) This means, among other things, a higher priority to loans for the exploitation of internationally demanded natural resources, the development of export-oriented manufacturing, the expansion of tourism and the provision of suitable accommodation for retired people from rich countries, and for projects which, though they do not earn foreign exchange directly, are required by heavy foreign exchange earners or savers.

It is particularly important that the Bank Group assist the semi-industrialized low-income countries to develop efficient capital goods industries, since these tend to be labor-intensive. These countries are eminently suited for the production and export of capital goods, such as machine tools, and technologically advanced labor-intensive products, such as electronics equipment."[2] IFC can be very helpful by encouraging firms in rich countries to share in joint ventures with private firms and governments in these low-income countries to develop capital goods industries.

The Bank Group can also increase the credit-worthiness of its low-income borrowers by including in the provisions of loans to them increased preferences to domestic suppliers and to suppliers in other low-income countries. The preference should not be too high, however, or continued over too long a period of time, as this could result in a misallocation of resources. A proper degree of protection of these suppliers would have to take account of a country's industrial development policy as reflected in its tariffs, exchange rates and controls, import quotas and licensing, export subsidies, tax and price policies, and government rules on procurement.

Since a flow of private investment to low-income countries can increase their credit-worthiness, provided that the investment is for high priority projects and is made on appropriate terms and conditions, and since the purpose of IFC is to be a "catalyst in mobilizing finance for private ventures in the developing countries,"[3] the Bank Group should expand greatly IFC's scale of operations in those countries requesting assistance from IFC. In the first four years of McNamara's presidency, the volume of IFC's operations was two and a half times greater than in the preceding four years, an increase from an average of $40 million a year to that of $106 million. The volume should, by 1980, have reached a level of at least $200 million a year in 1972 dollars if IFC is to have carried out its purpose of seeing "that no economically justifiable and worthwhile private project in the developing countries fails to move because of lack of finance."[4]

At the same time as it increases its volume of operations, IFC should press ahead vigorously with the efforts it has been making under the direction of its executive vice-president, William Gaud, to persuade foreign private investors (particularly the multinational corporations) to share the ownership and control of their industries in a developing country with citizens of that country. "It is not," Gaud has said, "foreign investment that most of [the developing countries] object to, but foreign ownership and control. If ownership and control could be shared more widely, I am confident we would see a rapid and marked change for the better in the overseas investment climate. Some foreign investors will not take kindly to this suggestion. But if they are not prepared to yield to local interests a measure of ownership and control, I frankly feel they will be better off at home. For in my judgment absentee landlordism in industry has had its day."[5] IFC should continue, by exhortation and example, to press this argument.

On questions relating to the nationalization of foreign property by its borrowing member countries, the Bank Group must steer a careful course. The Bank Group has always recognized the right of any government to nationalize foreign property, but it has insisted that a nation which expropriated foreign property cut itself off from receiving Bank Group loans unless it was proceeding at reasonable speed to give reasonable compensation. The Bank has taken this line since one of the purposes of the Bank, as set forth in its articles of agreement, is "to promote private foreign investment" and nationalization by a developing country not followed by efforts to reach a fair and equitable settlement with the foreign owners discourages the flow of private investment, not only to that country, but also to other developing countries. This does not, however, mean, as stated in one Bank Group publication in 1971, that the Bank, before lending to a country which has expropriated foreign-owned property, "must first be satisfied that the government is making serious efforts to reach a fair and equitable settlement *and that there are good prospects that the matter will be cleared up satisfactorily*" (italics added).[6] There may not be good prospects of the matter's being cleared up satisfactorily, not because of action or inaction by the expropriating government, but because of unreasonable demands by the company whose property has been nationalized. Good prospects of its being cleared up satisfactorily should not therefore be a condition of lending by the Bank Group. The condition should be that the expropriating government is proceeding at reasonable speed to give reasonable compensation. It is also important that the Bank assume to a greater extent than in the past the responsibility of strengthening the position of its borrowers against unreasonable demands by foreign owners of nationalized property by making a thorough review of the entire question of what is reasonable compensation. This review should be submitted to the board of executive directors of the Bank Group for their consideration. What, for example, is reasonable compensation to a foreign company for a plant nationalized ten years after it started operations if the company had been able to repatriate the full amount of its invested capital in the first three years of operation, which is by no means unusual? The Bank Group should discuss the result of its review with the Development Assistance Committee of OECD, as representing the principal lending countries.

A country's credit-worthiness can be increased if Bank Group lending results in the provision of free foreign exchange to the government, since this foreign exchange can be used to service old or new debt. In its lending to countries allowing very little importation of luxury goods, having reasonably effective control over the export of capital, having a good record of mobilizing their own resources for development, and using them effectively, the Bank Group should increase greatly its financing of local costs (as described above, pages 43 to 45).

The Bank Group should encourage its rich members to improve the terms of their loans and discourage its borrowers from incurring debts and credits on hard or inappropriate terms. In particular, it should do even more to discourage, not only its borrowers from accepting aid for low priority projects, even if this aid is on soft terms, but also its donor members from giving official development assistance, export credits, or guarantees for such projects, even if the aid is on soft terms. A gift to a developing country to finance a white elephant project will cost that country more than a loan at high interest to finance a first rate project.[7]

It is therefore to be hoped that the rich member countries of the Bank Group will agree that the Bank's periodic economic reports on a country contain frank evaluations of each of the main programs directed to that country, whether from the Bank Group, the regional banks, national aid agencies, or national export credit agencies. If a government agency has financed a low priority project, the Bank should say so. If the aid-receiving country has accepted loans and credits on terms which are too hard or has accepted aid for low priority projects even on soft terms, the Bank should say so. The agencies or persons at fault will object to these disclosures but it is to be hoped that governments will be far-sighted enough to over-rule their objections on grounds of long-run national interests. It is not in the long-run interests of either aid-giving or aid-receiving countries that resources devoted to development be wasted.

In undertaking the assessment of projects which donor governments are financing, the Bank Group would be carrying one step further what it is already prepared to do for projects not yet accepted for financing by any aid-giving agency: "to assist a recipient country in making up a project list for presentation to the [aid] coordinating group . . . [to] [i]dentify . . . projects on the list which seem *prima facie* to deserve serious attention by the donors, . . . to state any reservations it may have about a project . . . [and to] [i]ndicate projects which, in the Bank's judgment, are clearly of low priority, or otherwise not ready for consideration."[8]

The next decade may well be a decade of debt crises. The damage these crises will do to the flow of resources to middle-income and low-income countries, and thus to their credit-worthiness, will be reduced the greater the distinction made between losses suffered by the bad lender and the good lender. If all suffer equally in debt settlements, the lender for good projects on soft terms bails out the lender for bad projects on hard terms, and the bad lender is not penalized for his bad behavior. The Bank Group should therefore try to work out with the Development Assistance Committee of OECD agreed techniques and procedures for implementing the principle that, in debt negotiations, the harder lenders for the poorer projects should bear the major part of the burden, or even in some cases the whole burden, of rescheduling or writing down of debts, and the softest lenders for the best projects should bear less or even none of the burden. This would discourage lenders from making improvident arrangements with middle-income and low-income countries which reduce the credit-worthiness of these countries.

Projects which any reasonable man would have recognized at the time of their inception were going to give a low or negative rate of economic and social return on the investment should be written down in debt negotiations. Projects which any reasonable man would have known at the time of their inception were thoroughly bad should be written off. This would penalize the creditor who extended credit for projects built in the wrong places at the wrong times to make the wrong kind of goods in the wrong quantitites. It would be the responsibility of the borrowing government to fine or imprison those, whether ministers or officials, who had accepted loans for what they knew were thoroughly bad projects.

This policy of selective default on a project basis would, for example, have been appropriate to a number of projects in Ghana financed by suppliers' credits from 1962 to 1964. A four-lane limited access highway was built from the northern outskirts of Accra to the northern outskirts of Tema, a route which is little used because it is about ten miles inland, whereas the Accra-Tema traffic is generated close to the coast. Facilities at the port of Tema and for a dry dock and shipyard were constructed well in excess of foreseeable requirements, and financed by British suppliers' credits totaling over £18 million. Yugoslavia provided suppliers' credits of almost £5 million for a naval harbor and base when adequate berthing facilities were already available at Tema.

Efforts to search for remedies, once a difficult debt situation has arisen, should be accompanied by an intensification of the efforts the Bank Group is already making to reduce the likelihood of difficult debt situations emerging. This the Bank Group tries to do through the advice it gives, often in the framework of country economic reports and aid coordination groups, on the composition of investment programs and on appropriate terms of financing. Here the essential requirement is appropriate management by the borrowing country. Appropriate management by lending countries is also required. It is particularly important that lending countries be more scrupulous in granting suppliers' credits to their exporters to middle-income and low-income countries. The

Bank Group should make a thorough review of the criteria which govern the granting of these credits, and should discuss the results of its review with the Development Assistance Committee in an effort to persuade exporting countries to refuse suppliers' credits for exports not meeting these criteria.

One important question about international negotiations on the debt crises of developing member countries remains to be dealt with. This is the contribution the Bank should be expected to make to debt negotiations, apart from good advice and good offices. If other creditors must agree that their debts be written down, should the Bank ask for exemption? The argument for its having a preferred position is that it will have to raise a very large amount of new money in the next ten years from the capital markets of rich countries, and the difficulties of raising this amount of money would be increased if it were to cast doubt on the value of its accounts receivable. It is argued that, even if the Bank were able in these circumstances to raise the amount required, it might have to pay a higher interest rate on its borrowings and its borrowers would have to pay higher interest rates on Bank loans. If, on the other hand, the Bank Group were to ask for treatment no more favorable than that granted to other creditors, it is likely that, like other good lenders for good projects, its debts would not be written down though they might be rescheduled to smooth out payments or to extend them over longer periods. Under its articles of agreement, the Bank is authorized to reschedule its debts by modifying the terms of amortization, extending the life of the loan, and by accepting payments in the debtor's currency for a period of up to three years.[9]

On balance it would seem wise for the Bank to agree that in debt negotiations the same criteria would be applied to its debts and those of other creditors. This would have the advantage of forcing the Bank, not only to press hard in the negotiations for the adoption of criteria serving the long-term interests of both lending and borrowing countries, but also to bear constantly in mind the danger that a great increase in its own volume of lending, unless carefully controlled, may help to precipitate debt crises.

CHAPTER NINE

Tourism and Retirement Villages

From 1965 to 1969, the number of foreign tourists doubled in many developing countries, including Spain, Portugal, Morocco, Tunisia, Mexico, Colombia, and Venezuela. In 1970, gross receipts from foreign tourists amounted to more than one-fifth of the total value of merchandise exports in Greece, Portugal, Morocco, Tunisia, and Kenya. In Spain, Lebanon, Mexico, and many Caribbean islands, tourism had by 1970 become the most important single export. It is expected that the flow of tourists to developing countries will double in the seventies.[1] The great increase in the past two decades in the expenditures in developing countries by tourists from rich countries has had five main causes: higher income in the rich countries; longer holidays; increased facilities for air travel; relatively low costs of package tours; and more and better tourist accommodations. If developing countries, with the assistance of the World Bank Group, were to take proper action, there could be a great increase in the next two decades in the expenditures not only of tourists but also of "permanent tourists"[2]—retired people who take up permanent residence abroad. There are five main reasons for assuming that a large number of retired people from rich countries would make their homes in a developing country with a pleasant climate if the proper facilities were available. Because of increased population and lower retirement ages, the number of retired people in rich countries has increased and continues to increase. The great increases in average real income in rich countries and advances in social legislation have meant an increase in the number of retired people in rich countries entitled to pensions on which they could live comfortably abroad where the cost of services is relatively low. As the "three-generation" family has gradually given way to the "two-generation" family, retired people have been forced to live by themselves, or in "senior citizens" apartments, retirement villages, or nursing homes. In rich countries, the cost of personal services mounts even faster than the cost of goods, putting them beyond the reach of most older people at the very time they need them most. As people grow older, they find the cold of winter more trying.

Most retired people in Western Europe or North America would when first presented with the possibility of living in a retirement village in a country such as India, say that they would not want to live so far away from their own country, their familiar neighborhood, their friends, children, and grandchildren. Distance, however, is not to be measured in miles but in hours and costs of travel. In the early seventies, it takes a quarter of the time and costs about the same amount of money to travel from New York to New Delhi as it cost in time and money in the early thirties to travel from New York to San Francisco. In 1972 it took 21½ hours to travel from New York to New Delhi and cost $450 for the return fare. In 1930 it took four days to travel by train from New York to San Francisco at a cost of $125 for the return railway fare (not including berth or meals); and $125 in 1930 equals between $375 and $500 in 1972.

For its first twenty years, the Bank Group resolutely refused to have anything to do with tourism, not even permitting national development banks to finance it from the proceeds of Bank Group loans. If the Bank had from the early fifties onward been developing creative expertise in tourism and had been giving sensible advice and substantial loans for tourist development in those of its developing members that asked for them, much of the tourist development which took place in the fifties and sixties in developing countries might have resulted in greater economic benefits to the developing countries, with fewer unpleasant social consequences. It should not repeat this error in dealing with the present opportunity to help the poorer countries attract retired people from rich countries as permanent residents.

An influx of tourists and retired people from rich countries to low-income countries will inevitably have unpleasant social consequences; it can, if not properly controlled, have *highly unpleasant* social consequences. One of the tasks of the Bank Group is to help low-income countries work out ways by which these consequences are reduced to the minimum and the economic return increased to the maximum. The low-income countries can then decide whether the economic benefits are worth the social costs.

The economic benefits from a well-thought-out, well-administered scheme of retirement villages could indeed be great. By 1980 there will probably be about 60 million people of sixty-five or over in the rich non-Communist countries of the world and average income in those countries is likely to be at least $5,000 in 1972 dollars. Perhaps some 3 million of those people could afford to pay an annual fee of $4,000 for membership in a retirement village if this membership covered all living expenses and medical and hospital care. If only one in ten of these 3 million moved to a retirement village in a low-income country, the income from their fees alone would be $1.2 billion. They would spend money in addition to their fees. They would be visited by friends and relations. One writer has estimated that in Mexico the long-term economic impact of expenditures by retired people has been over seven times their expenditures.[3]

If such villages turned out to be successful, accommodation could be provided at lower rates. In the longer run, as low-income countries acquired experience in running these villages, and as the level of minimum payments by the governments of rich countries to their older citizens rose, there might even be villages established for old people from the richest of the rich countries who have no income other than their social security benefits and who would be able to live in their own countries only at a very low standard. In a well-organized retirement village in a low-income country, they would be able to live at a level which they could attain at home only at twice their income.

Even in the most wealthy countries, tourists from other wealthy countries are not generally popular. Most people don't like tourists. Most people don't export well. They behave better at home than abroad. When wealthy white people travel in the poorer countries, the social costs are much greater than when they travel in other wealthy white countries: The revulsion of the wealthy white visitor from the poverty of the poorer countries is accompanied by a revulsion of the poor people of the poorer countries against the wealth of the visitors. Moreover, "Tourism is an industry where the host workers of the poorer countries are made to feel servile to the paying guests from the richer countries, and can come intensely to dislike them."[4] Doctors, dentists, and nurses in the low-income countries will be attracted to work for the wealthy visitors, and there will be even fewer of them to serve their own fellow citizens. (If they were not able to work in retirement villages, they might, of course, emigrate to rich countries.)

For these reasons, the missions which the Bank group sends out at the request of a low-income country to study the possibilities of developing tourism and retirement villages should devote considerable time to working out with the government of the country measures to reduce the social costs. Some measures are obvious: tourist hotels and retirement villages must not monopolize the best beaches; to reduce the danger of their feeling servile, the workers should be helped to form strong trade unions; tipping could be replaced by a service charge; the proportion of foreigners in the management of the facilities should be constantly reduced as local nationals are trained to take their places. In some way—perhaps by earmarked taxes—it should be made clear to the poor people of the host country that the money brought into the country is being used to improve their living conditions.

Great expertise is required if a developing country is to secure the maximum economic benefits, including maximum employment and maximum foreign exchange earnings, from the development of tourism and retirement villages at minimum social cost. Great financial resources are required because the large expenditures on the facilities for the tourists and the retired people must be complemented by large related expenditures on water and sewerage, and on improved transportation facilities. These expenditures must, if they are to result in maximum benefit to the developing country, be accompanied by financial and technical help to local farmers, fishermen, merchants, and others, so that they can provide locally made goods of high quality to the tourist hotels and the retirement villages and directly to the tourists and the retired people. For all these reasons, it is essential that the Bank, IDA, and IFC play an increasingly active part in helping the developing members of the Bank Group with good prospects of large development of tourism or retirement villages to work out and finance soundly based projects.

The problems the poorer countries face in trying to establish soundly based development for visitors from rich countries are many and difficult. Understandably, many of the officials in the poorer countries who were given responsibilities for tourist development at the beginning of the boom in tourism in the fifties were not experts in gauging the requirements of the potential customers. As a result, they wasted scarce money building the kind of facilities they thought the foreigner most wanted, not the kind he in fact most wanted. Tourist officials in Kashmir proudly demonstrated to me in the mid-fifties the water closets in cottages they had just built for tourists, but the view from the cottages was not of the majestic surrounding Himalayas but of an unattractive village. A third-rate ugly hotel was built at the entrance to Petra, where a first-rate attractive hotel fitting into the environment would have been a compelling tourist attraction. Tourist authorities in these countries needed advice from people with expert knowledge of what foreign tourists wanted. Now they need expert advice on what retired people from rich countries want most in retirement villages.

But, if the local officials made errors, the foreigners who built tourist facilities in the fifties and sixties in the poorer countries made far more serious ones. In constructing and operating the facilities, they used capital-intensive methods and they did not use as much local labor and goods as they could have. They did not try hard enough to build up local sources of supply for the goods they needed, or to train nationals of the host country to take over gradually the operation of the facilities. The governments of the countries where these foreigners operated would have got a better deal from the foreign developers of tourist facilities had they been able to get impartial, well-informed, creative, expert advice from an agency such as the World Bank Group, and the support of that agency in driving a better bargain with the foreigners; a better bargain in the sense that it would have increased the long-run economic return to the host country and lessened the unpleasant social consequences.

There is no simple formula the Bank Group can apply to all tourist projects and all projects for retirement villages which come before it, but there are methods with which it could experiment. It should encourage member countries with a good potential for the development of tourism or retirement villages to request it to send an expert mission which, together with experts appointed by the government, would undertake a thorough study. The sector mission should include representatives of the regional bank, the UNDP, and the ILO. The study should deal, not only with such matters as the airports, roads, transport facilities, and water supply and sewerage development needed to support a large-scale expansion of the tourist industry, but also with the improvement of fishing, farming, brewing, and distilling to provide food and drink of acceptable quality, and with the training of hotel staff. Schools should be established for training cooks in both the western and the local traditions. Schools should also be established for training the management staff of hotels.

The mission should make recommendations on measures to insure that an increasing proportion of the goods consumed by the visitors is produced in the host country. It should consider the nature and extent of the credits and technical assistance to be made available to farmers to assist them in producing meat, dairy products, fruit, and vegetables of the required quality and kind. Fishermen should also be given credits and technical assistance. Special livestock farms and abattoirs might be established to supply high quality meat. The Bank Group should also, through local intermediary institutions, make credits and technical assistance available to local residents wishing to establish or improve facilities for visitors: restaurants, for example, or shops, handicraft industries, and agencies to run local tours.

One of the conditions of Bank Group loans for tourist hotels should be that a reasonable preference is given to local materials and labor in constructing them. To encourage a labor-intensive rather than a capital-intensive type of tourist development, another condition should be that the entrepreneur pay, in interest on the loan or in taxes or in some other way, a charge for the capital used in his tourist development equivalent to the real or shadow price of capital in the country. In most countries, this would be at least 10 per cent plus the annual average rate of shrinkage in the real value of the local currency.

In the five years ending in mid-1973, the Bank Group will probably have sent out sector missions to 34 countries to make studies of tourism, compared with only 3 in the preceding five years. This is a substantial achievement. It is clear, however, from the chapter on tourism in the Bank Group's book on its operations published in 1972, that none of these missions had terms of reference as wide as those recommended above. That chapter on tourism is indeed noteworthy for its omissions. It might have been written in the pre-McNamara age. It does not mention opportunities which tourism presents for building up local agriculture, fisheries, and industry for processing food and making drinks. It does not mention the opportunities to build up locally owned restaurants, shops, handicraft industry, and agencies to run local tours. It does not mention the importance of labor-intensive, capital-saving tourist development.

Perhaps the best form of national organization to run retirement villages would be an autonomous foundation established by the national government with a board of directors consisting half of nationals and half of outside experts. Such a foundation would be the intermediary institution to which the Bank and IDA would grant loans. It would issue all the contracts to the clients of the villages. After a two-

or three-year trial period, the clients should have the right to receive contracts good for the rest of their lives—to cover accomodation, food, medical and dental services, hospitalization, doctors' and oculists' prescriptions, and recreational facilities. A contract good for life would have to provide that the real value of the annual payments—expressed in terms of the purchasing power of the currency of the client's country—could not be increased. Thus, for a United States citizen, the contract might provide for an annual payment of a certain number of United States dollars of the value of U.S. dollars during the year in which the contract was signed; if the cost of living in the United States went up by 3 per cent a year, the annual fee would also go up at the same rate a year. This would mean no increase in the burden for the client on the assumption that pensions in all rich countries will by then be automatically adjusted to increases in the cost of living.

There can be no large development of retirement villages in developing countries unless the governments of the rich countries are prepared to cooperate. It will be necessary for them to agree that persons receiving pensions from them may continue to draw their pensions while living in these villages, and to help protect retired people living in these villages from increases in taxation which would make it difficult or impossible for them to meet their annual payments under their contracts. The Bank Group might decide, after studying the question, that the best solution would be a multilateral convention to be concluded between rich countries and developing countries desiring to establish retirement villages, in which effort it could seek the cooperation of the Development Assistance Committee of OECD. (Special concessions granted by rich countries could be restricted to low-income countries and not extended to middle-income countries.)

The governments of the countries of residents in the retirement villages might be perturbed by the drain of successful schemes on their foreign exchange, but, since this would come gradually, they would have time to adjust to it. Moreover, they would be able to offset against it their gain from not having to provide medical and hospital care for their older citizens living abroad. Increasingly, in rich countries, older people will be getting free medical and hospital care; the costs of this care to the state will be constantly and rapidly mounting.

This review indicates the great importance to a number of developing countries of a thorough exploration by the Bank Group of the possibilities of large programs for retirement villages. We have here, of course, not a question alone of the interests of the developing countries but pre-eminently a question of the interests of the older people in rich countries who are potential members of these villages. Well-organized retirement villages in developing countries would make possible much happier years of retirement for many of these older people.

CHAPTER TEN

Management Skills and Technology

In almost all developing countries, the scarcity of management ability, administrative resources, and entrepreneurial energy creates serious obstacles to economic growth; in many, these obstacles are more serious than those created by the scarcity of foreign or domestic capital. Just as detrimental to economic growth in almost all developing countries is the inappropriateness of so much of the technology of rich countries to the needs of the poorer countries, and the profound lack of interest of almost all firms in both rich and developing countries in spending money on research into adapting the technologies of the rich countries to the needs of the poorer.

The Bank Group can do much to help its developing member countries to surmount or find a way around these obstacles. It has a special responsibility to do so, because of its great intellectual and financial resources. That responsibility is especially heavy in countries where the Bank Group has made large investments, for the more help the Bank Group can give its borrowers in dealing with these obstacles, the greater will be the value to them of the investments the Bank Group has made, and the greater their capacity to meet the interest and the amortization payments on the loans from the Bank, IDA, and IFC. IFC has an important role to play because of its links with private industry in both the rich and the developing countries. But the Bank Group can work effectively in this field only if it works in close cooperation and harmony with the ILO, FAO, WHO, Unesco, the UNDP, the UN Industrial Development Organization, DAC, and the regional banks.

The most important way by which the Bank Group can help its developing member countries to increase their managerial and administrative resources is by aiding them to establish or strengthen national or regional institutes for training in management and business administration, and for carrying out practical research. There are now only a very few of these institutes in the developing world; many more, formal and informal, are needed because:

A rapid industrialization in some countries, an important development of export and import trades in others, and a replacement of expatriates by nationals in private and public enterprises in most of the former colonies have increased the demand for skilled middle level and high level managers.[1]

The most important way by which the Bank Group can help its developing member countries in the task of technological adaptation and innovation is by aiding them to establish or strengthen national or regional research institutes. These should undertake practical work of a high standard in adapting labor-saving techniques and technologies of rich countries to the local environment where capital is scarce and labor abundant. In their adaptation, these institutes would be guided by local needs and cultural values. Their task of adaptation would include transformation, which "involves reducing the scale of production, simplifying some processes, and improvising to meet the dearth of maintenance and support facilities,"[2] and creative innovation. These research institutes would maintain close communications with the governments, universities, and industries of the nation and region. Their work would be addressed to the practical problems of local industry; they would disseminate the results of their research; they would make certain that potential users received from them all the information they required.[3]

In developing countries, effective coordination between research institutes on technological adaptation and innovation, and local governments, universities, and industry is essential on the national and regional levels. On the international level, effective coordination is similarly required between the World Bank Group and the other international and national agencies concerned with helping the developing countries to establish both these institutes and also those for training managers and administrators, and for conducting research on problems of management and administration.

The Bank Group should be prepared to provide considerable financial assistance toward the establishment and effective operation of these institutes as a supplement to assistance from local governments, local industry, and from other international or national agencies. Sometimes the financial assistance from the Bank Group would take the form of grants, sometimes of Bank or IDA loans. The Bank Group should also, in association with the developing countries, determine why almost all the existing industrial research institutes in these countries have almost no relationship with the local industrial community, and why the local industrial community spends so little on research and development and is so little interested in developing labor-intensive, capital-saving technologies. This inquiry might well lead to the conclusion that changes in the nature of the research institutes will be inadequate unless they are accompanied by changes in incentives resulting in local industry's being willing to spend more on research and development, and to cooperate closely with the government-sponsored research institutes in promoting technological adaptation and innovation.

Under McNamara's presidency, the Bank Group has made a start in the right direction. Thus, in 1971 for the first time in its history, it helped to finance an institute of management (in a loan to Turkey), and announced that it "expects . . . to finance formal as well as non-formal training institutions in business administration and management."[4] It has contracted with the Asian Institute of Technology to analyze berth operations in the port of Bangkok. It is encouraging the University of East Africa to study how to increase the labor content and reduce the capital content of road-building, and to monitor the results of a Bank Group project for building feeder roads in Tanzania.[5] It is collaborating with agencies of the Indian Government in a comprehensive research project on substituting labor for capital in civil works in that country. It has been collaborating with the Korean Institute of Science and Technology on the programming of mechanical engineering industries. It established in 1972 an office of science and technology with a staff of two professional officers. But these are only short steps in the right direction.

The other ways by which the Bank Group can help its developing member countries to surmount or find a way around obstacles to economic growth are more directly related to the traditional roles of the Bank Group. Thus, it should give higher priority than in the past to loans calculated to make an important contribution to building up these scarce factors of production, and to stimulating the transfer or adaptation of appropriate technology. It should press harder for the inclusion in other loan agreements of provisions calculated to have these effects. It should modify its rules and practices on international competitive bidding to stimulate the growth of local contracting firms. It should take much greater care than in the past to insure that it does not itself give positive encouragement to the introduction of inappropriate technology to its developing member countries.

Missions sent out by the Bank Group to appraise projects should be instructed by the president of the Bank to attach greater importance than in the past to working out, with the member country or the company concerned, modifications that would increase the contribution the project would make to the transfer or adaptation of technology and the building up of management ability, administrative resources, entrepreneurial energy, and skilled labor. The contribution IFC can make to this can be especially helpful. In the past the Bank Group's approach to a particular project has tended to be, "How can we do this project as well and as efficiently as possible?" There should now be much greater emphasis on the question, "How can we implement this project in a manner so as to increase the technological and managerial competence of the country in which the project is located?"

Since insistence on international competitive bidding for projects which can make effective use of substantial local resources can impede the growth of local industry, the Bank Group should generalize and expand the precedent set in the 1971 loan for agricultural research in Spain, which required for certain goods produced locally, not international competitive bidding, but local procurement under the standard competitive procedures of the national government. At present, in comparing bids under international competitive bidding, the Bank Group allows a preference of 15 per cent to local suppliers over foreign contractors. The Bank Group should establish as its objective that a reasonable proportion of Bank Group contracts go to local suppliers and contractors to build up their competence, engage them in international competition, and expand the size of their potential market. To implement this policy, the Bank Group should increase the level of preference in selected countries for defined periods of years.

The Bank Group has been paying special attention in recent years to building up the capacity of local contractors to undertake road projects and other construction projects financed by the Bank Group. Thus:

. . . it has tried in one country to assist local contractors . . . by financing consulting services to advise them in bid preparation, costing and the like. In another country it has stimulated an investigation into ways of developing the local contracting industry.

Believing that complementary measures which can be taken by the governments of developing countries

. . . are more important to development of the local [*contracting*] *industry than any steps the Bank can take . . . the Bank has recently started a research study to explore . . .* [*such measures as the adoption of*] *a clear policy of putting road construction and other work out to contract . . .* [*and the reviewing of*] *existing taxation and contracting procedures which are unfavorable to contractors.*

The Bank Group's sector working paper on transportation, from which these quotations are taken, goes on to say:

The Bank believes that more could be done. It will explore further what technical assistance might be given to local firms through consultants or in other ways. Recognizing that in some countries shortage of equipment and of the foreign exchange to purchase it have hindered the growth of local firms, the Bank might consider financing equipment for the use of local contractors. This might be possible on a rental or hire-purchase basis through a government department or development bank.[6]

Governments of both rich and developing countries should give the management and the staff of the Bank Group every assistance and encouragement they can to press ahead with these efforts, since this is one of the best ways to help developing countries build up management ability and entrepreneurial energy.

It is also important that the Bank Group do what it can to strengthen local consulting and designing firms in developing countries, since these firms can contribute much to the creative adaptation of foreign techniques and technologies to local conditions. These firms "have hardly made their appearance in developing countries, even in those which have gone in for machine fabricating capacity. . . . [The development] will eliminate the need for repetitive import of technology and also help improve the productivity of imported technology."[7] In selecting consulting and designing firms, the Bank Group should give great weight to the advantages in the longer run of using local, rather than foreign, firms. The ability of local contractors and of local consulting and designing firms to compete against foreign firms will be increased the more the Bank Group is able to work out with its borrowers, whenever this is appropriate, standards and specifications for its projects which are labor-intensive, capital-saving, and foreign-exchange-saving. Local firms normally have more experience with projects of this kind than firms from rich countries. To strengthen the capacity of these firms, the Bank Group often requires them, as a condition of receiving contracts for projects financed by the Bank Group, to employ consultants approved by the Bank Group. Most of these consultants come from private industry, and from consulting and designing firms and institutes of management in the industrialized countries. To provide some protection against possible biases or conflicts of interest in consultants from the private sector in industrialized countries, the Bank Group should be able to supplement these consultants with consultants from its own staff. It should therefore add to its professional staff a number of technical innovators and experts in industrial research and development and in management, who would be available to consulting and designing firms in middle-income and low-income countries.

In approving consultants and in appointing consultants to its own staff, the Bank Group should take much more care than in the past to guard against the danger that these consultants will strengthen the tendencies already strong in most developing countries to import inappropriate techniques and technologies from rich countries. In the past, insistence by aid agencies on the employment of foreign architects and consulting engineers has, as Dudley Seers has pointed out, often resulted in the adoption of techniques of construction and technologies appropriate to their own countries but inappropriate to countries suffering from severe shortages of capital and dangerously large surpluses of labor. It is not only foreign architects and engineers, however, who have been at fault. Local engineers "who had at least part of their training overseas on courses not adapted to the needs of countries with surplus labor"[8] "mostly have an in-built tendency to prefer the capital-intensive methods of production with which they are familiar."[9] They do not realize that while the task of technology in rich countries is to save manpower, the task of technology in the poorer countries is to save capital. Indeed, the authors of the Bank Group paper on urbanization published in 1972 state: "While the authorities of developing countries are sometimes more aware than foreign consultants of the need to tailor standards to local conditions, the reverse situation of local agencies favoring the highest standards in use in developed countries appears more general."[10]

Two striking examples of outside technical assistance experts recommending inappropriate technologies are given in Dudley Seers' report on Ceylon:

In 1959 a visiting expert advised the Government of Ceylon to reduce drastically the amount of labour input used in quarrying operations in the cement industry. His argument was mainly based on the fact that a factory of similar size in the United States showed about one-fifth of the number of man-hours per ton spent in quarrying operations in Ceylon . . . The automatic conveyor belt and luggage sorter at Colombo International Airport is an example of unsuitable equipment supplied under an aid programme.[11]

Ernest Stern, formerly assistant administrator for program and policy of the United States Agency for International Development, and now senior adviser on development policy in the World Bank, has given a damning indictment of the support which aid agencies have given in the past to the introduction of "inapplicable technology" to developing countries, meaning by technology "all aspects of the transfer of technologic concepts, ranging from engineering advice on a specific project to assistance to institution building in education and the training of individuals from developing countries":

All these channels have tended to provide advice which has reduced the employment creating potential of investment. Engineers, educators, administrators, agricultural advisers and economists from the developed countries think in terms of their labor-scarce, capital-abundant economies when they are transplanted to the developing countries. In some ways one could expect nothing else. Nonetheless, the relatively uncritical acceptance of their advice has reinforced the bias in favor of sophisticated, high standard, labor-saving equipment. It has placed a misguided emphasis on constructing new schools to "modern" specifications rather than utilizing ones which are consistent with the availability of local materials and skills; it has led to the conviction that large-scale farming is necessarily more efficient, whereas the facts suggest the contrary; it places emphasis on increasing productivity per man instead of per acre; it leads to the introduction of computer data processing in service industries, (particularly banks).[12]

So that these costly errors of the past will not be repeated, all members of the professional staff of the Bank Group concerned with what Ernest Stern calls "all aspects of the transfer of technologic concepts" should be given special training in working out techniques and technologies appropriate to capital-scarce, labor-surplus developing countries. They could then protect developing countries against the well-meaning but expensively inappropriate advice of other outside experts and of foreign-trained local experts who still do not realize how profound must be the process of creative adaptation and innovation before the labor-saving technologies of rich countries can be made appropriate to developing countries.

Since, even if all the proposals set forth in this chapter are implemented, many years will pass before developing countries have enough local technical experts of the required quality, a large crash program is probably necessary to cover the intervening period. The main responsibility would fall on international agencies other than the Bank Group, but the Bank Group would, as I. G. Patel has suggested, have important responsibilities. In a speech in 1968 he said:

What is needed if the business of world economic development is to be taken seriously is a massive effort whereby hundreds and even thousands of technical experts are hired by some international agencies and made available for actual employment to different developing countries. I cannot help feeling, for example, that if the World Bank is serious about a substantial increase in fertilizer production in the developing world, it will have to begin by training and employing hundreds of fertilizer technicians and assign them for designing, erecting and even managing fertilizer projects in different parts of the developing world. It will not be [enough?] *merely to assume that the transfer of know-how and skills is the business of private foreign investment. For, however desirable such investment might be, it would be mere wishful thinking to assume that such investment could be the wave of the future for large parts of the developing world.*[13]

The agricultural development service which the Bank Group maintains in East Africa, associated with its permanent mission in Nairobi, is a prototype of the kind of large development service I. G. Patel has suggested the Bank Group establish. It "is a corps of experienced personnel who can be made available, on a reimbursable basis, to manage new project organizations, especially in the early years."[14]

All this would go some distance to meet the plea made in December 1971 by the finance minister of India when he said:

There is one area where the quest for a genuine world partnership has hardly even begun . . . the whole question of the transfer of technology from the developed to the developing countries. . . . It seems to be taken for granted that whereas the technology for agriculture or family planning should be transferred freely from one country to the other, the technology for industry, transport, mining and the like is the preserve of private business which can be transferred only on the basis of commercial collaboration with such business. Collaboration with private foreign business has certainly a role to play. But I cannot help feeling that on this basis alone the transfer of technology to the developing world would be so slow and expensive as to be of little avail in satisfying the legitimate aspirations of the people. I have no ready-made solutions to offer in this area. But I think the time has come when our international agencies like the UNDP and the World Bank will have to show greater imagination and boldness in chalking out new paths for the transfer of technology to the developing world.[15]

And not new paths just for the transfer of technology but also for the creative adaptation of technology.

CHAPTER ELEVEN

On Giving Advice

Robert McNamara has spoken of the kind of advice on policy the Bank Group gives to its borrowers as "advice leading to sound social and economic development programs."[1] This advice is based on the periodic assessments the Bank Group makes of the development programs of countries wishing to borrow from it. These assessments are made in the reports of the Bank Group's country economic missions, in its studies of sectors of a country's economy, and in its reports appraising projects submitted to it for financing. For an international agency dominated by rich givers of aid to make assessments of the development programs of poor receivers of aid is a delicate, difficult, and hazardous affair. It will become less so, the more the domination of the agency by rich countries is reduced and the more the agency assesses the aid performance of rich aid-givers, as well as the development performance of poor aid-receivers. But, even at the present time, responsible receivers of aid recognize that, while it is seldom pleasant to have one's performance assessed by others, the burden is bearable. I. G. Patel said in a public lecture in India at the beginning of 1968:

[T]here is no reason why we should object to an assessment of our plans and policies by the aid-giving countries and institutions and much less reason why we should suspect something sinister in every honest advice rendered to us. As long as we ourselves are clear about where we stand and what we wish to achieve, there is no reason why we should fear a dialogue with other people.[2]

Coming from I. G. Patel, this statement has particular importance. When he made the statement, he was the senior official in the Indian government concerned with aid matters. He has had long experience in dealing with aid-givers. He is well known for his firm opposition to what he would consider to be intervention by the Bank Group in India's affairs. He is a distinguished Indian, and Indians are particularly sensitive about being given advice by rich white nations or agencies controlled by rich white nations. The history of the last two hundred years gets in the way—the humiliation of being the only great Asian nation to have been conquered and occupied by the West and ruled by it for many generations, the cultural arrogance of the conqueror, the racial discrimination he practiced.

A Bank Group assessment of the development programs of a government must determine whether they are best calculated to advance development quickly, given the special conditions of the country, and how far modifications might speed up the rate of development. The question at which McNamara has been hammering is how should advance in development be measured in a particular country. In terms of the annual rate of growth in GNP per capita in constant prices? In terms of social, as well as economic, advance? Or in terms of the rate of progress in providing the goods and services required to raise the consumption of every man, woman, and child in the nation to a minimum level of nutrition, clothing, education, housing, and medical care?[3] Should the Bank Group's assessment of a borrowing country's development program discuss the wisdom of that country's adopting measures which would result in some increase in the pace of progress toward meeting the minimum consumption needs of the poorest two-fifths of the population even if this should mean some slowing of the rate of growth in constant prices in GNP per capita?

The overriding requirement of any Bank Group assessment is that it be first-rate. No assessment would be first-rate if limited to assessing short-run effects. It must take longer-run effects into account. Therefore, even if the Bank Group's assessment is limited to judging a development program by the sole criterion of how far it is likely to lead to the highest possible rate of increase in GNP measured in constant prices, the Bank is under an obligation to the government of the borrowing member country to take into account the degree to which in that country failure to advance on the social front is likely in the longer run to hold up advance on the economic front.

Thus, if the Bank Group's studies of a particular country lead it to conclude that a continuation of existing government policies will perpetuate or result in a distribution of income among regions and classes so inequitable that it is likely in the long run to lead to a slower rate of economic growth than possible alternative policies, the Bank is in duty bound to inform the member government and to suggest changes in its policies which it might consider. These changes might include the substitutions, in certain types of projects, of labor-intensive for capital-intensive technologies, or a higher priority for labor-intensive projects (such as small industries and rural development works), so that there would be substantial increases in the number of people getting proper pay for performing productive work. This would result in a more equitable distribution of the benefits of economic growth and in more social justice, in higher levels of consumption of the basic necessities of life by the mass of the people, and, in the longer run, in more political power for the masses.

It is in moving from this to measures calculated to increase the pace of advance toward social justice at the cost of some slowing down of the pace of economic advance that the problem becomes more difficult for an outside aid agency. The question of what action, if any, a national government should take to increase social justice at the expense of decreasing the potential production of useful goods and services lies at the core of government policy in every country, rich or poor; and the poorer the country, the greater the real cost of any slowing down in the rate of economic growth. It would be one thing for the United States, with income per capita of about $5,000 a year, to decide that it would prefer no economic growth and more social justice to a 5 per cent rate of economic growth and less social justice; it would be an entirely different thing for Upper Volta, in which income per capita is probably about $60 a year, to so decide. Equality of income in Upper Volta means equality in misery. If the economy of Upper Volta is to be capable of providing the means to meet the basic minimum needs of its people, if it is to be capable of providing the basis for reducing the unhappiness implicit in high rates of maternal and infant mortality, its production of essential goods and services must be doubled, trebled, quadrupled. This will not of itself insure that the people of Upper Volta have their basic needs met, since the government may divert a considerable part of the additional resources into its own pockets and those of its friends and supporters (by selling some of the additional production abroad and transferring the proceeds into bank accounts n Switzerland). But, without a doubling, trebling, and quadrupling of the production of essential goods and services, no government in Upper Volta, however noble its motives and however efficient its operations, could meet the basic minimum needs of the people. Such increases are necessary to social advance, although they do not guarantee it.

Moreover, Bank Group assessments of the national development programs of its borrowers are drafted by people with no direct and immediate personal experience of the kind of poverty implicit in figures of per capita GNP of not more than $150 a year, the level of more than half the peoples of the world. Indeed, most, if not all, the people who draft these assessments are, judged against a world scale of income distribution, extremely wealthy. They probably belong to the wealthiest 2 per cent of the population of the world. No matter how great their expertise, their creative imagination, their respectful sympathy for people suffering from the kind of poverty endemic to half the people of the world, they are so remote from the realities of that kind of poverty—and this is just about as true of staff members from the poorer countries as of staff members from the rich—that it is almost impossible for them to comprehend the feelings or share the attitudes of these people; it is almost impossible for them to make useful judgments on whether these people would consider themselves better off with a little less economic growth and a little more social justice. When they try to make such judgments, the danger is that they will apply their own values and their own priorities; and this would indeed be to use aid as an agency of cultural imperialism.

Thus, the poorer the country, the less appropriate it is that the Bank Group, in its assessment, make recommendations entailing a slowing down in the rate of healthy economic growth. Rather, it should concentrate on the task of proposing to the government measures to speed up the rate of healthy economic growth and, at the same time, to increase employment on productive jobs at proper pay. It would, nevertheless, on occasion be appropriate for the Bank Group to state in its assessment, no matter how poor the country, that such-and-such a change in its development program would likely result in a considerable advance in social justice at the cost of a modest reduction in the rate of economic growth. The Bank Group would then do its best to be precise about the extent of the real economic cost of the slow-down in the rate of growth. Moreover, though the Bank Group should not urge poor countries to sacrifice economic growth to social justice, it need have no hesitation in concurring in decisions of the government of the country to make a relatively small sacrifice of economic growth in return for a substantial increase in social justice.

The problem in any event is not pressing or acute or important at the present time in the Bank Group's relations with most of its low-income borrowers, particularly with the very poor countries with per capita GNP's of not more than $150 a year, which contain 60 per cent of the population of all the developing member countries of the Bank, since it is likely to be a long time before the Bank Group has, in its assessments of the development programs of these countries, exhausted the possibilities of making recommendations which would result in progress toward social justice, without in the long run slowing down the real rate of growth in the production of essential goods and services.

One of the main purposes of this kind of an assessment is to provide the basis for a dialogue between the Bank Group and the government of the borrower. The Bank Group and other lenders have thought of this dialogue as providing an opportunity for them to put to the government of the borrower arguments for that government's making changes in its development program. They have hoped that from the dialogue would emerge an agreed strategy of development. The borrower has thought of the dialogue in terms similar to those I. G. Patel used in 1968 of the consortium on India, which the Bank Group had organized and chaired. "The Consortium," he said, "began [in 1958] perhaps as a rescue operation. But it soon emerged as a forum for getting our plans endorsed by the donor countries as a first step towards having our foreign exchange requirements underwritten jointly by the members of the group."[4] Certainly skilled Indian representatives at consortium meetings have usually been able to turn the meetings into a sort of seminar conducted by them on India's development plans and policies, its difficulties, and its financial requirements.

Thus, after the 1963 meeting of the aid-India consortium, I wrote as follows on May 10 to Prime Minister Nehru in my capacity of director of the South Asia and Middle East department of the Bank:

This was the first time India had been represented at a Consortium meeting. The atmosphere was not, as some people had feared, one of the Indian representative being in the dock, but rather of his conducting a seminar on the problems of Indian economic development. This does not mean that the governments represented on the Consortium did not take advantage of the opportunity to make known their misgivings over some of the policies and procedures of the Indian Government which seemed to them to reduce the value to India of the aid they gave. They did bring up these misgivings. Similarly L. K. Jha [*the Indian representative*] *took advantage of the opportunity to stress the need for the members of the Consortium to make changes in their own policies in order to help India with the task of development.*

An assessment by a Bank Group mission of a borrowing country's development program has often been followed by prolonged and arduous negotiations between the Bank Group and the borrower. In these negotiations, the Bank Group has in the past often maintained that it would be easier for it to make loans to that country, and to persuade other aid-givers to do so, if it could be more convinced that the plans and policies the borrowers proposed to follow would result in economic development. It might add that certain changes in these plans and policies recommended in the Bank Group's assessment would lead to the necessary degree of conviction. The Bank Group might say that in this it was not trying to buy policies it liked by making aid contingent on the borrower's acceptance of the Bank Group's advice, since there was a fine but genuine distinction between trying to buy with aid the policies favored by the Bank Group, and coming more generously to the assistance of policies that promised growth. The Bank Group might argue that to support a borrower less strongly when prospects for using aid effectively are poor, and more strongly when they are more promising, is a method of using its scarce resources in a systematic way to encourage the borrowing country's growth. This, the Bank Group might say, challenges the sovereignty of the borrower no more than any mutual accommodation among sovereign nations.[5]

The traditional approach of the Bank Group to its dialogue on development with its borrowing member countries was that it would try, by its so-called leverage—gained from its ability to increase or decrease the volume of its lending—to secure changes in the borrower's policies resulting in a higher rate of economic growth. (Leverage is the term applied to the practice of linking development loans with requirements for changes in the policies of the borrower.) The new approach, which McNamara has been advocating, is that the Bank Group use its leverage to secure changes in the borrower's policies which would result, not only in growth, but in a more equitable distribution of the benefits of growth among the people of the borrowing country. The degree to which either of these approaches to the use of Bank Group leverage has a reasonable chance of success depends mainly on the extent to which the Bank Group and other aid-givers will in fact come more generously to the assistance of governments which pursue policies promising growth, or growth plus a more equitable distribution of its benefits, than of governments which do not. The record of the past is not encouraging. The World Bank in 1964 and 1965 made a major study to determine why the pace of economic advance in India had slowed down in the first half of the sixties. The Bank produced a ten-volume report containing about eight fairly precise recommendations on changes in Indian policy which the Bank mission considered would lead to more rapid growth. The recommendations were related mainly to policy on the exchange rate, to the administrative controls over imports, and to the relative neglect of agriculture. In its discussion of these recommendations with the Indian government in 1965 and 1966, it can be assumed that the Bank Group was wise enough not to promise that more aid would be forthcoming if India accepted the recommendations. It can also be assumed that the Bank Group told the Indian authorities that if India were to accept the recommendations, the chances of more aid from the Bank Group and from the other members of the aid-India consortium would be greatly increased. After prolonged, difficult, and at times abrasive negotiations, India agreed to make the recommended changes in policy, but this agreement was not followed by more aid. Indeed, the transfer of resources to India from the members of the aid-India consortium fell steadily after India accepted the Bank Group's recommendations.[6] (The fall might, of course, have been greater if India had not accepted the recommendations.) Even the Bank Group was unable, because of delays in the second replenishment of IDA, to provide India with the additional program aid both India and the Bank Group had expected would follow acceptance of the recommendations. Thus, the Bank Group was not able to reward India's performance. It did not, in fact, possess the leverage it had claimed. This well-known failure of the Bank Group has ever since weakened the Bank Group's bargaining position in negotiations with its borrowers.

The ability of the Bank Group and of the other members of the international aid community to persuade the poorer countries to use their own scarce resources in ways best calculated to promote both development and a more equitable distribution of the benefits of development depends in the long run on the ability of the international aid community itself to use its own scarce resources in ways best calculated to promote development and a more equitable distribution of its benefits. The ability of the Bank Group to use its resources in these ways is limited by its dependence for funds on the governments and capital markets of rich countries. The Bank Group must always be looking over its shoulder to find out whether a particular modification in its policy would prejudicially affect its capacity to raise funds. The more important the Bank Group becomes, the greater the danger that it will be subjected to political pressures from its rich member governments. That is why it is so important that there be a great reduction in the proportion of the Bank Group's financial resources which depends on the attitude of governments and capital markets to changes in its policies.

(The ability of the international aid community to use its scarce resources in the best interests of the developing countries also, of course, depends on the willingness of the aid-giving governments to accept as a basic principle of their bilateral aid policy that the purpose of their development aid is development and a more equitable distribution of its benefits, and nothing else. For, insofar as they attempt to use their development aid for other purposes, whether political, economic, diplomatic, or strategic, they diminish the ability of the international aid community to persuade the poorer countries to make wise use of their scarce resources. They reduce the leverage of the international aid community. Another way of putting this is to say that to import into bilateral negotiations on aid considerations other than development strengthens the bargaining position of those developing countries which are willing and able to deliver some political *quid pro quo*, such as votes in the UN, or support of the donor government's policy on East Germany, Vietnam, Cuba, Quebec, China, Hungary, or Czechoslovakia in return for more aid. Developing countries prepared to make bargains of this kind are not necessarily the countries which put development money to the best use.)

The ability of the Bank Group to use its control over financial resources as carrots and sticks with which to persuade borrowing countries to do more for the poorest two-fifths or so of their population depends, of course, on how many carrots are available and on how tough the Bank Group is in withholding them from countries not prepared to adjust their development strategies so that they result in improved standards of living for those two-fifths. The Bank Group's bargaining position or leverage has been increased by the doubling of its volume of lending in the first five years of McNamara's presidency.

There are some countries in which Bank Group lending can help to distribute a greater share of national income to the poor, even if the borrowing government does not make changes in its development strategy apart from putting up to the Bank Group projects designed to help the poor. In Iran the poorest 30 per cent of the population, about 10 million people, receive about $1,000 million a year, a sum well below 10 per cent of the total national income; and their share of the growing national income is not rising. If the Bank Group were to lend $200 million a year to Iran on projects costing about twice that amount which are biased to the poor, this could be of tremendous direct benefit to them.

* * *

The most effective way for the Bank Group to give advice to one of its borrowers on the general lines of its program of economic and social development—its development strategy—is to hold periodic discussions with the borrower based on the Bank Group's economic reports on the country and on a personal and confidential letter from the president of the Bank to the minister of finance of the country transmitting the report. This letter can be franker than the economic report circulated to the governments of all the member countries of the Bank. It should be given very limited circulation within the staff of the Bank Group on a need-to-know basis, and not be made available to anyone not on the Bank Group staff. The Bank Group follows this procedure with many economic reports. The practice should become general.

The value of the dialogue between the Bank Group and a borrowing country is likely to be enhanced if both sides can keep the discussions confidential. Then the ultimate agreement will look, not like a compromise between conflicting points of view, but like a shrewd reappraisal by both sides. The difficulty, of course, is that those in the borrowing country who consider a suggestion put forward by the Bank Group in these confidential discussions as not in the national interest will be tempted to leak it to the press in order to stir up opposition based not on the merits of the suggestion but on its having been put forward by intervening outsiders.

L. K. Jha, the Indian ambassador in Washington, who as a senior official of the Indian government has been concerned for fifteen years or more with relations between the Bank Group and India, has put this point well. He said in 1971:

If the World Bank's influence gets beyond a certain point, if it begins to look like pressure, even if it is something desirable in itself or something desired by the country itself, the fact that the World Bank has been putting pressure to achieve it can be a very deadly political weapon. The World Bank is a source of external finance to India, and it is very easy, when an unpopular measure is taken, for its critics to argue that the country has either been bribed or blackmailed into a policy measure. Unless there is a degree of political sensitivity [*on the part of the World Bank*], *one may get a situtation where the whole relationship between the World Bank and the recipient country can get awkward.*[7]

The dialogue between the Bank Group and a borrower, based on a confidential letter from the president and on the economic report on the country, should be conducted on the Bank Group side by a member of the management or of the senior staff. For talks with the dozen or so principal borrowers from the Bank Group, the president of the Bank might appropriately represent the Bank. He would be assisted by the head of the regional office and the head of the resident mission. It seems probable that the principal borrowers from the Bank Group in the mid-seventies will be Argentina, Bangladesh, Brazil, Colombia, India, Indonesia, Iran, Korea, Mexico, Nigeria, Pakistan, Turkey, and Yugoslavia.

The president and his colleagues from the staff would learn much from these discussions: some of the facts and the analysis in the Bank's report would be questioned; some of the assumptions, and of the diagnoses and prescriptions in the report, would be challenged; weaknesses in the report would be exposed. The president and his colleagues would become more aware of the nature and the extent of the obstacles in the country to adopting what to outsiders (and they are outsiders) would appear to be obviously the best development strategy.

The president of the Bank is in constant danger of being insulated from adverse criticism of his ideas and policies and of the operations of the Bank Group. A wise president would use these discussions as an opportunity to elicit from the Bank Group's principal borrowers criticisms of his ideas and policies and proposals for changes in the policies, programs, projects, and administration of the Bank Group. In an atmosphere of give and take, the discussions would take on more and more of the quality of a real dialogue. Those who ask for aid and those who give aid are entitled to the dignity of dialogue, not a dialogue of the deaf or between two solitudes, but a dialogue of partners. As L. K. Jha has put it, a healthy relationship between the Bank Group and a borrowing country is one in which influence flows both ways. India, he asserts with justification, has influenced Bank Group policy in many ways. He instances "the birth of the consortium approach, financing projects in the public sector, and giving non-project aid."[8]

In a federal state, the dialogue constantly going on between the federal government and the governments of the constituent states is the more productive the more the representatives of the federal government treat the representatives of the state governments as their equals in status and dignity. This is equally true of the international aid community. The dialogue between the World Bank Group and its borrowing member countries will be the more productive the more the representatives of the Bank Group, from the president down, treat the representatives of the borrowing members as their equals in status and dignity.

This dialogue is even more difficult than that between the federal government and the government of a member state of the federation because of the differing bases of legal power. A parallel would be found in the United States, for example, if in the election of the president of the United States a citizen of a rich state had many times the number of votes of the citizen of a poor state. This anomaly would greatly lessen in the minds of citizens of the poor states the legitimacy of the federal government. The very great power of the rich countries in the World Bank Group, compared with that of the poorer countries, engenders doubt in the minds of many citizens of the poorer countries concerning the legitimacy of the World Bank Group.

As emphasized earlier in this book, the task of giving advice by the Bank Group to its developing member countries wishing to borrow from it would be easier, and the advice probably more effective, if it were given within the framework of an international aid community where aid-receiving and aid-giving countries would have the right to review the performance of the other, and where the international aid community would advise its rich member countries on ways of improving their aid and trade performance, just as it would advise its poorer member countries on ways of improving their development performance. Two principal advances could be made. The first relates to the analysis of the aid and trade performance of rich countries, the second to the provision of a forum in which aid-receiving countries could review the aid and trade performance of the rich countries.

The DAC publishes in its annual reviews the best studies now available of the extent, nature, and value for development of the assistance given by each aid-giving country. These studies are improving every year. But the fact that they are produced by an agency consisting entirely of aid-givers cannot but arouse the suspicion that the definitions of aid used in compiling the statistics, or the application of these definitions, serve to exaggerate the quantity and probably the quality of the help given. Surely there is something questionable in statistical studies (such as those published in the DAC review for 1972) which show Portugal as first in all four rankings of the comparative aid-giving performance of the sixteen DAC countries in 1971. Gunnar Myrdal, indeed, goes so far as to suggest that this may indicate that the DAC secretariat "seems to lack an ordinary sense of humor."[9] Studies of the aid performance of governments should not only be reliable but should be seen to be reliable. This requires that they be produced by an independent, objective, expert body representing both aid-givers and aid-receivers.

The statistics prepared by the Bank Group on the net transfer of official development assistance from each aid-giving country and institution and on the net receipts by each aid-receiving country should be supplemented by Bank Group assessments of the quality of the projects and programs financed by each donor. (See above, page 63). The Bank Group should also include in each of its country economic reports information about the difficulties faced by the country in gaining access to markets in certain specified rich countries. (See below, page 98).

Aid-coordination groups (which bring together representatives of the aid-receiving country and the principal givers of aid to that country) now review the development performance of receivers of aid. DAC, comprising representatives of the principal non-Communist givers of aid, reviews the performance of givers of aid. Thus, aid-givers review the performances of one another and of the receivers of aid; but the receivers of aid have no forum in which to review the performance of the aid-givers. The concept of partnership in the international aid community would be enhanced if the receivers of aid were provided with opportunities to review the performance of the givers of aid in discharging the commitments they have voluntarily made on aid and related matters. On this the Pearson Commission said:

The most important advantage of the multilateral process is the fact that it is mutual. It gives recipients an opportunity to monitor donors, and donors to monitor other donors, as to the performance of their commitments, the quality and terms of proffered aid, the criteria of performance, and the ties and strings attached to aid. Foreign aid becomes a matter of mutual cooperation between many partners, and not as it has sometimes been, an awkward political relationship between two countries.[10]

The two possible forums in which they might have this opportunity are aid-coordination groups and DAC. The advantage of DAC over aid-coordination groups is that the representatives of givers of aid at DAC meetings are likely to be more influential in determining general government policy on aid than the representatives of aid-givers to aid-coordination groups. Thus far, the member governments of DAC have insisted that aid-receivers should not participate in its annual reviews of the aid programs of giving countries. But, once governments are seized with the importance to the whole international aid effort of emphasizing equality of status between the giving and the receiving members of the international aid partnership, it should be possible to get the DAC governments to agree that just as they have the right to assess the development performance of aid-receiving countries, so aid-receiving countries should have the right to assess the aid performance of aid-giving countries. The aid-receiving countries could be represented at the annual DAC reviews by the regional economic commissions for Asia and Africa and by the Inter-American Committee for the Alliance for Progress (CIAP) or on a rotating basis.

A number of changes could be made in Bank-sponsored aid-coordination groups to make them more effective agencies for the giving of advice by aid-givers to aid-receivers. One change would be to remove any vestigial remnants of inequality of status between the aid-givers and the aid-receiver, such as excluding the aid-receiving country from some of the meetings of the group. All members of all aid-coordination groups should be invited to all meetings of the group. The chairman of an aid-coordination group will sometimes wish to have private meetings with the aid-receiving country between sessions of the group. Similarly, he will sometimes wish to have private meetings with the representatives of the aid-givers. The appearance of inequality between the aid-givers and the aid-receiver would be further reduced if the aid-receiver were represented around the table at meetings of the group by three or four representatives, while each aid-giver were restricted to one. The appearance of confrontation at the meetings would be reduced if the Bank Group ceased to provide the chairman, as well as the secretariat, of the group. The chairman would instead be an outsider of considerable prestige, known and respected in the aid-receiving country. He would be appointed by the Bank Group and would receive a fee for his services. In addition to chairing the meetings, he might travel from time to time to the capitals of the aid-giving governments represented on the group of which he is chairman, in an effort to persuade them to improve the volume and quality of their assistance.

* * *

Finally, there is the question of the way in which officers of the Bank Group, from the president down, should set about the delicate task of giving advice.

Most of the Bank Group's contacts with its borrowers are through its professional officers. They talk to ministers, businessmen, and officials in the borrowing countries about identifying and appraising projects. They negotiate the conditions of loans. They supervise their execution. They man the economic missions, the pre-investment survey missions, the sectoral missions to the country, and the resident missions in the country.

Officers who deal with low-income countries will do more harm than good if they are racially or culturally arrogant; if they are unable to comprehend the depth of the poverty of most of these countries, the values and virtues of civilizations other than their own, the need to reconcile the importance of a rapid growth in the production of essential goods and services with efforts to improve the economic and social conditions of especially poor regions and especially poor people, and to maintain and enrich local cultural and social values; if they cannot understand why it is so much more difficult for governments in low-income countries to step up the rate of savings and to choose between a little more or a little less economic growth, a little more or a little less social justice, than for governments in rich countries; and if they cannot enter into the feelings of the people they deal with in low-income countries who have to ask for aid or deal with aid-givers and who, in order to get aid, must submit to searching investigations of their affairs by outsiders and advice from them. Officers must realize that development diplomacy is one of the most difficult of all diplomacies to master, and that when they have to give advice, they should give it in the least abrasive, the least corrosive way possible. They should be aware that the success of a development diplomat is measured, not by the wisdom of the advice he gives, but by how much of his wise advice is accepted. Officers of the Bank Group who come from the upper classes of highly stratified low-income countries may find it even more difficult to grasp this than many officers from rich countries.

Officers of the Bank Group who deal with borrowing countries, especially with the poorer borrowing countries, should constantly remind themselves that human judgment is fallible—hence even the experts of the World Bank Group can be mistaken; that unequivocal answers are seldom possible to the complex questions of development strategy; and that humility and caution are therefore essential in exploring the enigmas of development. Luck or providence or the unpredictable plays a large role in development. Outsiders cannot pull the low-income countries out of the morass of their poverty; they must save themselves, and to save themselves, they must be proud. They must retain their own self-respect, and their governments must retain the respect of the governed. It is good that poor people have more to eat and to wear, better places to live in, more and better trained nurses, doctors, and teachers, and less illness. It is better that they have these without sacrificing those ancient values of their societies which can preserve for them a sense of belonging to a group, a sense of dignity, and a hope of serenity.

The Bank Group can properly expect to be kept fully informed by the governments of the countries which borrow substantial sums from it on all aspects of their programs of economic and social development.

As a result of its appraisal of these programs, the Bank Group may properly encourage these governments when they are proposing to embark on what seem to the Bank Group to be wise courses of action and, conversely, may properly warn them against the consequences of what seem to it to be unwise courses of action. But the encouragement and the warning should be given cautiously and without condescension.

While the talks between the Bank Group and a borrowing country based on the latest economic report (prepared every year for the largest borrowers and every two to four years for the smaller borrowers) should be conducted by a member of the management or senior staff of the Bank Group, the constant discussions in-between can best be conducted by the head of a resident Bank mission in the country, particularly since he and his staff have better opportunities than the staff at the headquarters of the Bank to acquire an understanding of the political and social restraints which inhibit a government from adopting what appear to outsiders the ideally best programs and policies of development. The restraints may be politically powerful groups in the country: large landowners, trade unions, big industrialists, or the local Pentagon. Or the obstacles may exist because the dominant local value judgments or moral judgments are not identical with those of the president of the Bank or of his advisers.

The Bank now maintains twelve resident missions to individual member countries and two regional missions, one to East Africa and one to West Africa. The twelve missions are in Afghanistan, Bangladesh, Colombia, Ethiopia, Ghana, India, Indonesia, Nigeria, Nepal, Pakistan, Thailand (which also covers Malaysia), and Zaire. The number of resident missions could usefully be increased, provided that the Bank is able to staff them with officers expert both in development and in the diplomacy of development. The twelve existing missions include missions to six of the thirteen countries likely to be the principal borrowers from the Bank Group in the mid-seventies: Bangladesh, Colombia, India, Indonesia, Nigeria, and Pakistan. If the other seven were added (Argentina, Brazil, Iran, Korea, Mexico, Turkey, and Yugoslavia), the Bank's nineteen resident missions would probably cover from three-fifths to two-thirds of the total borrowings from the Bank Group. (In the four years ending in mid-1972, over three-fifths of the loans of the Bank and IDA went to these countries.) McNamara might therefore sound out these seven countries on whether they would welcome resident missions from the Bank.

The head of a resident Bank mission should be considered as an ambassador accredited by the president of the Bank to the government of the country. He should be an officer with wide experience and considerable influence in the Bank. He should be able to win the confidence and respect of the leading cabinet ministers, officials, and others concerned with development. He should have a profound grasp of the problems of the economic and social development of the country and be passionately concerned with the success of the country's program for economic and social advance. He should be able to conduct continuous informal and confidential dialogues on behalf of the Bank and the aid-coordination group with cabinet ministers, senior officials, and leaders in politics, industry, banking, trade unions, agriculture, and education. He should shun publicity and have a passion for anonymity. He must be a master of the art of quiet development diplomacy. His principal task should be the diplomatic one of applying tact to the conduct of relations between the Bank Group and the government to which he is accredited.

One of his tasks should be to assist visiting Bank Group missions and to exercise effective control over them on behalf of the president of the Bank. He should always be consulted on the dispatch of missions, their membership, their terms of reference, and the timing of their visits. By making efficient arrangements in advance of the mission's arrival, he will reduce the length of the visits, often by half. He should report to the president personally once or twice a year on the value of visits of Bank Group missions and of individual officers with suggestions on how, in the light of experience, the number of visits, the size of missions, and the length of their stay in the country could prudently be reduced to lighten the burden they impose on the host country and to reduce the cost of Bank Group administration. Another of his tasks should be to advise project appraisal missions on how they can best formulate conditions of loans so that they will be both effective under local conditions and also as little distasteful as possible to the borrower.

As resident missions acquire the confidence of the borrowing country and of the headquarters of the Bank, more and more authority can usefully be entrusted to them, beginning with information and research activities (including the preparation of country economic reports), and going on to the appraisal of the smaller and more routine projects, the loan negotiations on these projects, and the supervision of all projects. This would reduce drastically the numbers of Bank Group missions to a country, numbers which are now so great as to impose a heavy burden on officials of the receiving country. In the early seventies, there were once six Bank Group missions in Ethiopia at the same time, and Ethiopia borrowed less than $25 million a year from the Bank and IDA in the four years ending in mid-1972.

All this emphasizes that the professional staff of the Bank Group must understand the art of development diplomacy. The Bank Group, however, provides its staff with little or no organized training in this art. According to one officer who attended two orientation and training programs in 1970, this aspect was entirely missing from these programs.

The art of development diplomacy is more difficult to master than the art of most other types of diplomacy. The main reason is the strain arising from a relationship between the representative of a giver and the representative of a receiver, a strain normally absent from inter-state diplomacy, which is usually concerned with working out agreements from which each side benefits, or with a mutually beneficial exchange of information or of opinions. But, there are other subsidiary reasons. An obvious one is that most of the poorer countries have hot climates; are usually riddled with diseases a visitor is in danger of contracting through drinking impure water or eating infected food; and are distant from the World Bank's headquarters. A person irritated by heat, suffering from dysentery, or worried about contracting it is apt to have a short temper, particularly if he has recently flown across many time zones.

Again, a young, inexperienced officer from the Bank Group may be assigned to a project appraisal mission where he will be discussing the project with an experienced senior official of the borrowing country. The senior official can find this extremely irritating, particularly if he belongs to a society very conscious of status, as are the societies in most of the developing two-thirds of the world. The opposite situation can be equally irritating. The Bank Group officer may find himself discussing a project with relatively junior local officials on the spot, who may believe that part of their job is to minimize difficulties in the way of the success of the project. This usually becomes clear very soon to an experienced officer, and can make him short-tempered. Or, sometimes a project is so obviously essential and also so obviously surrounded by difficulties of implementation, which an outsider will believe could be removed but which probably won't, that the officer may become arrogant.

Moreover, the officers of the Bank Group are not protected, as are national diplomats, by the consciousness of belonging to a profession which has worked out codes of conduct to ease the strains of inter-state relations, particularly the rule that it is never wise for a diplomat to allow himself to become irritated, bad-tempered, or arrogant, though it may sometimes be wise for him to pretend to be. In London in the autumn of 1945, I worked under great pressure for week after week at meetings of the executive committee of the preparatory commission of the UN. At this conference I usually wore an ordinary business suit, but if, when I awoke in the morning, I felt that my temper was likely to be short, I put on the diplomatic armor of short black chancery coat and striped trousers. Then, when at the conference I felt irritation mounting in me, I would look down at my striped trousers and remember that I was a diplomat and expected to behave like one. The development diplomat has no such armor, no such easy way to remind himself of the codes of conduct of his new profession of development diplomacy, particularly the rule that if it is necessary for him to give advice, he should give it with humility and caution.

I remember that once when I was an officer of the World Bank I was visiting an agricultural university, for which IDA had already given an interest-free loan and for which the government had requested a second loan. It was the only agricultural university in the country. As I walked with an official through the university buildings, I was surprised to see no students. I asked why. He said they were on vacation. When pressed, he admitted that they were on strike because they considered it unfair that when they graduated and got jobs at the capital, they were paid less than graduates in economics. (Apparently the university was not training people to work with the farmers but training civil servants for the head office of the department of agriculture.) Walking along the corridor of the men's residence, I could see through the bedroom windows that the rooms were filthy. Why? Because when the students went on strike they had taken the keys to their rooms with them. We then passed a common room. It was equally filthy. The students had certainly not taken away the keys to it. I looked out through one of the windows, and there, next to the wall, was a veritable moat of stagnant, dirty water two feet deep. Why couldn't the water be drained off? Because the drainage plan for the university had not yet been agreed to. (All that had to be done to drain the water away from the building was to dig a couple of drainage ditches to the edge of a slope about thirty feet away.) Later in the day, I found out from a well-informed foreign expert that the student body was composed, not of the brighter sons of the farmers in the country, but of the sons of those larger landowners who had the most influence with the government. Admission to the university was part of the system of government patronage. Very few of the students had ever dirtied their hands farming. Very few ever intended to dirty their hands.

I was exasperated by the problem of what I should recommend the Bank Group do with the government's request for money to expand this university. The Bank Group would obviously have to insist that any buildings it helped to finance be properly maintained, which meant they could not be surrounded by stagnant water. The Bank Group's appraisal mission to be sent in a few months would make intelligent suggestions about the curriculum and the training of future teachers for the university. It would try to persuade the university and the government to improve the quality of the student body. But I was sure that the forces of inertia and of political patronage were so powerful that if we were to help the country improve its university training in agriculture, we would have to be satisfied with a very slow pace of advance.

I am afraid that during my visit I displayed more irritation, bad temper, and arrogance than I had ever displayed as a diplomatic representative of my own country. I learned then how much more difficult the art of development diplomacy can be than that of inter-state diplomacy.

I have one final thought on how to make the advice-giving function of the World Bank Group more useful and more palatable to the poorer member countries of the Bank Group.

These countries cannot help but resent the fact that they, because of their poverty, must submit to inquisitions by outsiders into their domestic affairs before they can go ahead with that part of their development programs which depends on outside financial aid, whereas rich countries, because of their wealth, do not. Might it not be helpful if some of the rich member countries of the Bank Group were voluntarily to submit to similar inquisitions by asking the Bank Group to investigate, at its expense, some aspect of its domestic anti-poverty programs?

The more closely these resembled those the Bank Group has had experience in investigating in the poorer countries, the better. This means that the programs should be concerned with areas or subregions in rich countries "where poverty is so wide-spread that its elimination can be treated in many ways as an area problem. In the United States, considerable attention has been focused on one such area, the Appalachian Region. In Canada, large parts of Eastern Quebec and the Atlantic Provinces could be looked at in the same way."[11]

It would also be best if the Bank Group's investigation of such a program in a rich country resembled, in character, investigations by the Bank Group into the development programs of poorer countries. Thus an investigation by the Bank Group into Canadian anti-poverty programs in the Atlantic Provinces (made at the request of the Canadian government, concurred in by the governments of the Atlantic Provinces) might be similar to the investigation the Bank Group made in 1964-65 into the development programs of India. This would mean a mission of about twenty experts, who would spend about six months in the field and another four months preparing their report. The governments of Canada and the Atlantic Provinces would learn from this experience a little of what it is like to have outsiders—no matter how intelligent and well meaning—probing into sensitive areas of the national life, asking embarrassing questions, demanding precise information. This would give them an insight into the problems of the relationship between the Bank Group and its borrowers. They would find out, not only how helpful a report by Bank Group experts can be, but also the limitations of a report by outsiders. This would enable them to give valuable advice to the president of the Bank on what he might do to remedy some of the deficiencies in Bank Group investigations in the developing countries.

Most important of all, the work of an expert Bank Group mission in investigating aspects of anti-poverty programs in a rich country would help to break down the barriers now separating those in rich countries working on these programs from those who are working on the development programs of the poorer countries. Each group has much to learn from the other. At present, each is not learning enough from the other. In most countries the two groups, whether in government or in universities, are working in pretty water-tight compartments. The rich countries which are conducting domestic anti-poverty programs might well find that they would get a big return on their past investments in the World Bank Group if they were to tap in this way the knowledge and wisdom the Bank Group has accumulated in the past twenty-five years through its studies of the failures and successes of anti-poverty programs in the poorer countries, for this might well save them from making some of the expensive mistakes they are now making—mistakes the more knowledgeable of the poorer countries ceased to make five or ten years ago.

CHAPTER TWELVE

More Trade

A large sustained international aid effort is required, in which the Bank Group can and should play a central role. This aid effort must be complemented by a large sustained international trade effort to help the developing countries increase their earnings from their exports of goods and services. It would be folly to believe that in the next ten years or so the large net transfer of real resources required from the rich countries to the developing countries will be entirely in the form of grants and of loans with a large grant component. A considerable proportion will consist of loans with little or no grant component. If the developing countries are to be able to service their past debts, incur new debts, and purchase the additional imports needed to support higher rates of growth of income and output, they must have much better opportunities than they now have to sell more of their goods and services to the rich countries at remunerative prices.

The following figures indicate the comparative orders of magnitude of the flows of real resources resulting from increased aid from rich countries to developing countries and from higher returns from the exports of developing countries to rich countries. The net transfer of resources from all the non-Communist rich countries to all the developing countries resulting from official development assistance amounted in the early seventies to about $6,000 million a year.[1] The establishment of free trade in one commodity alone, sugar, would probably increase the export earnings of developing countries by $1,000 million a year in 1970 dollars.[2] If, as a result of commodity agreements, the prices of tea, coffee, and cocoa went up by 3 per cent a year for ten years, and if this increase in prices did not affect the volume of sales, the earnings of developing countries from their exports of these three commodities would be, at the end of the ten-year period, about $1,750 million more a year in 1970 dollars than if prices had remained stable.[3]

Figures for net transfer of resources resulting from official development assistance and figures of export earnings are not, of course, equivalent, since a developing country must use its domestic resources to produce exports, and net transfers resulting from official development assistance are an addition to domestic production. This does not mean, however, that an increase in exports will always mean a decrease in production for domestic use, since the increased exports may result from using land and labor which would otherwise have been idle. Moreover, increased export earnings can result not from an increase in the volume of exports but from an increase in the prices of the exports, as a result of arrangements such as commodity agreements.

The Bank Group was not established by the nations of the world for the purpose of helping the developing countries gain access for their goods and services to the markets of the rich countries. But the Bank Group is the principal banker of many of the developing countries, and an important banker for most of the others. As such it has a direct and immediate interest in the capacity of its borrowers to service Bank Group loans by making foreign exchange available for amortization and interest payments. The ability of its borrowers to obtain foreign exchange is dependent on their ability to export goods and services. Consequently, it is appropriate that the Bank urge, as it has been doing, that the nations of the world recognize to a much greater extent than at present, not in words but in actions, the urgent importance of the developing countries selling more goods and services at remunerative prices to the rich countries. The Bank should emphasize that this imposes obligations on rich countries, on low-income countries, and on international lending agencies. The Soviet Union recognizes that when it lends money to a low-income country, it shares with that country an obligation to work out ways by which it can export goods to the Soviet Union and thus pay the debt. Rich western countries should recognize a similar obligation by opening their markets to the goods and services of the low-income countries, and by helping them exploit these markets. By doing this they will stimulate the development of the low-income countries and, at the same time, provide themselves with cheaper supplies and stimulate their own exports to those countries. The low-income countries should so adjust the productive structure of their economies as to increase their foreign exchange earnings. Lenders, whether rich countries or international agencies, should, in selecting projects, attach much greater importance than in the past to potential foreign exchange earnings.

The Bank Group should do even more than at present to help its developing member countries, particularly its very poor members, to expand their exports both of traditional and of new goods. This means, as pointed out above in Chapter Eight, that the Bank Group should give a high priority to loans for financing the discovery and exploitation of internationally demanded natural resources, to loans for the development of export-oriented manufacturing, and to loans for projects which, though they do not earn foreign exchange directly, are required by heavy foreign exchange earners. The Bank Group should insure, if necessary by financial support, that more and better research is conducted on new uses of such primary products as jute and rubber, and on lowering the costs of production and improving the quality of primary products. It should also insure that its low-income borrowers are provided with technical assistance in building up and expanding profitable export markets for traditional and new goods. It should assist low-income countries to set up national export financing facilities to help their exporters of capital goods compete on equal terms with exporters from rich countries who benefit from medium- and long-term credit facilities provided by their governments. These credit facilities frequently amount to subsidies on exports. The export financing facilities of low-income countries might be set up within their national development finance companies.

The Bank Group should press ahead vigorously to implement rapidly the decisions it took in 1969 to help solve the commodity problem as it affects the economic development of developing countries. It then decided to help these countries diversify their production, strengthen the competitiveness of primary products in world trade, and participate more effectively in international commodity arrangements aimed at stabilizing world prices at remunerative levels. The Bank Group should devote particular attention to tea, coffee, and cocoa.

Hitherto the Bank has, in its periodic country economic reports, tended to confine its criticisms of trade policies to the policies of the developing countries. It has quite properly criticized them for paying more attention to promoting high-cost home-made substitutes for imports than to promoting low-cost exports. Henceforth, the Bank should in these reports be equally outspoken in criticizing the failure of rich countries to offer new sales opportunities in their markets for the products of low-income countries. The Bank has, in some of its most recent reports, noted, on the basis of information furnished it by GATT, difficulties faced by the country in gaining access to markets in certain specified rich countries. This should become a general practice.

The president of the Bank has been stressing in his speeches and in the publications of the Bank Group the importance of the rich members doing much more than at present to assist the low-income members to increase their earnings from their exports. He should continue to do this. He could usefully emphasize the following points. Low-income countries need, not only the prospect of a lowering of the barriers to their exports, but also the certainty that barriers will not be raised against one of their exports once that export begins to surmount the existing barriers. If they do not have this certainty, they cannot afford to use scarce resources of skills and capital to build up an efficient export industry. The interests of the low-income countries would be served best by the rich countries agreeing to move progressively over a certain fixed period, perhaps ten years, toward the abolition of all tariff and non-tariff barriers to all exports of low-income countries: manufactured goods, semi-manufactured goods, raw materials, and agricultural products in raw or processed form. The non-tariff barriers are now more important than the tariff barriers. They include subsidy techniques, safeguard or emergency mechanisms, regulations on government procurement, countervailing duties, and so-called voluntary restraints imposed on the exporting countries by the importing countries.

Demolishing barriers to the manufactured goods of low-income countries would cause some industries in rich countries to close down unless they could move into new types of production. The industries which are particularly vulnerable are labor-intensive manufactures such as textiles, wearing apparel, and footwear. Free access for sugar would close down beet-sugar production. The green revolution will probably result before long in an increasing number of the low-income countries being able to produce surpluses of wheat and rice and of other grains for sale in world markets at world prices. Free access for these grains would mean that the rich countries would not only grant free access to their own markets but would also refrain from pre-empting other markets by offering their own grains at subsidized prices. Free access for the grain exports of low-income countries would in time result in structural changes in agriculture in rich countries.

The domestic problems rich countries face in granting easier and ultimately free access to their markets for the goods of low-income countries are so great that progress in lowering barriers has been very slow. Three steps could be taken to lessen the difficult domestic problems of the rich countries. First, the rich countries should, as McNamara has been emphasizing, enact effective legislation to help domestic interests suffering from increased imports from low-income countries to move into other types of production; particularly generous assistance should be given to the workers in the industries affected. Second, the rich countries should be given about ten years to make the necessary structural changes in their economies before completely free access becomes effective. Third, free access should be given to the exports of low-income countries only; the exports of rich, so-called developing countries and of middle-income countries should not be given this concession. The low-income countries do not include Argentina, Greece, Hong Kong, Israel, Mexico, Portugal, Singapore, South Africa, Spain, and Venezuela. The elimination of countries such as these from the benefits of trade preferences or free entry was recommended by the Committee for Development Planning, though the Committee did not define precisely the countries it considered should be eliminated. Its report on its session held in January 1970 stated:

In such matters as granting preferences by developed countries to developing countries and providing them with financial resources, it seems inappropriate to have a sharp demarcation line between the two country groups. For, were such a demarcation line maintained, it would mean that at a point of time in the future a country would be considered to have shifted suddenly from the developing to the developed country group, and as such would experience a setback by virtue of the new obligations it was suddenly asked to assume in place of the assistance previously received. It seems desirable to introduce an intermediate group of countries which would not have to undertake obligations towards developiing countries but at the same time would no longer, as a rule, receive assistance or preferences. The Committee has given some thought to the complex problems involved in defining such a group of countries. It believes that a study needs to be made to determine what variables or characteristics would be appropriate for this purpose. The work underway in a number of organizations may well yield fruitful indicators.[4]

Thus, when a low-income country moved into the ranks of middle-income countries, it would no longer be entitled to the special trade preferences extended to low-income countries, but it would not have to grant trade preferences to low-income countries.

The Bank Group can do much to help its low-income members increase their earnings from exports, but it is not appropriate that it be the major international instrument for facilitating and encouraging the conclusion of international agreements to abolish the tariff and non-tariff barriers to the movement of goods from low-income to rich countries. UNCTAD, under the leadership of its secretary-general, Perez Guerrero, appears to be the agency best fitted to assume this task. UNCTAD would, of course, work closely with the General Agreement on Tariffs and Trade (GATT), OECD, the UN Committee for Development Planning, and the World Bank Group.

CHAPTER THIRTEEN

The Volume of Lending by the Bank Group

In the autumn of 1968, six months after he took office as president, Robert McNamara announced that his goal was that the volume of Bank Group lending during his first five years of office would be double what it had been in the preceding five years. By mid-1972 it was clear that he would surpass this goal in terms of current dollars and almost reach it in terms of stable dollars. But, in spite of this great increase in the volume of lending, the Bank Group was not able to do much in the four years ending in mid-1972 for its very poor member countries, compared with what it was able to do for the better-off (the middle-income and the poor countries). In terms of the volume of loans per inhabitant, the very poor countries received only a third as much as the better-off countries. The better-off received $2.10 per inhabitant, the very poor only 72 cents. And it is the very poor member countries which most need help. Their GNP's grew during the sixties at a rate in real terms of only 3.7 per cent a year, compared with 6.2 per cent in the better-off member countries. If these rates of growth continue, the better-off will double their GNP's in twelve years, the very poor in twenty.*

Hollis Chenery, a vice-president of the World Bank, and its principal adviser on development policy, said in 1970, "India . . . is the outstanding example of aid shortages contributing to reduced growth."[1] The Bank and IDA did not do much in the four years ending in mid-1972 to relieve these shortages. They lent India only 55 cents a year per head of population, compared with $2.10 to the better-off developing countries. Chenery went on to say: "In general there should be a presumption that aid is provided for the purpose of accelerating growth, which would result in the highest per capita amounts going to countries in the income range of $100–$300. At higher income levels, exports and private investment should be able to finance imports, and adequate domestic savings are mainly a question of government policy."[2] In the

*These and other statistics in this chapter on past lending by the Bank Group are derived from Table 3, page 237.

four years ending in mid-1972, lending by the Bank and IDA was distributed in the diametrically opposite way from that recommended by Chenery. The countries he recommended should get the highest amounts per capita got 63 cents a year for every inhabitant. Countries at the income range of $440 to $1,400 received $2.16 a head, almost three and a half times as much.[3]

For most developing countries, what is as important or even more important than the volume of loans received for development is the net transfer of resources resulting from the loans, net transfer meaning the disbursements on the loans less the interest and amortization payments. In the four years ending in mid-1972, the net transfer from the World Bank and IDA to the very poor countries was only $173 million a year, or 16 cents a head a year. The better-off developing countries received $283 million, or 38 cents a head. The net transfer of resources to the better-off developing countries was not very great. The net transfer to the very poor developing countries was small.

The explanation of the Bank Group's inability to give as much help to its very poor member countries as to its better-off developing member countries is, of course, that most of Bank-IDA lending to its developing member countries (over 70 per cent in the four years ending in mid-1972) comes from the Bank, not from IDA, and that the Bank's articles of agreement stipulate that it shall in its lending "pay due regard to the prospects that the borrower . . . will be in a position to meet its obligations under the loan." This means that the Bank can lend only to countries it considers credit-worthy, and it quite properly does not consider many of the very poor countries to be very credit-worthy. Thus, in the four years ending in mid-1972, only 15 per cent of Bank lending went to the very poor countries.

The distribution of IDA's resources between the better-off developing countries and the very poor was the exact opposite to that of the Bank. The Bank's resources were distributed 85 per cent to the better-off and 15 per cent to the very poor. IDA's resources were distributed 80 per cent to the very poor and 20 per cent to the better-off. IDA was the main source of Bank Group funds for the very poor countries. In the four years ending in mid-1972, they got twice as much from IDA as they got from the Bank. If, as Hollis Chenery urges, the Bank Group is to be able to do more for its member countries in the income range of $100 to $300 than for those with higher levels of income, lending by IDA must increase at a much faster rate than lending by the Bank.

The senior officers of the Bank Group are unanimous in believing that the needs of the very poor member countries of the Bank Group for interest-free loans from IDA are so great that the Bank Group should urge its rich members to support great increases in the resources of IDA. Almost all believe that IFC is unlikely to be able to do much more than double its annual investments in terms of constant dollars by the end of the seventies. Most of the senior officers approve of the increases in lending by the Bank proper, which are taking place under the McNamara regime. A minority of the senior staff, however, are doubtful about the wisdom of the doubling of lending which took place during the first four years of McNamara's presidency; they have even greater doubts about the wisdom of the Bank's continuing to lend in this volume, and are opposed to raising Bank lending above its present level. The opponents of the policy of extensive increases in Bank lending fear that these increases will encourage the borrowers to load themselves up with so much foreign debt that they will not be able to meet the interest and amortization payments on it, and will run into debt crises. They are not impressed by the Bank's studies of debt and credit-worthiness which support substantial increases in Bank lending. This skepticism does not, however, appear to be shared by the member governments of the Bank, not even by the governments of the rich countries. They had opportunities, during the annual meeting of the Bank in the autumn of 1972, to express reservations about the wisdom of the big increase in Bank lending during the previous four years, and to urge caution in the next six years. None of them did.

The differences of opinion within the staff of the Bank Group on the appropriate level of lending by the Bank are not surprising, since, as pointed out in Chapter Eight, the ability of a borrowing country to service ten or twenty years from now loans contracted today depends on a host of factors, of which many of the most important are beyond the control of the borrowing country.

Keeping in mind the discussion of credit-worthiness in Chapter Eight, and the imprecision of efforts to forecast what level of lending by an institution such as the World Bank would be appropriate, we shall look in turn at each of the four main groups of borrowers from the Bank —middle-income countries, poor countries, India, the other very poor countries—and set down what seems to be a reasonable target for Bank lending to each group by the fiscal year 1983. We shall not consider loans by the Bank to its rich member countries, since it is assumed that they will have ceased to borrow before the end of the seventies. We shall then examine what kind of distribution of the combined funds of the Bank and IDA would result in 1983 from this level of Bank lending on the basis of various assumptions about the volume of lending by IDA.

The pace at which it will prove possible and wise to advance during the next ten years toward the targets of lending set for 1983 will depend in the main on four factors. The first is the ability of the Bank and IDA to raise the necessary funds. The second is the ability of the Bank Group to recruit qualified professional staff and to make substantial improvements in its administration. The third factor is the degree of success of the Bank Group in building up the credit-worthiness of its borrowers for Bank loans. To improve a borrower's credit-worthiness, some of the Bank's lending will have to be conditional on the borrowers' agreement to restrain their dependence on short-term and medium-term borrowing for purposes of long-term investment, and to refrain from taking on any kind of debt on inappropriate terms, such as excessive interest rates. The fourth factor is the importance attached to speedy movement toward the qualitative goals of Bank Group lending. It seems clear that a rapid advance in the fiscal years 1974, 1975, and possibly 1976 depends on reducing the volume of Bank Group lending in those years. Because of the urgent needs of the very poor IDA-worthy countries, this reduction would have to be in Bank lending, not IDA lending. Therefore, if it is thought desirable that Bank lending go up in the next ten years, the increase should take place from 1976 or 1977 on.

As a background to this discussion of the appropriate levels of Bank and IDA lending in the next ten years or so, it is useful to look at the level of lending by each of the three Bank Group institutions from 1965 on, and at the probable level of lending in the three years from mid-1971 to mid-1974, if lending by the Bank in the fiscal years 1973 and 1974 is maintained at the level reached in 1972. These are the years of the third replenishment of IDA, when IDA is expected to be able to lend at a rate of $1,000 million a year, the level attained in the first year of this three-year period. To remove distortions caused by inflation, the statistics of lending from 1965 to 1972 are expressed in terms of constant dollars. The unit is the dollar with the purchasing power of a dollar in the fiscal year 1972.* From now on, this dollar is called the 1972 dollar.

BANK GROUP LOANS 1965–1974 (constant 1972 dollars)

	Average 1965, 1966 1967, 1968 ($ million)	*Average 1969, 1970 1971, 1972* ($ million)	*1972* ($ million)	*Average 1972, 1973 1974* [*estimate*] ($ million)
Bank	1,069	1,885	1,966	2,000
IDA	324	698	1,000	1,000
IFC	49	116	116	125
Total	1,442	2,699	3,082	3,125

This table shows that the average lending in the first four years of McNamara's presidency (1969–72) was almost double what it had been in the four years before he took office (1965–68). It shows an increase of 84 per cent in Bank lending between 1965–68 and 1972–74 and a trebling of IDA lending in the same period.

The next table shows the distribution of lending by the Bank and IDA in current dollars in the four-year period 1969–72 among the various categories of developing member countries—middle-income, poor, and very poor, with the category of very poor subdivided into two groups with precisely equal populations. One group consists of India. The

*The deflator index is given in Table 1, page 223.

other group embraces all the other very poor member countries. (Bank loans to rich countries averaged $40 million a year in this period. These loans are not shown in this table.)

BANK-IDA LOANS 1969–72 (annual average in current dollars)

Countries	*Popn. in mid-1970* (million)	*Bank*	*IDA* ($ million)	*Total*	*Per cap* ($)
Middle-income	236	509		509	2.16
Poor	502	916	126	1,041	2.07
Very poor					
India	538	35	258	294	.55
Others	538	217	259	476	.88
Total	1,076	252	518	770	.72
Developing	1,814	1,678	644	2,320	1.28

The following table gives in current dollars the average annual net transfer of resources to developing countries in the four-year period 1969–72 resulting from Bank and IDA loans:

Countries	*Popn. in mid-1970* (million)	*Bank*	*IDA* ($ million)	*Total*	*Per cap* ($)
Middle-income	236	82		82	.35
Poor	502	160	43	203	.40
Very poor					
India	538	-37	78	41	.08
Others	538	43	89	132	.25
Total	1,076	7	166	173	.16
Total	1,814	249	209	457	.25

In the discussion of levels of future lending in the rest of this chapter, the unit used is the 1972 dollar unless otherwise stated.

The following are the average annual borrowings from the Bank of the middle-income members in the years 1969, 1970, and 1971, and in 1972:

	GNP per cap ($) *1970*	*Average Annual borrowing 1969–71*	*Borrowing 1972*
		[*current dollars* ($ million)]	
Ireland	1,360	15	28
Argentina	1,160	106	
Greece	1,090	20	25
Spain	1,020	47	50
Venezuela	980	29	28
Hong Kong	970		
Cyprus	950	7	12
Singapore	920	14	10
Trinidad/Tobago	860	5	2
Uruguay	820	9	11
South Africa	760		
Panama	730	14	23
Chile	720	10	
Mexico	670	96	277
Jamaica	670	8	
Portugal	660		
Yugoslavia	650	78	75
Gabon	630	2	
Lebanon	590		
Costa Rica	560	11	33
Peru	450	10	
Saudi Arabia	440		
Total		488	574

The application to these countries of the normal criteria for creditworthiness would appear to justify the conclusion that almost all of them are, or could become, capable during the seventies of bearing a good deal heavier burden of debt than they now bear, provided that they follow reasonably sensible economic and social policies and that other countries behave sensibly toward them. Romania, which joined the Bank in December 1972, will also be a borrower. Perhaps annual Bank lending to middle-income countries could therefore rise gradually from about 1976 on to a level of $1,100 million a year by 1983. (It is assumed that until there are changes in the regimes in South Africa and Portugal, they will continue to receive no loans from the Bank.)

The poor countries which borrowed on the average more than $5 million a year from the Bank from 1969 to 1971 or in 1972 were:

	GNP per cap ($) *1970*	*Average Annual borrowing 1969–71*	*Borrowing 1972*
		[*current dollars* ($ million)]	
Nicaragua	430		31
Brazil	420	147	437
Zambia	400	29	
Taiwan	390	74	
Iran	380	95	125
Malaysia	380	35	32
Guatemala	360	3	16
Dominican Rep.	350	8	
Colombia	340	128	65
Iraq	320		40
Turkey	310	56	137
Ivory Coast	310	21	18
Papua/N. Guinea	300	9	10
Honduras	280	4	12
Tunisia	250	25	41
Korea (South)	250	63	33
Liberia	240	5	1
Senegal	230	1	6
Morocco	230	43	39
Philippines	210	31	30
Thailand	200	27	42
Bolivia	180	8	
Cameroon	180	10	
(Others)		22	2
Total		845	1,127

The UN's recognition in 1971 of the government in Peking as the government of China very properly resulted in the Bank's ceasing to lend to the government in Taiwan, even though that government continued to occupy the Chinese seat in the Bank. Brazil is unlikely to be able to continue for the rest of the seventies to borrow at the rate of its borrowing in 1972. A number of the other poor countries, however, such as Iran, Tunisia, and Morocco, probably will be able to increase their borrowings. On balance, therefore, Bank lending to its poor member countries might be expected to remain from about 1976 on at about the 1972 level of $1,100 million.

In the three years 1969, 1970, and 1971, India borrowed only $27 million a year from the Bank. In 1972 this went up to $60 million, only $10 million more than what India was repaying to the Bank on past loans. India's credit-worthiness for Bank loans is not at present high. It would be substantially increased if the flow of IDA funds to India were substantially increased. On the assumption that by 1982 India will be receiving at least $600 million a year from IDA and that a good deal of this, say 40 per cent, will be for local expenses and thus available for servicing foreign loans, Bank lending to India by 1983 could safely reach a level of $250 million a year.

The very poor countries other than India which borrowed on the average more than $5 million a year from the Bank from 1969 to 1971 or in 1972 were:

	GNP per cap ($) 1970	*Average Annual borrowing 1969–71*	*Borrowing 1972*
		[*current dollars* ($ million)]	
Kenya	150	28	32
Uganda	130	9	3
Guinea	120	25	
Nigeria	120	51	120
Pakistan	120	52	
Botswana	110	11	
Sri Lanka	110	16	
Tanzania	100	21	3
Bangladesh	80	6	
Ethiopia	80	9	11
(Others)		5	
Total		234	167

Loans to very poor countries would have reached about $220 million in 1972 if lending to Pakistan had not been suspended during the crisis in Bangladesh. On the assumption that lending to Pakistan will by 1983 have reached at least the pre-1972 level of about $50 million a year and that lending to Nigeria, Kenya, Ethiopia, and Guinea will average at least $200 million a year, lending to all the very poor countries might be about $300 million a year by 1983. This assumes that the very poor countries will by 1983 be receiving at least $600 million a year from IDA, and that a good deal of this will be for local expenses.

This would mean total lending by the Bank in 1983 of $2,750 million —$1,100 million to middle-income countries, $1,100 million to poor countries, $250 million to India, and $300 million to the other very poor countries.

If these changes in Bank lending take place, and if IDA's resources are at the same time increased by 1983 to $1,500 million a year, and if these resources are distributed in the same proportions among the poor countries, India, and the other very poor countries as in the four years ending in mid-1972 (20 per cent to poor countries, 40 per cent to India, and 40 per cent to the other very poor countries), the results in 1983 would be:

	Popn. (1983)[4] (million)	*Bank*	*IDA* ($ million)	*Total*	*Per Cap* ($)
Middle-income	310	1,100		1,100	3.55
Poor	710	1,100	300	1,400	1.97
Very poor					
India	710	250	600	850	1.20
Others	745	300	600	900	1.21
Total	1,455	550	1,200	1,750	1.20
Total	2,475	2,750	1,500	4,250	1.72

The disparity between the Bank Group's treatment of its very poor member countries and its poor member countries would be much less than at the beginning of the seventies, though it would still be considerable; but the disparity between the treatment of the very poor and the middle-income countries would remain the same. The very poor countries would still be getting only one-third as much per head of population as the middle-income countries. The disparity in the net transfer of resources (disbursements less interest and amortization payments) would, of course, be less, since the greater the proportion of Bank money which countries receive from the Bank Group, the greater is the burden of interest and amortization payments. But the figures demonstrate that the Bank Group would not be able to give as much help to its poor and very poor member countries as it would be giving to its middle-income member countries unless IDA's resources were increased substantially above $1,500 million a year, perhaps to the point at which they enabled IDA to lend as much as the Bank, or about $2,750 million a year.

It should not be too difficult for the Bank Group to raise $1,500 million for IDA by 1983, since this would be an increase of only 50 per cent over the level of ten years before, and the GNP's of the rich member countries will probably have increased by about 60 per cent in real terms during those ten years. It would, however, in all probability be almost impossible for the Bank Group to raise $2,750 million a year for IDA unless IDA were to receive interest-free special drawing rights (SDRs) from the International Monetary Fund (see Chapter Fifteen).

There is another way to increase Bank Group lending to those of its poor and very poor member countries which are IDA-worthy: to use IDA money to pay the interest for the first ten years on Bank loans to these countries. Most poor and very poor countries which are eligible for IDA loans do not qualify for substantial Bank loans because their creditworthiness is low; some of these countries are likely in ten years' time to have a much greater ability to service Bank loans. Their worthiness to receive Bank loans would therefore be increased if some or all of the Bank loans to them had a ten-year grace period for both amortization and interest payments. Under this scheme, some of the allotment of IDA money to the country would be used to pay to the Bank the present value of the interest payments for the first ten years on loans to it from the Bank. If the interest rate on Bank loans were 7 per cent, the present value of ten years' interest would be almost exactly half the amount of the loan. Thus $50 million of IDA funds, if used for this purpose, could generate $100 million of Bank loans. If a country received $100 million a year of IDA funds, and if the Bank and the country agreed that $50 million of the $100 million should be used to finance Bank loans in this way, the resources available from the Bank Group to finance Bank Group projects and programs in that country would be greater by $50 million a year than they would have been if all the country's allocation of IDA money had been used to finance IDA projects and programs. A high proportion of these IDA-subsidized Bank loans could wisely be devoted to projects and programs to improve the borrowing country's ability to service its foreign debts in ten years' time.

In making calculations of credit-worthiness for ordinary Bank loans of, say, thirty years' duration (the period recommended in Chapter Fourteen for loans to low-income countries), the Bank must estimate the borrower's capacity to service the loan during the entire period of its duration. The difference between the calculations for ordinary Bank loans and those for IDA-subsidized Bank loans would be that in making its calculations for the latter, the Bank would disregard the country's capacity or incapacity to service loans during the first ten years of the loan, and would base its calculations on estimates of capacity during the last twenty years. Because of the large element in economic and social development of chance, political wisdom or stupidity in aid-giving and aid-receiving governments, and wars and rumors of wars, the calculation of credit-worthiness for most ordinary long-term Bank loans is a heroic exercise in creative imagination. The calculation of credit-worthiness for IDA-subsidized Bank loans would be no more heroic; it might indeed be less. The IDA-subsidized loans would go only to countries which clearly had good prospects in the longer run (because of their natural resources, their skilled or adaptable people, and their location), but which were poor risks for Bank loans on conventional terms (because of their existing debt or because the programs and projects which required financing would not bring results for about ten years).

If $200 million of IDA's resources were used to subsidize Bank loans to poor countries, $50 million to subsidize Bank loans to India, and $50 million to subsidize Bank loans to the other very poor countries, and if the interest rate on Bank loans were 7 per cent, Bank lending would go up by $600 million a year, from $2,750 million to $3,350 million. This would mean that Bank lending would have gone up from a little under $2,000 million in 1972 ($1,966 million) to $3,350 million in eleven years, an increase of 70 per cent. On these assumptions, total Bank Group lending in 1983 to countries (other than China) which are now middle-income or low-income members of the Bank Group would be a little more than double in real terms what it had been in 1972. The figures would be:

	1972 ($ million)	*1983* ($ million)
Bank	1,966	3,350
IDA	1,000	2,750
IFC	118	200
Total	3,084	6,300

McNamara almost doubled the volume of Bank Group lending in the four years from 1968 to 1972. It is suggested here that the volume be doubled in the eleven years from 1972 to 1983.

The distribution of the lending by the Bank and IDA would be as follows:

Countries	*Popn.* (*1983*) (million)	*Bank* ($ million)	*IDA* ($ million)	*Total* ($ million)	*Per cap* ($)
Middle-income	310	1,100		1,100	3.55
Poor	710	1,500	550	2,050	2.89
Very poor					
India	710	350	1,100	1,450	2.04
Others	745	400	1,100	1,500	2.01
Total	1,455	750	2,200	2,950	2.03
Total	2,475	3,350	2,750	6,100	2.46

A comparison of this table with the table on page 109 shows substantial differences. The very poor countries, instead of getting per head of population only a third of what the middle-income countries were getting, would get almost 60 per cent. The very poor countries would get per head of population, not 60 per cent of what the poor countries received, but about 70 per cent.

In terms of net transfer of resources resulting from Bank and IDA loans, rough equality of treatment might well result from this pattern of Bank-IDA lending, for the higher the proportion of IDA loans to Bank loans which a country receives, the lower are its debt charges in relation to its total borrowings from the Bank Group. The very poor countries, under this pattern of lending, would get about three-quarters of their total borrowings from IDA, whereas the poor countries would get only a little over a quarter. Therefore, this pattern of lending in the early eighties might mean that by the late eighties the net transfer of resources per head resulting from Bank and IDA loans would be roughly the same for the very poor countries and the poor countries. If Bank lending to the middle-income countries remained stable at a level of $1,100 million a year, it would not be many years before the middle-income countries would be paying to the Bank in interest and amortization as much as the Bank was disbursing on past loans to them. There would then be no net transfer of resources from the Bank to the middle-income countries. We would thus have reached the kind of allocation recommended by Chenery in 1970.

Bank Group lending of $6,300 million a year by 1983 would probably result by 1985 in a net transfer (disbursements less interest and repayment of principal) of about $3,500 million.[5] This would probably be about one-twelfth of 1 per cent of the combined GNP's of the rich member countries of the Bank, which by that time would probably have reached a level of $4,000 billion ($4,000,000 million).* If lending by the regional banks were then resulting in a net transfer of two-thirds of this amount, the combined lending of these multilateral agencies would result in a net transfer of about one-seventh of 1 per cent of the combined GNP's of the rich member countries. The Pearson Commission set the target of seven-tenths of 1 per cent of the GNP's for the net flow of official development assistance which should be reached by 1975, but in no event later than 1980. Net flow is disbursements less repayment of principal. Net transfer is net flow less payments of interest. A net flow of seven-tenths of 1 per cent might turn out to be much the same thing by 1985 as a net transfer of six-tenths of 1 per cent. If net transfer had reached six-tenths of 1 per cent by 1985, a net transfer of one-seventh of 1 per cent resulting from lending by the Bank Group and by the regional banks would mean that these agencies would be responsible for about a quarter of the total transfer. This is not much above the proportion of one-fifth which the Pearson Commission considered would be reasonable for the last half of the seventies.

The projections given above of Bank Group lending in 1983 are of loans to members other than China. It is suggested in Chapter Twenty that if the Soviet Union and the Eastern European states become members of the Bank and if the Peking government takes over the Chinese seat in the Bank, Bank lending to these countries might amount by 1983 to about $550 million a year. It is further suggested that China's borrowings from IDA might by 1983 be about $1,000 million a year. If lending to other countries were not to be scaled down, Bank lending would have to go up from $3,350 million to $3,900 million and IDA lending from $2,750 million to $3,750 million. Lending to other possible new members—North Korea, North Vietnam, Mongolia, Albania, and Cuba—might increase each of these totals by $100 million, to $4,000 million; and $3,850 million.

Apart from the possibility that Peking takes over the Chinese seat in the Bank and IDA and that the other Communist countries become

*The projections of GNP, population, and GNP per capita which are used in this chapter are set forth in Annex Five, pages 250 to 253.

members, there remains the question of what increase would be appropriate for Bank Group lending during the rest of the eighties. Perhaps all that can usefully be said is that after 1983 Bank Group lending might increase at the rate required to keep the net transfer of resources resulting from that lending stable in terms of its relationship to the combined GNP's of the rich member countries. Since the ratio which the return flow of interest and amortization payments on past Bank Group loans would bear to Bank Group lending would constantly increase, this would mean that the volume of Bank Group lending would increase at a higher rate than the rate of increase in the GNP's of the rich member countries.

By the second half of the eighties, given reasonably sensible behavior by all concerned and a reasonable run of good luck, all or almost all the countries now in the middle-income category may well be able to raise from the capital markets of the world on reasonable terms almost all the foreign capital they need to maintain a high rate of development. Bank lending to these countries might therefore be expected to fall sharply during the second half of the eighties and to cease during the nineties. As disbursements on Bank loans tapered off, these countries would be paying to the Bank more in interest and amortization than the Bank would be disbursing on loans to them. They would thus increasingly become a source of funds for the Bank.

Before the end of the century, therefore, all or virtually all the lending by the Bank and IDA would be to countries which are now poor or very poor. These countries are likely to have a total population in the year 2000 of about 4,700 million, amounting to about three-quarters of a total world population of about 6,300 million. Most of the countries now poor or very poor might well have achieved before the end of the century a pace of economic and social advance substantially higher than that achieved in the sixties; but it is highly unlikely that any except the oil-rich countries would have achieved a level of economic and social development which could be considered satisfactory by any reasonable person.

Certainly, barring a miracle, the standard of living the great majority of the very poor countries will have achieved by the end of the century will still be very low. India, in the middle ranks of the very poor countries, can be taken as a representative of the very poor countries. In the sixties, GNP in India increased in real terms at a rate of 3½ per cent a year. This increase was a great improvement over the record in the half-century or so preceding independence, when the rate was only about 1¼ per cent a year.[6] If India were able in the last thirty years of this century to maintain a 7 per cent growth rate, this would be an extraordinary achievement; it could come about only as the result of much better performance at home and of much more aid from abroad. The most optimistic forecast of India's population in the year 2000 is 948 million. This, according to the study of population projections in *World Bank Operations*, "can be attained only if considerable effort is applied to changing present attitudes toward high fertility" among the people of India.* But, even if India were able to do both these things, income a head in India in the year 2000 would be only $460 a year (in 1970 dollars), about the level Peru had reached in 1970. This level could scarcely be regarded by the governments and peoples of rich countries as an indication that India had reached a satisfactory level of economic and social development, particularly since by that time average real income a head in the rich countries of the world might be three times what it had been in 1970. Average income a head in the rich countries, both Communist and non-Communist, was probably about $2,800 in 1970. In the year 2000 it could be $9,500 in 1970 dollars.

In 1970, the gap between average income a head in India and average income a head in the rich countries of the world was about $2,700. On very optimistic assumptions about progress in India, the gap in the year 2000 may be about $9,000. The situation of India is not unique. The income of the average person in virtually all the other very poor countries of the world at the end of the century is not likely to be much better than that of the average person in India. It may be worse. And the total population at the end of the century of the countries which are now very poor is likely to be about 3,600 million, almost three-fifths of the population of the world.**

The Bank Group is likely to have enough to do not just for decades but for generations.

* See Annex Five.

** The estimates in Annex Five of GNP per capita for rich countries and for India (on very optimistic assumptions) are, in 1970 dollars:

	1970	*2000*
Rich countries	$2,790	$9,570
India	110	460
Gap	2,680	9,110

CHAPTER FOURTEEN

The Terms of Lending by the Bank and IDA

In the first half of the sixties the rate of interest charged by the Bank to its borrowers was about $1\frac{2}{5}$ percentage points more than the rate of interest it had to pay on its bonds. When the cost to the Bank of its borrowings rose from 4 per cent in 1964 to 8 per cent in 1971, the rate of interest charged by the Bank did not rise to the same extent. It increased only from $5\frac{1}{2}$ per cent to $7\frac{1}{4}$ per cent. The result was that in the fiscal year 1971, instead of a positive spread of about $1\frac{2}{5}$ percentage points between the cost of borrowing and the rate of lending, there was a negative spread of about $\frac{4}{5}$ of 1 percentage point. In the fiscal year 1972, the cost to the Bank of its borrowings fell to $7\frac{2}{5}$ per cent, with the result that the negative spread fell to $\frac{1}{8}$ of 1 percentage point. The existence of a negative spread meant that the Bank gave a subsidy to all its borrowers, whether they were rich, poor, or very poor countries.*

(Not all the members of the Bank would agree that the subsidy element in Bank lending is the difference between the rate of lending and the cost of current Bank borrowing. Some would say that the cost of money to the Bank on the basis of which the Bank's rate of lending should be calculated is not the cost of current Bank borrowing but the average cost of all the money it has available for lending, and this includes its interest-free endowment and its reserves. In 1972 this average cost was 4 per cent. Others would say that the cost of lending by the Bank should include not only the cost of current Bank borrowing but also the costs of administering the lending program. The annual cost of administering the Bank is about $\frac{1}{2}$ of 1 per cent of the loans outstanding. It is further argued that the cost to the borrower of a Bank loan is not the interest rate on the loan but the interest rate less the annual rate of inflation.)

Under its articles of agreement, the Bank is precluded from granting a loan unless it "is satisfied that in the prevailing market con-

*Table 1, page 223, gives for each of the years from 1960 to 1972 the current cost of borrowing by the Bank and the interest charged by the Bank on its loans.

ditions the borrower would be unable otherwise to obtain the loan under conditions which in the opinion of the Bank are reasonable for the borrower" (Article III.4.ii). This provision has to be read along with the statement in the first of the articles of agreement that one of the purposes of the Bank is, "when private capital is not available on reasonable terms, to supplement private investment by providing, on suitable conditions, finance for productive purposes." In practice, these provisions have been interpreted to mean that the Bank is precluded from lending to countries which can raise sufficient resources under reasonable conditions on the world's capital markets. This makes all but a few of the rich member countries of the Bank (countries with per capita GNP's in 1970 of at least $1,600 a year) ineligible to receive Bank loans. Some rich members have contended that, while they can raise some private capital on reasonable terms, they cannot raise it in sufficient volume on reasonable terms, and that they are therefore eligible to borrow from the Bank to supplement their borrowings from private capital markets. The Bank has recognized the validity of this contention and has lent and continues to lend to them, though in relatively small amounts. In the four fiscal years 1969 to 1972, the Bank lent about $40 million a year to its rich member countries. These countries, in descending order of GNP per capita, were New Zealand, Finland, Iceland, and Israel.

The Bank decided in 1965 that countries able to raise most of the capital they needed on the world's private capital markets but unable to raise sufficient private capital on reasonable terms should be charged an interest rate of up to 1 percentage point higher than the prevailing standard rate, then 4/5 of one percentage point above the current cost of Bank borrowing. This meant that the rate to these countries would be up to 1 4/5 percentage points above the current cost of Bank borrowing. The Bank called these countries "market-eligible." Only two loans were made at market-eligible rates, both in the fiscal year 1965, one to Italy for $100 million and one to Japan for $75 million. In 1967, presumably as the result of the rise in the current cost of Bank borrowing, the Bank abandoned the special market-eligible rate of interest. Since then, it has charged market-eligible countries the same rate of interest as its other borrowers.

The argument advanced in 1965 for setting the interest rate for market-eligible countries at up to 1 4/5 percentage points above the current cost of Bank borrowing was that this rate would approximate the rate at which these countries could borrow on the market, that to charge them less than this would tend to discourage them from trying to raise all they could from the market, and that this would be contrary to the statement in the articles of agreement that one of the purposes of the Bank is, "*when private capital is not available on reasonable terms,* to supplement private investment by providing on suitable conditions finance for productive purposes" (italics added). This argument would appear to be as valid now as in 1965.

The rich members of the Bank, which borrowed from the Bank in the fiscal years 1969 to 1972, are clearly market-eligible countries; as soon as they are able to raise all the capital they need on reasonable terms in the world's capital markets, they will become ineligible to receive further Bank loans. The DAC annual review for 1971 stated that the main developing countries, according to the DAC definition of developing, which raised capital during the sixties by issuing bonds in DAC countries were Argentina, Israel, and Mexico, "who are now well-established in the market." The DAC review went on to say, "Thirteen more countries are approaching the same category having made several issues of bonds: Jamaica (9 issues), Venezuela (7 issues), Brazil, Spain, the Philippines, Peru (6 issues each), Ivory Coast, Gabon, Malaysia, Colombia (5 each), and the Netherlands-Antilles, Panama, Trinidad and Tobago (4 each)."[1] Mexico, Argentina, and these thirteen countries borrowed a total of $832 million from the Bank in 1971 and $961 million in 1972. The average annual borrowings from the Bank of this group of countries are likely to increase over the next ten years or so. Their borrowings during the ten fiscal years 1974 to 1983 inclusive might average at least $1,000 million a year (in 1972 dollars). If all these loans were made at a rate of 1½ percentage points above the current cost of Bank borrowing, the gross profit on these loans at the end of ten years would be $150 million a year. This profit could be used to increase both the reserves of the Bank and the help it gives to its poorest member countries by transfers of Bank profits to IDA or in other ways.

The Bank might wisely, therefore, re-establish a differential rate of interest for those borrowers which are market-eligible. The rate might be 1½ percentage points above the current cost of Bank borrowing. Whether a country were or were not market-eligible would be a question of fact. The test would be whether the country could raise a part but not all of the capital it needed on reasonable terms in the world's private capital markets. (This is a broader definition than that adopted by the Bank in 1965, that market-eligible countries would be those which cover their external capital needs mainly in private markets.) In charging one group of borrowers a higher interest than another, the Bank would be following the practice of the Inter-American bank in its concessional loans. It charges its "more advanced member countries" 3 or 4 per cent and its "relatively less developed" member countries 1 per cent during the first seven to ten years of the loan, and 2 per cent thereafter. The countries coming in-between these two categories are charged 2 per cent throughout the period of the loan.

A related question about the terms of Bank lending is whether the Bank should re-establish a positive spread between its current cost of borrowing and its standard interest rate and, if so, what the positive spread should be. Decisions on this matter can affect greatly the size of Bank profits and therefore the size of the Bank's reserves and of the assistance it can give to its poorest member countries. If, over the ten-year period 1974 to 1983 inclusive, Bank lending to member countries which are not market-eligible were to average about $1,750 million a year (in 1972 dollars), and if the interest rate were 4/5 of 1 percentage point below the current cost of Bank borrowing, as it was in the year 1971, Bank profits at the end of the ten-year period would be about $225 million a year less than they would have been if the interest rate had been ½ of 1 percentage point above the current cost of Bank borrowing, as it was in 1967.

Because of the importance of increasing the reserves of the Bank and its ability to help its poorest members, the Bank should return to a positive spread between the current cost of borrowing and the standard interest rate. Perhaps the spread might be ½ of 1 percentage point. If this change were made when the current cost of Bank borrowing was above 6 per cent, the standard interest rate would have to rise from its present level of 7¼ per cent. Since this would create difficulties for the Bank in its relations with those member countries not eligible to receive a blend of Bank loans and IDA credits, the Bank should postpone the establishment of a positive spread of ½ of 1 percentage point until the current cost of Bank borrowing has fallen below 6¼ per cent; the standard interest rate would then be maintained at a rate of ½ of 1 percentage point above the current cost of Bank borrowing. If the current cost of Bank borrowing were to rise above 8 per cent, the present standard rate of 7¼ per cent should be increased *pari passu*.

The differences in interest rates on Bank loans should be accompanied by differences in maturities and in grace periods before repayments of principal begin. As a general rule, loans to market-eligible countries should be for 10 to 15 years, with grace periods of 1 to 5 years; loans to middle-income countries should be for 20 to 25 years, with grace periods of 1 to 10 years; and loans to low-income countries should be for 30 years, with 10-year grace periods. The grace periods on loans to market-eligible countries and middle-income countries should be related to the gestation period of the project financed by the loan.

The articles of agreement of IDA state that IDA "shall not provide financing if in its opinion such financing . . . could be provided by a loan of the type made by the [World] Bank" (Article V. 1. (c)). A strict interpretation of this provision would prohibit IDA from granting credit to a country until that country had completely exhausted its credit-worthiness for Bank loans. Any country which was credit-worthy for Bank loans would *ipso facto* not be IDA-worthy. IDA has in practice departed from this strict interpretation. It has granted IDA credits to countries which are still receiving Bank loans. Nevertheless, it is clear that the main criterion for determining IDA-eligibility must be either lack of or low credit-worthiness for Bank loans; in general, the poorer the country, the less credit-worthy it is likely to be. The present cut-off point for IDA-eligibility is "a per capita income of around $300 per annum."[2] Only 4 per cent of the IDA credits granted in the four years which ended June 30, 1972, were to countries with per capita GNP's of more than $300 a year in 1970.

Guesses about the credit-worthiness of a country thirty years or more from now are subject to wide margins of error. In the late forties,

Libya was a very poor country, and, if an IDA had existed then, Libya would have received interest-free loans from IDA repayable over fifty years. By the early seventies, Libya had become one of the rich countries of the world. By the mid-seventies, GNP per capita in Libya will probably be higher than in the European Economic Community. There will be other Libya's, countries now very poor and clearly IDA-worthy, but whose foreign exchange earnings will go up rapidly as the result of unpredictable developments. Indonesia may turn out to be such a country. So may Egypt. IDA needs greatly increased resources. To get these resources, there must be much more parliamentary and public support for IDA in the rich countries. The emergence of a Libya among the recipients of IDA loans would weaken this support. This is the kind of event which incenses legislatures and taxpayers. There would be attacks on the management of IDA for its improvidence in granting to the new Libya loans which were not only interest-free but which did not have to be repaid for fifty years.

To avoid this danger, it would be wise to give IDA credits, all of which go to low-income countries, the same maturity recommended for Bank loans to low-income countries, that is, 30 years. However, unlike Bank loans, these would be renegotiable in the twentieth year at the request of the borrower. If at that time the borrower's credit-worthiness was still low, the credit would be extended for another 10 or 20 years, making its total length 40 or 50 years. If IDA credits had a maturity of 30 years, 2½ per cent a year might be repayable in the second decade, and 7½ per cent a year in the third. If, as a result of renegotiation, the loan was extended to a total length of 40 years, the annual repayments in the last years of the loan would be 3¾ per cent; if extended to a total of 50 years, 2½ per cent. This would in effect create three types of IDA loans: 30-year loans, 40-year loans, and 50-year loans.

The immediate reaction of low-income countries to this proposal on the terms of IDA loans is likely to be unfavorable. What will impress them is that it will increase the cost to them of servicing IDA loans, that it will reduce the grant component in these loans, But, what is more important to low-income borrowing countries than the cost of servicing loans, whether from IDA or any other source, is the net transfer of resources resulting from the loans (net transfer being what is left when the cost of servicing loans is deducted from the disbursements resulting from them), and in the longer run, the adoption of this proposal is likely to increase the net transfer of resources. It is likely to have this result because it will lessen the danger that the emergence of a new Libya will reduce the resources of IDA and therefore its disbursements. Moreover, the reduction in the length of some IDA loans from 50 to 40 or 30 years will increase the resources of IDA by increasing its income from amortization payments.

The adoption of these proposals would result in a wide range in the terms of Bank-IDA lending. Thus, if the current cost of Bank borrowing were to fall to 6½ per cent, market-eligible countries would pay 8 per cent interest on Bank loans with maturities of 10 to 15 years; middle-income countries which are not market-eligible would pay 7 per cent, with maturities of 20 to 25 years; and low-income countries (those with per capita GNP's of less than $440 a year) would pay 7 per cent, with maturities of 30 years; the poorer of them would be eligible to receive IDA credits which would be interest-free (though bearing the ¾ of 1 per cent service charge) and have maturities of 30 years but which could be extended to 40 or 50 years. Further flexibility would be provided by adopting the proposal discussed in Chapter Thirteen, that some of the Bank loans to IDA-worthy countries be free for 10 years of both interest and amortization payments, the interest charges during these years being paid out of IDA funds.

CHAPTER FIFTEEN

The Sources of Funds for the Bank Group

About three-quarters of the Bank Group's financial resources comes directly or indirectly from the capital markets and the governments of its principal rich member countries (the United States, Britain, Germany, France, Japan, and Canada), and almost the whole of the remainder from other rich countries. This dependence inevitably imposes limitations on the freedom of action of the Bank Group to do its best for its poorer member countries. One indication of this was the attitude of many of the rich countries to some of the principal recommendations of the Pearson Commission relating to the Bank Group. One such recommendation was that IDA should "seek in its policies to offset the larger inequities in aid distribution"; but, most of the rich countries did not want the allocation of their bilateral aid, which is based in part on considerations other than the economic development of the poorer countries, to be offset by allocations of IDA loans. Another was that there should be "balanced and impartial reviews of donor aid policies and programs"; but, most of the rich countries did not want their aid policies and programs to be subjected to an impartial, expert examination. A third was that "in regard to the possible excessive use of export credits, a strong 'early warning system' based on external debt reporting should be evolved by the OECD and the World Bank"; but, most of the rich countries were opposed to this because it would limit their freedom of action in granting export credits, though they would, of course, deny that they wanted freedom to finance third-rate or thoroughly bad projects or an excessively large volume of export credits or credits on inappropriate terms.[1]

A strong indication of the power of the rich countries is that until recently the Bank Group has had to proceed very cautiously in increasing its lending for the local costs of projects—that is to say, for costs incurred in local currency, not costs resulting directly or indirectly in a drain on foreign exchange. Only, however, by lending large sums for local costs can the Bank Group help its poorer member countries to finance large-scale programs of rural development works and large-scale development of small industries, two of the most promising ways to promote growth with jobs and justice. Some of the most influential rich member countries have opposed great expansion of local-cost financing largely because they want Bank Group money spent whenever possible on the purchase of capital goods from their own manufacturers.

Another indication of their power is that the Bank Group has diverted more of its resources than it otherwise would to countries in which one or more of its important rich member countries was especially interested, whether for political reasons or because loans to those countries would likely result in increased exports from those rich countries. Thus the great efforts the Bank Group has made to increase its lending to francophone Black Africa arise in part from the importance of getting the French government to support increased resources for the International Development Association. The interest of the Bank Group in Indonesia since the establishment there of an anti-Communist government is in part the result of the interest of Japan and the United States in that country under its present leadership. The high level of Bank Group loans to Taiwan, Thailand, and South Korea in the sixties was related to the high level of United States political interest in those countries.[2]

The Bank Group would have been able to do more for its poorer member countries if the opposition of some rich member countries and some senior members of the staff from rich countries had not resulted in its being slow to do the following things. In allocating its funds among the poorer countries, it would seek to offset the larger inequities which result from the concentration of bilateral aid in certain countries for political, strategic, or historical reasons. It would augment greatly the proportion of its loans which finance essential imports, including industrial raw materials needed to make full use of existing industrial capacity, and reduce the proportion of its loans used to finance capital goods required for the expansion of industrial capacity. In evaluating competitive bids on projects in low-income countries which it helps to finance, it would give local suppliers and suppliers in other low-income countries a higher preference over foreign suppliers than the 15 per cent now allowed them. It would complement its expert and impartial studies of the development policies and performance of aid-receiving countries with equally expert and impartial studies of the aid policies and performance of aid-giving countries (and aid means trade, as well as loans and grants). It would take action making it more difficult for rich countries to use their export credits in ways which harm the developing countries. It would help low-income countries to establish export finance facilities for their own exporters as effective as those provided by rich countries to their exporters, so that they could compete on equal terms.

The limitations on the Bank Group's ability to do its best for its poorer member countries will be reduced the less it is dependent for its finances on its rich member countries. This dependence will be reduced the greater the proportion of its finances which it itself generates, the greater the proportion flowing from long-run contractual agreements with its member countries and from changes in the international monetary system, and the more resources it receives from a sort of international taxation system.

The Bank

The internal sources for the generation of Bank resources are the investment of its paid-in capital and its reserves, and the spread between the interest rate it charges on its loans and the cost of the borrowings required to finance these loans. Usable paid-in subscriptions now amount to about $2,200 million. The argument for doubling the capital of a lending agency which has doubled its volume of lending is strong. If governments were to agree that the Bank's capital be doubled and 10 per cent of the new capital paid in, this would provide the Bank with an additional $2,200 million of interest-free capital. Bank reserves created from transfer of profits will probably amount by 1975 to about $2,000 million. Thus, by the mid-seventies, the Bank could have interest-free resources totaling about $6,500 million. The return to the Bank would, at present interest rates, be over $400 million a year. As the Bank's reserves increased, this return would go up, though only in terms of current, not constant, dollars.

Ten years after the establishment of a spread of 1½ percentage points between the current cost of Bank borrowing and the interest rate charged to market-eligible countries, and of a ½ of 1 percentage point spread for other borrowers, the Bank might be making a gross profit of over $225 million a year on the loans it had granted in the preceding decade. It would also be receiving a profit on some of its earlier loans.

These calculations indicate that by the middle of the eighties the gross profits of the Bank could be running at a rate of over $600 million a year (in 1972 dollars), and, if its net administrative expenses (gross expenses less payments received for services rendered to other agencies, etc.), which were $66 million in 1972, were not to increase to more than about $150 million, its profits could be about $450 million a year (in 1972 dollars). Of this, $250 million a year might be used for research (see Chapter Six) and $200 million transferred to reserves.

In the first four and a half years of the McNamara regime, the borrowings by the Bank from the central banks of its members and Switzerland, by the sale of Bank bonds to them, increased from $1,065 million on June 30, 1968, to $2,400 million on January 1, 1973. Of this, over $1,600 million was from the central banks of Japan ($853 million) and Germany ($766 million). The structural changes which will be made in the international monetary system in the seventies will undoubtedly result in the special drawing rights of the International Monetary Fund, constituting an ever-increasing proportion of the reserves of central banks, until before long they will constitute the major reserve asset. Could not the structural changes also include an arrangement under which each of the central banks of the member countries and of Switzerland (whether these countries are rich, middle-income, or low-income) would hold a certain proportion of its reserves—possibly 5 per cent—in special World Bank bonds? When its reserves went down, the World Bank would buy back the surplus holdings of these bonds over the agreed proportion. When its reserves went up, it would buy more of these special bonds from the World Bank. (This would not affect the right of central banks to hold other issues of World Bank bonds in addition to these special bonds.)

In December 1972 the reserves of the members of the International Monetary Fund were $155 billion. Five per cent of this would be about $8 billion. The suggested arrangement between the World Bank and the central banks might include a provision that the World Bank would re-lend to the regional banks one-third of these borrowings from the central banks. Thus the World Bank would keep, out of the $8 billion raised from the sale of special bonds to central banks, $5⅓ billion for its own use and pass on $2⅔ billion to the regional banks. As a result of experience in working this scheme, the central banks might be prepared in the eighties to increase their holdings of special World Bank bonds from 5 per cent of their reserves to, say, 10 per cent. By the time that point had been reached, the Bank might be re-lending half of the proceeds to the regional banks, if by then their total volume of nonconcessional lending was about the same as that of the World Bank. But, even if central banks were holding only 5 per cent of their reserves in special World Bank bonds, and the Bank was re-lending a third of the proceeds to regional banks, these borrowings from central banks plus increased profits would substantially diminish the extent of the dependence the Bank would otherwise have on selling its bonds on the capital markets of rich countries.

IFC

IFC began its operatons in 1956 with a share capital, subscribed by governments, of $100 million. As a result of increases in membership, its share capital on June 30, 1972, had increased to $107 million. In addition, it had a reserve against losses of $73 million derived from accumulated earnings. Its resources were increased in 1965 by an amendment to the articles of agreement of the Bank and of IFC under which, provided IFC does not incur any other debts, the Bank may lend it up to "four times its unimpaired subscribed capital and surplus." Since at least $25 million of the reserve against losses could be transformed into surplus, this means that the Bank could lend IFC about $500 million. So far the Bank has lent it $260 million.

The Peterson task force on international development recommended to the President of the United States in March 1970 that the paid-in capital of IFC should be increased "to perhaps $400 million."[3] One result of this would be to enable the Bank to lend IFC about $1,700 million instead of about $500 million. IFC can use its share capital and its reserves for investment in equities. It can use its borrowings from the World Bank only for loans. Thus, if its share capital were increased to $400 million, it could increase its investments in equities from the present level of less than $120 million to about $475 million; its increased borrowings from the World Bank would enable it to increase its loans from the present level of about $300 million to about $1,700 million. Because this sort of distribution of investments in a ratio of about 2 to 7 between equities and loans is too heavily weighted in favor of loans for an investment agency such as IFC, and because there may be delay in increasing the share capital of IFC, it would seem wise to amend the Bank's articles of agreement in order to permit IFC to use the proceeds of Bank loans both for equity investment and for loans.

Until IFC's capacity to invest is increased, either by an increase in its share capital or by an amendment to the Bank's articles of agreement, the only way by which it can secure additional funds for equity investment is by loans from member governments for this purpose. The Netherlands government made such a loan in 1971. Other governments might wisely follows its example.

IDA

IDA at present generates internally a very small flow of resources. It charges no interest but only a service charge of ¾ of 1 per cent a year on the disbursed portion of each credit. Further, there is no repayment of capital in the first ten years and only 1 per cent a year in the next ten years. (The repayment of capital in the succeeding thirty years is at a rate of 3 per cent a year.) It is likely that, as the volume of credits disbursed increases, the service charge will be reduced, so that it would no more than cover the administrative expenses of IDA. This would mean that IDA's net income would consist only of the amortization payments and of interest on sums received from its member governments but which it had not disbursed. As time goes on, however, the amortization payments would be substantial, particularly if, as has been recommended above (Chapter Fifteen), the initial period of IDA credits were reduced from fifty to thirty years and the amortization payments in the second decade of the credits increased from 1 per cent to 2½ per cent a year.[4]

In Chapter Thirteen, it is suggested that IDA might in part be financed in future by special drawing rights of the International Monetary Fund. Certainly it is greatly to be hoped that this will be one result of the substantial structural changes to be made in the seventies in the international monetary system. The president of the World Bank has been reluctant to take a public position on this matter, since it is a direct responsibility of the International Monetary Fund, not of the Bank. It is therefore important that in 1972 McNamara publicly associated himself with proposals to link the financing of aid, "either directly or indirectly, to future issues of Special Drawing Rights."[5]

To establish a direct and operational link between the issuance of special drawing rights and the replenishment of IDA (and UNDP and the soft-loan funds of the regional banks), it would be necessary to amend the articles of agreement of the International Monetary Fund to permit the Fund, at the time of the periodic allocation of SDRs, to allocate some proportion of newly issued SDRs to these development agencies, to be used in their operations on the basis of internationally established rules. "This could be done by a new statutory provision (in the articles of agreement of the IMF) which stipulated that a given proportion of SDRs created should be made available to development agencies, with the remainder being allocated to participants (that is, members of the IMF) on the basis of quotas. This approach would entail fluctuations in the flow of SDRs to development agencies, in accordance with variations in the decisions on the need for global SDR creation. Alternatively, the amount to be put at the disposal of development agencies could as far as possible be kept stable in the short run, with allocations to participants absorbing any variations in amounts created."[6] This quotation comes from the report on the reform of the international monetary system which the executive directors of the IMF made in 1972 to the board of governors.

There is some misgiving that the establishment of a direct and operational link between the issuance of SDRs and the financing of soft loans and grants by international development agencies would result in the creation of too many SDRs, and this would add to the inflationary forces in the world, already too strong. The countries which would be eligible for the soft loans and grants would be mainly those whose GNP per capita is not more than $300 a year. These countries have about 17 per cent of the votes in the IMF,* and an affirmative vote of 85 per cent is required to make the necessary amendments in the articles of agreement of the IMF and to make the periodic decisions on the creation of SDRs. These countries could, therefore, if they presented a united front, veto reforms in the international monetary system desired by the rich countries if the reforms did not include a link between SDRs and development finance. The existence of this veto probably insures that there will be some link. But, once the link is established, they could not use their veto power to insist on what most of the rich countries considered to be an excessive creation of SDRs without running the risk that none would be created. The bargaining power of the poorer countries in discussions of the volume of SDRs to be created is therefore not likely to be great.

A stronger argument against the link is that a reformed international monetary system will have to rely heavily on the SDR; to play its part successfully the SDR must be considered by governments and central banks to be a first-class international reserve asset, one in which they have complete confidence; the chances of their having such confidence will be lessened if the SDR is both a reserve asset and a means of financing the poorer countries.

Some experts believe that the establishment of a link between SDRs and development assistance would not increase the volume of aid but would result merely in substituting SDRs for direct contributions

*See Table Four, pages 238 to 244.

which governments would otherwise have made. Harry Johnson, a leading proponent of this view, said in 1970 that the proposal for a link between SDRs and development assistance "is essentially a proposal to provide development assistance by inflationary world monetary expansion, based on the naive assumption that the governments of the advanced countries can be tricked by exploitation of the mysteries of money—which they can understand at least as well as the proponents of the scheme—into accepting a larger volume of aid commitments than they would be willing to provide by democratic budgetary vote."[7]

It is surely not, however, a question of tricking governments. Governments know that the effect of linking SDRs to development assistance would be to transfer real resources from rich countries to poorer countries in the form of unrequited exports. The question before the governments of rich countries is whether, if they want to increase the transfer of real resources to the low-income countries, this is for them an easier way of doing it than other possible ways, easier because once accepted by legislatures, it would not be necessary for the governments to go back to them every year, easier because, as I. G. Patel has said, it ought to be "somehow easy to convince ordinary citizens that if they get something for nothing, they should be willing to share a part of it with less fortunate people."[8] And, to ordinary citizens, SDRs will seem like something for nothing.

Since this is an easier method of transferring real resources from rich countries to low-income countries, it is reasonable to assume that governments would probably provide more real resources by an easier method than they would by the more difficult method of asking legislatures to vote money. This is not to say that all the resources deriving from SDRs would be additional to what governments would otherwise have provided. It is an assertion that, given the nature of politics in the rich, democratic, aid-giving countries, a substantial proportion of the resources deriving from SDRs would be additional to what governments would otherwise have provided.

Experience certainly suggests that not all democratic governments share Harry Johnson's aversion to providing resources for international development by means other than what he calls "democratic budgetary vote." The Canadian government treats its contribution to IDA as a loan, not as a grant. In the public accounts of Canada for the year 1971-72, the total Canadian contribution to IDA of $215 million is listed among the assets of the government, even though the present value of an interest-free loan repayable in full at the end of fifty years is about one cent on the dollar, on the assumption of a discount rate of 6 per cent and an inflation rate of 2 per cent. A high official of the German government told me in 1960 that his government did not expect repayment in full of the development loans it was then making to developing countries, but that it was easier to get the German parliament to agree to loans than to grants.

The Canadian government's method of dealing with the Canadian contribution to IDA and the German government's method of financing development in the early sixties could be described as methods to trick parliaments. The device of providing IDA with some of its financial resources by using SDRs would not be a trick. Parliaments would be asked to approve the necessary amendments of the articles of agreement of the IMF, and the discussion in parliaments of the amendments would make clear that one of the purposes of the amendments was to transfer real resources from rich countries to the poorer countries.

How great a source of income might SDRs provide for IDA and the regional banks? One possible formula might be that development agencies would receive one-third of the allocations of SDRs. Another is that they might receive one-half of the allocation which would otherwise have gone to rich countries. In 1970, 1971, and 1972, when the allocation was $3 billion a year, these formulas would have resulted in the development agencies receiving $1 billion in each of the three years. They would have received nothing in 1973, since there was no allocation of SDRs that year.

IDA and the other development agencies would clearly prefer the formula mentioned above, under which "the amount to be put at the disposal of development agencies could as far as possible be kept stable in the short run, with allocations to participants absorbing any variations in amounts created." But, even this formula would not protect them against a shortage of funds in years when there was no, or a very small, allocation. In those years, they would have to reduce the volume of loans they granted, as IDA has had to do when the United States has been slow in appropriating funds for it.

Perhaps the member governments of the IMF will agree that, beginning in 1975, an average of $1 billion a year (in 1972 dollars) of interest-free SDRs might be made available to IDA, and $500 million a year to the regional banks, to be used by them in granting interest-free loans to countries below a certain level of per capita income. This would bring IDA's resources to at least $2,250 million a year on the assumptions that by 1975 governments will be giving IDA $1,200 million a year (in 1972 dollars), compared with $800 million a year in the preceding three years, and that IDA also receives $50 million from transfer of Bank profits, and miscellaneous income, including amortization payments.

By the mid-eighties, SDRs will presumably have become the major international reserve asset, all additions to reserves (apart from the 10 per cent used to purchase special World Bank bonds) will be in the form of SDRs, and it is likely that the rate at which SDRs will be created will be at least half the rate of increase in international trade. It is also probable that the Soviet Union and all the eastern European Communist states will have become members of the IMF and of the Bank Group, and that the government in Peking will have taken the Chinese seats in those institutions. It is therefore possible that by the mid-eighties the volume of SDRs made available every year to IDA and the regional banks may be about $3,000 million (in 1972 dollars). Since by then the activities of regional banks should have gone up at a faster rate than the activities of the Bank Group, this $3,000 million might be divided equally between IDA and the regional banks.

Even if by the mid-eighties governments have not increased their contributions to IDA above $1,200 million a year, though it is reasonable to expect this, IDA would, on this calculation, have resources of about $2,800 million a year—$1,200 million from governments, $1,500 million from SDRs, and $100 million from miscellaneous income, including amortization payments. (IDA would no longer, under the proposal made in Chapter Seven, receive transfers from Bank profits. These would be used for research.) The estimate given above (Chapter Thirteen) of an appropriate level of IDA lending by 1983 to the low-income members of the Bank, other than China, was $2,750 million a year.

There are other possible sources of income for IDA. Of these, the most promising is the proposal made by the governments of the United States and Canada in 1970 and 1971 that royalties derived from the exploitation of the sea bed outside the national jurisdiction of any country be used for international development.

President Nixon set forth his proposal about the sea bed in his message to Congress on foreign aid on September 15, 1970. He suggested that "to add a new dimension to the international aid effort insuring a more permanent and enduring source of funds for the low-income countries . . . all nations enter into a treaty to establish an international regime for the exploitation of . . . [the vast economic resources of the sea bed], and that royalties derived therefrom be utilized principally for providing economic assistance to developing countries participating in the treaty." Six months later, the Canadian government proposed that, since it would probably take some time to reach international agreement on the contentious issue of the extent of the sea bed under national jurisdiction, the nations of the world might agree on a determination "of the minimum noncontentious area of the sea bed beyond the limits of national jurisdiction; the simultaneous establishment of an interim international machinery for that area; and the simultaneous creation of an "international development fund" to be derived from voluntary contributions made by the coastal states, on the basis of a fixed percentage of revenues accruing from off-shore exploitation beyond the outer limits of their internal waters." 9

When President Nixon spoke of the vast economic resources of the sea bed, he must have been referring to the so-called manganese nodules which are scattered over millions of square miles of ocean floor. These nodules are of unknown origin. Some are as small as peas, others as large as baseballs. They consist primarily of manganese but also contain copper, nickel, cobalt, and other metals. They would be mined by dredging the ocean floor with a relatively simple continuous bucket system. The quantities of nodules are said to be so vast that they could be mined at a rate of 400 million tons a year indefinitely. Some experts forecast that they will be mined at a rate of 100 million tons a year within ten or twenty years. One hundred million tons of nodules would produce one-quarter of the present annual production of copper in the non-Communist world, three times the production of nickel, six times the production of manganese, and twelve times the production of cobalt. And all this, according to some experts, at costs of production one-fifth and less of current prices.

The nations of the world should conclude a treaty on the lines of the Nixon proposal promptly. The longer they delay, the more difficult the task; vested interests will have been established, vested interests of governments which are constantly extending the area of the sea bed over which they claim jurisdiction, vested interests of the dozen or more national and multinational corporations and consortia already actively working on the problem of how to mine the nodules. At the end of 1972, \$50 million to \$100 million had already been spent or committed, mostly by United States companies, for nodule mining, and at least a dozen national or multinational corporations and consortia were actively working on the problems.[10]

Three proposals for financing the development of the poorer nations of the world by a sort of international taxation system have been made by the UN Committee on Development Planning. A majority of the members of the Committee have supported a proposal for a "world solidarity contribution." The tax authorities of each country participating in this scheme would levy a special international development tax of, say, ½ of 1 per cent on the purchase price "of a limited number of goods, the possession of which is at present indicative of a relatively high level of living by the purchaser: for example, cars (and aircraft and pleasure boats), television sets, refrigerators, washing machines and dishwashers." Each participating government would devote the revenue collected by this tax to financing such international development expenditures as it selected. It is to be hoped that most participating governments would agree to transfer the revenues to IDA, the regional banks, and UNDP. One attractive feature of this scheme is that it would tax the well-to-do minority in the low-income countries, as well as the great majority of people in rich countries. It would be the beginning of an international system of taxation based on the comparative ability not of countries but of people to pay. The two other proposals the Committee thought merited "particular attention" were the "introduction of special contributions by multinational corporations operating in developing countries" and "activating widely voluntary contributions by companies, public organizations and individuals, if necessary through provision of tax concessions."[11]

This sort of move toward an international system of taxation could properly be interpreted as a recognition that the transfer of resources from the well-to-do of the world to the poor of the world is an act not of charity but of justice, just as the redistribution of income within countries for the advantage of the poor by national taxation systems is now generally agreed to be an act not of charity but of justice. Certainly the more this principle is recognized by deed as well as by word, the healthier will be the aid relationship between the rich and the low-income nations. Ultimately—perhaps by the end of the century—international royalties and taxation, the provision of concessional resources through the International Monetary Fund, the purchase of World Bank bonds by central banks, and the revenues of international aid agencies from past loans and from their reserves could well become the sole sources of outside funds directed to speeding up the economic and social development of the low-income countries.

The international lending agencies would no longer be dependent on the sale of their bonds on the capital markets of the world, or on gifts from national governments. Hence, they would no longer have to keep constantly in mind the danger that the adoption of a new policy in the interest of their low-income member countries would offend the Wall Streets of the world, and thus make it more difficult for them to sell their bonds; or that it would offend the governments of one or more of their rich member countries, and thus endanger the flow of funds from governments for IDA, or make it less likely that governments would allow the Bank to sell its bonds on their capital markets.

CHAPTER SIXTEEN

The United Nations

The UN Charter sets forth a grand design for a world-wide, coordinated, massive, and sustained effort by the nations of the world, operating through the UN and its specialized agencies, to achieve "higher standards of living, full employment, and conditions of economic and social progress and development" and "solutions of international economic, social, health and related problems." The member states of the UN pledged themselves in the Charter to cooperate with the UN organization to achieve these objectives, and hence with the principal organs of the UN, the General Assembly, the Economic and Social Council, and the Secretariat. The UN organization, acting through the General Assembly, was instructed by the Charter to "make recommendations for the coordination of the policies and activities of the specialized agencies."[1] If this grand design of the founders of the UN had been implemented, the Bank Group would today be a member of a community of international agencies, organized under the leadership of the General Assembly and the Economic and Social Council of the UN. In this community, each agency would be equal to the others in status and dignity, though differing from them in function.

There were two main arguments for the creation of ECOSOC, one founded on prudence and one on hope. The argument of prudence was that the UN Security Council, like the League Council, might be a failure. Since the League Council had been in charge of all the work of the League, its failure in political and security affairs had resulted in a weakening of its economic and social work. To reduce the possibility of such a situation arising in the UN, there should therefore be two independent councils, one to deal with political and security affairs and one to deal with economic and social affairs. The argument of hope was two-fold. The first part was that if a community of international specialized agencies was established, it would, under the leadership of the General Assembly and ECOSOC, reduce the conflicts between nations over economic and social matters and so reduce the chances of war. The argument was not that these conflicts lead to war. It was that if nations are constantly quarreling over such matters as tariff and nontariff barriers to trade, competitive currency devaluations, aviation rights, and access to raw materials, they are less likely to be willing and able to cooperate in political and security matters to the extent necessary to preserve world peace. The second part of the argument was the so-called functionalist argument (essentially the argument later put forward by Jean Monnet in relation to European unity): that the way to build a world community is through building a series of functional international agencies, each of which would be the nucleus of a universal department of government. Thus ILO would be the nucleus of a universal department of labor, FAO the nucleus of a department of agriculture, WHO of a department of health, Unesco of a department of education, and the IMF of a universal central bank.

The grand design of the founders of the UN could have been realized only if each of the principal members of the UN had pursued coordinated policies in the specialized agencies, since a coordination of policy within each national government would automatically have resulted in a coordination of the policies and activities of the specialized agencies. But the governments did not do this. A government would pursue one policy in one agency and an inconsistent policy in another. Jealousies and struggles for power among departments of national governments were translated into jealousies and struggles for power among the various agencies and organs of the UN. The General Assembly and ECOSOC are emanations of national governments. If national governments refuse to coordinate their policies in the specialized agencies and organs of the UN, their representatives in the General Assembly or ECOSOC can do little to coordinate the policies and activities of those agencies and organs.

The two Bretton Woods institutions, the IMF and the World Bank, were particularly insistent in their early years on keeping ECOSOC and the other specialized agencies at a distance and on emphasizing the differences between them and these other agencies. Indeed, they conveyed the impression that they scarcely regarded themselves as specialized agencies of the UN. Their close relations with central banks no doubt contributed to this, for central banks are properly jealous of their autonomy and emphasize that they are not departments of government. It was therefore not surprising that the central bankers, who through their nominees on the boards of executive directors dominated the IMF and the Bank in their early years, insisted on the special characteristics of the IMF and the Bank which distinguished them from the other specialized agencies.

These special characteristics did exist. Because the IMF and the Bank began their operations with endowments given by governments in the form of capital subscriptions, and governments did not ask for dividends on these subscriptions, they were not dependent on governments for annual appropriations for administration, as the other agencies were, and they were therefore not as tempted to curry favor with governments by accepting second-rate national nominees for posts in their secretariats. Because they were well endowed, they could afford to pay salaries high enough to attract able people. Because they were not governed by assemblies in which each state had one vote, power in their governing bodies was not divorced from a capacity to contribute to the organization's purposes, as in other governing bodies. Because they did not have Communist members, except for Yugoslavia (and Czechoslovakia and Poland for a few of their early years), they were more homogeneous than the other agencies. It was therefore easier for their governing bodies to reach a consensus and for the professional staff of each to learn to work together as a team. Because they had concrete problems to handle and financial resources to deal with those problems, they were subjected to the discipline of translating objectives into specific actions, whereas the other agencies were largely limited to making recommendations for action to governments. Because of all this, and because they insisted from the outset on adhering to banking traditions, the World Bank was able to resist pressures by its member states to finance projects it considered to be of low quality.

These were sources of strength for the Bank. Some of them were also sources of weakness. The concentration of power in the hands of the rich white countries and their nationals was so great that it led to a feeling among many people in low-income colored countries that the Bank was not their bank but an agency of the white wealthy capitalist world. Many of the politicians and officials of these low-income countries who were dealing with economic development came to believe that agencies in which each state has one vote, or agencies based on regions, were apt to have a better understanding of their problems and their susceptibilities than the Bank Group; that the possession of large financial resources tended to make the Bank Group arrogant in its dealings with borrowing countries; and that the Bank Group's understanding of the problems of development had been greatly impaired by the absence of the Soviet Union and China from its council chambers, its management and staff. In the late sixties and the early seventies, an increasing number of the younger people of rich countries, interested in helping the development of low-income colored countries, came to share these feelings and beliefs.

By the middle of the fifties, some of the more sophisticated leaders of poorer countries had concluded, with some justification, that the more pressure they put on the rich countries to agree to the establishment of a special UN Fund for Economic Development (SUNFED), which would be dominated by the poorer countries, and to provide it with funds, the better were the chances that the rich countries would decide to counter this pressure by supporting the creation of a soft-loan affiliate of the World Bank and by providing it with ever-increasing financial resources.

Their efforts to establish SUNFED were abortive because the rich countries would not provide funds for an agency in which they would have little control over the disposition of funds. The most the rich member nations of the UN would agree to was the establishment in

1957 of the UN Special Fund which was amalgamated nine years later with the UN technical assistance program (which had been established at the very beginning of the UN) to form the UN Development Program. They agreed to the establishment of the Special Fund on condition that it was not to be used to finance capital projects, but would be limited to financing pre-investment studies. The establishment of UNDP and its gradual growth to a budget of $250 million a year amounted to a partial victory for the poorer countries. The poorer countries also won a partial victory in the establishment of regional development banks in some of which the voting power of the rich countries was sharply restricted, and in the establishment of the UN Industrial Development Organization. Another victory was the formation of the UN Conference on Trade and Development and its acceptance by the rich countries as the principal forum in which poorer countries could press their claims for more aid and better trade opportunities.

From the early sixties on, FAO, ILO, Unesco and WHO began to shift the emphasis of their work from research and discussion to technical assistance to developing countries. This shift brought them closer to the area of activity of the Bank Group. At the same time, the Bank Group was shifting its emphasis from development judged on purely economic criteria to development judged on social as well as economic criteria. This brought the Bank Group closer to the fields of activity and the concepts of development of the four socially-minded specialized agencies, FAO, ILO, Unesco and WHO. This would probably have resulted in the previously distant relations between the Bank Group and these agencies turning into conflicts, had it not been for the leadership of two successive presidents of the Bank, George Woods and Robert McNamara. George Woods was determined that the Bank Group should lend more for education and agriculture and try the experiment of close cooperation with Unesco and FAO. Robert McNamara was determined that the Bank Group should lend more for employment-maximizing projects and for populaton control and develop closer and more friendly relations not only with Unesco and FAO but also with ILO and WHO. The international strategy for the second development decade, adopted by the General Assembly of the UN in 1971, though general in its terms, helped put the relations between the Bank Group and the rest of the UN family into a new perspective. Thus, the relations between the Bank Group and FAO, ILO, Unesco, and WHO greatly improved from about 1963 on.

The pattern which has emerged in the generation since the founding conference of the UN at San Francisco in 1945 is of a weak ECOSOC, weak regional economic commissions, a financially and intellectually powerful World Bank Group, five regional development banks, the UN Conference on Trade and Development (UNCTAD), and five agencies or organs whose activities in international aid are financed in whole or in part by UNDP-ILO, FAO, Unesco, the UN Industrial Development Organization (UNIDO) and WHO. In this aid community, the World Bank Group, because of its intellectual and financial resources, has been thrust into a position of leadership on many aspects of aid problems. But its dependence on governments and capital markets in rich countries for almost all its financial resources makes it not the most appropriate leader for the international aid community. A more appropriate leader would be a reinvigorated Economic and Social Council, receiving guidance and direction for the UN General Assembly and operating directly and through the regional economic commissions, the UNDP, and the UN Committee on Development Planning.

ECOSOC began with eighteen members, increased first to twenty-seven, then to fifty-four.* Fifty-four is a reasonable number for a deliberative body but much too large for a body with executive responsibilities. The first step in the reinvigoration of ECOSOC should therefore be to create an executive committee of not more than twelve members. ECOSOC would presumably wish to elect the five permanent members of the Security Council to this committee (Britain, China, France, the Soviet Union, and the United States), leaving seven seats for other countries. It would be appropriate if five of these seven were held by developing countries, so that half of the committee would represent them. An executive committee of this size could be the nucleus of a committee on the specialized agencies to be established by the General Assembly. This committee would be charged by the General Assembly with the task of advising it on the recommendations it should make to governments under Article 48 of the Charter "for the coordination of the policies and activities of the specialized agencies." It would consist of the members of the twelve-member executive committee of ECOSOC, plus the heads of the ten agencies or organs especially concerned: UNDP, the UN Committee on Development Planning, UNCTAD, the Bank, the IMF, ILO, FAO, Unesco, WHO, and UNIDO. When the advisory committee discussed the policies or activities of any other UN specialized agency or organ, the head of that agency or organ would be invited to participate as a full member of the committee. The formation of this advisory committee would make unnecessary the continued existence of the administrative committee on coordination, consisting of the secretary-general of the UN and the executive heads of the specialized agencies.

The UN Charter makes clear the distinction between the kinds of resolutions on the specialized agencies which ECOSOC (or its proposed executive committee) is authorized to adopt and those which "the Organization" (in this context, the General Assembly) is instructed o adopt. ECOSOC, under article 63, "*may* coordinate the *activities* of the specialized agencies through consultation with and recommendations to such agencies and through recommendations to the General Assembly and to the members of the United Nations" (italics added). The Organization, on the other hand, under article 58, "*shall* make recommendations for the coordination of *the policies and activities* of the specialized agencies" (italics added). One provision is permissive; the

* On the assumption that the amendment of the Charter is ratified.

other is mandatory. One applies only to activities; the other extends to policies. The reason for the distinction was that the San Francisco Conference did not consider it fitting that a body such as ECOSOC, composed of only some of the members of the UN, should make recommendations on the policies of specialized agencies, of which all members of the UN might be members. The Conference did not hold the same view about the coordination of the activities of the specialized agencies. The combination of an executive committee of ECOSOC and of an advisory committee of the General Assembly, composed in part of the executive committee of ECOSOC, would put both ECOSOC and the General Assembly in a position where each could discharge the responsibilities conferred on it by the UN Charter, provided that this reform was accompanied by certain other changes. Thus a condition of the success of the advisory committee of the General Assembly and of the executive committee of ECOSOC would be that the twelve government members of the executive committee appoint as their representatives on the committee persons equal in status and authority to the executive heads of the specialized agencies. The General Assembly's advisory committee would receive reports from the agencies and organs represented on it, and from the regional banks and economic commissions. It would be assisted by a working committee, on which each of the members of the advisory committee would be represented by a senior official holding the confidence of the executive head of his agency or of his country's representative on ECOSOC. Another step which should be taken to strengthen ECOSOC is to improve greatly the qualifications of the professional staff in the economic and social department of the UN Secretariat who serve ECOSOC and its subsidiary bodies. This department includes some highly competent and devoted members, but, in general, the quality is not high enough. The quality would reach the appropriate level only if the secretary-general of the UN were to insist that the paramount consideration in appointing this staff should, in accordance with the directive set forth in the UN Charter, be the "necessity of securing the highest standards of efficiency, competence and integrity." This is to say that the secretary-general must be firm in resisting pressures from governments to appoint or promote persons not measuring up to these high standards. Unfortunately, the pressures from governments will probably remain great, for, as one former under-secretary-general put it in 1971, "Philosophically they may all agree that a sound international civil service eventually would benefit everyone, including themselves, but in the meantime they are likely to succumb to the temptation of demanding posts and other favors for their own nominees, and of retaining control over their 'representatives' and agents within the Secretariat."[2]

The establishment by ECOSOC of an executive committee of twelve countries; the appointment by the governments of these countries of full-time, able respresentatives on this committee; the participation of this committee in an advisory committee of the General Assembly together with the executive heads of the ten principal UN organs and agencies concerned; and the strengthening of the staff of the economic and social department of the UN would, in time, have two desirable results. ECOSOC would become able to conduct or to supervise central coordinating functions now performed by the World Bank Group, such as the preparation of the periodic reports on the state of development in the developing countries, and the chairing of aid-coordination groups. It would in time become the leader of the international aid community. The General Assembly would become able to discharge the responsibility conferred on it by the Charter to make recommendations for the coordination of the policies and activities of the specialized agencies.

As ECOSOC moves into a central position in the international aid community, and as the General Assembly begins to make recommendations for the coordination of the policies and activities of the specialized agencies, the member governments of the UN must bear constantly in mind that resolutions of ECOSOC and the General Assembly cannot compel rich and powerful governments to change the instructions they give their representatives in agencies such as the World Bank Group, and that the only strength possessed by a resolution passed by these bodies, in which each state has one vote, is the good sense of that resolution and the importance of the countries which voted for it. In the past, many resolutions relating to the work of the specialized agencies have failed to impress rich and powerful governments (or the managements of the specialized agencies) because these resolutions were impracticable.

CHAPTER SEVENTEEN

International Aid Agencies

Because of the inertia of governments and the strength of vested interests, the task of reinvigorating the Economic and Social Council is formidable, and progress is likely to be slow and difficult. In consequence, the World Bank Group must for some years continue to lead the international aid community on many aspects of aid. This makes it all the more important that it continue to improve its relations with the other international agencies concerned with aid, and that there be a more equitable balance of power in the Bank Group between the richer and the poorer member countries. In spite of the socially conscious image which Robert McNamara has given to the Bank Group and his efforts to improve relations between the Bank Group and the other agencies, the suspicion still lingers that the Bank Group is not really prepared to work in partnership with most of these agencies (other than with its sister institution, the IMF) and to treat them as its equals in status and dignity. The agencies are ECOSOC, UNDP, the UN Committee for Development Planning, UNCTAD, the regional economic commissions, the five regional banks for Asia, Africa, East Africa, Latin America, and the Caribbean, the Inter-American Committee for the Alliance for Progress (CIAP), four UN specialized agencies (FAO, Unesco, WHO, and ILO), and the UN Industrial Development Organization (UNIDO). Those in the other agencies and in national governments who continue to have these suspicions of the Bank Group believe that the majority of the officers of the Bank Group look down upon these agencies as, in varying degrees, much less efficient, much less knowledgeable, and much less responsible than the Bank Group. They believe that these officers are not really willing to share power or responsibility with the other agencies, but are constantly trying to extend the authority of the Bank Group over areas which are of primary concern to other agencies; and that when they talk to other agencies about aid coordination, they mean subservience to Bank Group policies, enforced by the fact that the Bank Group has large resources to lend and the others have not. The more these suspicions are dispelled, the better are the possibilities of greater cooperation between the Bank Group and other international aid agencies.

These suspicions would be largely dispelled if the Bank Group would intensify its efforts to create an increasingly healthier partnership between itself and the other aid agencies; and if governments took action to strengthen the other agencies so as to put them on a more equal footing with the Bank Group. Not only should the Economic and Social Council be so strengthened that it can in time become the leader of the international aid community, but the ILO, FAO, Unesco, WHO, and UNIDO should be strengthened so that they can take over from the Bank Group more and more of the responsibility for identifying, appraising, and supervising Bank Group projects.

The pace of the move toward a more decentralized system depends in large part on the willingness of governments to take measures within these agencies to make them more efficient. Partly because, with the exception of the International Labor Organization, they are governed by assemblies in which each state has one vote, regardless of the size of its population or the extent of its wealth, power, and influence, their standards of efficiency and competence are well below what is required of partners in an efficient international aid community. The Bank Group must become more international. The other international aid agencies must become more efficient.

Most of these agencies also must be modernized by changes in their constitutions embodied in the inter-governmental agreements which established them. The constitutions of most of them were drawn up in the second half of the forties or in the early fifties. Thus they reflect the thinking of a period when the rich nations were not so conscious as today of the needs of the low-income nations and of the urgent importance of dealing with their problems. Moreover, at the time when most of the agencies were established, much less was known of the complexities of the problem of how to speed up the economic and social development of low-income countries. Finally, very few of the low-income countries took part in the international discussions which led to the drawing up of their constitutions, and, since most of these constitutions were drafted when Europe was in eclipse and Japan under occupation, they reflect the thinking of only a small minority of the countries now members of them. They are mainly the creations of the United States and Britain.

Cooperation between the Bank Group and the other agencies has greatly improved in recent years, but there is room for further improvement. What the Bank Group itself said in 1972 of cooperation in industrial development can be applied to many other areas of possible cooperation:

While the framework of cooperation exists, instances of meaningful and significant collaboration in industry work between the Bank Group and other agencies concerned have been rare. The difficulties arise partly from the multiplicity of institutions interested in this area, partly from the disinclination of each agency to surrender the lead on projects it has under consideration, and partly from the severe financial and technical constraints under which some of the agencies have to operate.[1]

It is particularly important that the Bank Group and the agencies cooperate to reduce the demands they make on developing countries to supply information and to receive visiting missions. One developing country in the early seventies received within less than one month a questionnaire from the Bank, one from the IMF, and one from the Asian Development Bank, relating to the same data but presented in a slightly different way, so that separate work was required for all three. This resulted in an inexcusable waste of the scarce time of the few really able officers of the developing country. Missions arrive in a developing country from international aid agencies (and from national aid agencies) to cover much the same ground, and to ask much the same questions of the same officials; they expect to be received by the same busy officials and cabinet ministers. Agencies not skilled in assisting developing countries to prepare projects for submission to lending agencies conduct investigations into possible projects which take up the time of officials and other experts in the developing countries but result in reports considered by the lending agencies so incomplete that they must start almost from the beginning in their own investigations of the projects. The Bank Group hires so large a number of experts in education and agriculture that it is difficult to believe that it does not duplicate work being done by Unesco and FAO, or which could be done more effectively and economically by these agencies.

But greater cooperation between the Bank Group and the other agencies must not lead to the creation of a monolithic international aid community; for the one thing worse than uncoordinated policies is unanimity on wrong policies and coordinated action to implement them. The Gadarene swine which rushed headlong together over a cliff into the sea and were drowned gave an impressive demonstration of unanimity on policy and coordinated action. There must always be room in the international aid community for differences of opinion, for minority views, for aid programs to give effect to minority views. What is required is a coordinated but not a centralized international aid community. The foundations of the community must be equality and cooperation. Within every international aid agency all member governments, whether rich or poor, must be treated as equals. Within every agency there must be built up a partnership of the rich and the poorer countries. Each aid agency must treat every other agency as its equal. All agencies must be united by a common determination to wage successful war against world poverty.

A healthier partnership between the Bank Group and the other agencies requires a recognition by the governing bodies and the staff of the Bank Group (and this ultimately means the member governments) that the Bank Group needs the partnership of the other agencies to offset its weaknesses. These weaknesses result from the concentration of power in the Bank Group in the hands of rich countries and from the absence from the Bank Group of the Soviet Union and China. The other agencies need the partnership of the Bank Group to offset their own weaknesses.

There are seven principal means by which the World Bank Group could demonstrate that it wishes to establish an effective partnership with the other aid agencies. The first is to re-establish, in agreement with them, the Advisory Council, a council required by the Bank's articles of agreement. The second is that the Bank Group take the lead in arranging with the other agencies that their offices in developing countries be in the same building and share common services. The third is that the Bank Group seek more effective participation by the other aid agencies in all the various kinds of Bank Group missions: the country economic missions, the sectoral missions, the missions to prepare coordinated programs of pre-investment studies, and the missions to appraise and to supervise projects for which loans have been granted. The fourth is that the Bank Group seek more effective participation by the other agencies in aid-coordination groups. The fifth is to create a system for exchanges of staff. The sixth means is close cooperation in expanded research activities, and the seventh is to conclude formal agreements for cooperation.

Advisory Council

Article V, section 6, of the Bank's articles of agreement provides that:

> (*a*) *There* shall be *an Advisory Council of not less than seven persons selected by the Board of Governors including representatives of banking, commercial, industrial, labor, and agricultural interests, and with as wide a national representation as possible. In those fields where specialized international organizations exist, the members of the Council representative of those fields* shall be *selected in agreement with such organizations. The Council* shall advise *the Bank on matters of general policy. The Council* shall meet *annually and on such other occasions as the Bank may request.* (*b*) *Councillors shall serve for two years and may be reappointed. They shall be paid their reasonable expenses incurred on behalf of the Bank.* (Emphasis added.)

This Advisory Council was established in the early years of the Bank and held two meetings, one in 1948 and one in 1949. It was not a success, however, and a majority of its members expressed the opinion that "no Advisory Council appointed in accordance with the Articles of Agreement and entrusted with the functions there defined was likely to have a value commensurate with its cost in time and money."[2] As a result, when the two-year terms of its first members expired, no further appointments were made. It is now time that this decision, taken over twenty years ago, be reversed, since the re-establishment of the Advisory Council would now serve two important purposes. First, since the Bank's articles of agreement stipulate that the "representatives of banking, commercial, industrial, labor and agricultural interests . . . [would] be selected in agreement" with the specialized agencies concerned, this would place on the Advisory Council of the Bank a banking representative possessing the confidence of the IMF, a commercial representative possessing the confidence of GATT, an industrial representative possessing the confidence of UNIDO, a labor representative possessing the confidence of ILO, and an agricultural representative possessing the confidence of FAO. Presumably the Bank would also wish to add to the Council advisors approved by Unesco, WHO, and UNCTAD. This would give the eight agencies a feeling of more intimate partnership with the Bank; and the reality of more intimate partnership. Second, the leading authorities in the world would be honored to accept membership in this Council. Its establishment would therefore enable the Bank to draw upon the wisdom of these authorities, acting not as international or national officials, even if they were, but in their personal capacities, so that they would have no special vested interests to defend or promote. This arrangement would provide a useful counterweight to advice given by national governments (through executive directors or in other ways), by the specialized agencies, and by the experts on the professional staff of the Bank. Most of the members of the Council should come from low-income countries.

The international advisory panel of IFC, composed of five distinguished private bankers, which meets annually with IFC's officers and management to discuss IFC's activities and policies, has been helpful, not only to IFC, but also to the Bank Group as a whole, especially in correcting biases resulting from the dominance of United States thinking at the Bank's headquarters in Washington. This dominance arises in part from the very high proportion of United States citizens in the relatively small group of officers most influential in determining Bank Group policy, and in part from the fact that all the members of the staff and all the executive directors, whatever their origin, are daily subjected, since they live in Washington, to the impact of United States ideas. In the mid-sixties, IFC's international advisory panel was largely instrumental in persuading the Bank Group to relax its theological objections to government-owned banks and industry. In the seventies and eighties, an advisory council of the Bank might be equally helpful in persuading the Bank Group to modify other parochial United States attitudes.

Common premises and services

At present, in many developing countries, the offices of the Bank Group, the UNDP, the specialized agencies, and other development organizations are scattered throughout the capital cities. "The advantages of common premises at the field level have long been vaunted, but, despite many proposals and discussions the situation is still highly unsatisfactory. Progress on this front would undoubtedly do much more to achieve effective field coordination and cooperation between UNDP and the Agencies than all the principles and guidelines that either ACC [Administrative Committee on Coordination] or this Study [the Robert Jackson study on the UNDP] are ever likely to produce. . . . It is obvious that capacity could be increased and money saved if the various parts of the UN system made a determined effort to introduce common services to the maximum . . . ,particularly as regards the purchase of common user items, such as vehicles and office equipment and supplies and the adoption of standard forms for similar functions."[3] The Bank Group should do its best to assist in giving effect to these recommendations in capital cities where it has a resident mission. Since it has much greater financial resources than the other agencies, it might offer to construct an office building in each of these cities and to rent space to the other agencies on attractive terms.

Bank Group missions and reports

In the fifties and sixties, the resources allocated by the World Bank to country economic reports and sectoral studies were not adequate to make possible the preparation of comprehensive and thorough reports. Moreover, few of the reports were prepared after sufficient consultation with the other international agencies, such as the IMF, UNDP, FAO, Unesco, WHO, ILO, UNIDO, and the regional development banks. Because these missions usually did not set forth clearly the relative priorities of sectors and of projects and programs, they did not reduce to the extent they might have the pressure on donor governments to finance low-priority projects. Because they did not coordinate their inquiries closely enough with those of the principal donors to a country and of the other principal international agencies, they did not reduce to the extent possible the serious and unnecessary drains on the time, energy, and patience of the ministers and officials of aid-receiving countries caused by the visitations of many independent and uncoordinated missions of inquiry.

One of the most valuable decisions the World Bank has taken on the initiative of McNamara was therefore the decision, early in 1970, to improve greatly the Bank's country economic reports and its sectoral studies, since comprehensive and thorough reports of this kind can improve the aid performances of giving and receiving countries and of international agencies. In reporting to the UN Economic and Social Council in November 1970, McNamara announced that the Bank's periodic economic missions and their reports would assess: (a) the situation and prospects of a country's economy; (b) its development objectives and the major obstacles in the way of achieving them; (c) its domestic and external financing requirements and the possibilities of meeting them; (d) the principal pre-investment surveys and studies required to carry out the development program and the relative priorities of those requirements; (e) the available machinery for planning and for formulating economic and financial policy; (f) the problems of investment and resource mobilization and allocation, external debt prospects, appropriate borrowing terms, and credit-worthiness; (g) the country's population problem and program; and (h) the quality as well as the quantity of economic development, including analyses of income distribution, nutrition, literacy levels, life expectancy, and trends in employment. The Bank's expectation, McNamara said, was "that the end result of this effort will be to facilitate the adoption of realistic development strategies by our developing member countries, which can then serve as the basis for effective operational coordination of aid from all the various sources of development assistance. . . . The program is designed, on the one hand, to assist the government of the [developing] member country in planning and implementing its own national development strategy, and, on the other, to help interested multilateral and bilateral aid agencies to tailor their [technical and financial] assistance to the requirements of that strategy."[4]

McNamara said in this address that the Bank planned "to schedule regular annual reports on approximately 30 countries—countries containing more than 80% of the population of the developing member countries—and biennial or triennial reports on the remaining 60 countries." Later, however, he wisely decided that it was not necessary to devote scarce resources of skilled manpower to preparing comprehensive reports every year even for the thirty leading middle-income and low-income borrowers from the Bank Group; that it would be adequate if a comprehensive report on each of these countries were prepared only every three or four years and up-dated in the intervening years by relatively brief supplementary reports.

One other important development relating to the Bank's economic missions as a result of McNamara's initiatives is the increased participation in these missions of other international agencies. Thus, the UNDP resident representative is now associated with the work of the missions, and is expected to be particularly active in the areas of technical assistance and pre-investment. The Bank is getting cooperation from FAO, ILO, Unesco, WHO, and from the regional banks in providing information and technical staff to assist the missions. The Bank and the regional banks have agreed to coordinate their missions so that they will not conflict with one another. In Latin America, the Bank, the Inter-American Development Bank, and CIAP have agreed to establish joint economic missions. The Bank Group now gives to the UNDP, the regional banks, and the relevant specialized agency an opportunity to participate in its sector missions. The UNDP is invited to take part in missions preparing coordinated programs of pre-investment studies. FAO, Unesco, and WHO have provided staff members for appraisal and supervisory missions; it would be helpful if they and the ILO and UNIDO were encouraged to participate in all missions coming within their areas. It would also be desirable that the regional banks, as well as the specialized agencies, be invited to participate in Bank Group missions to appraise and to supervise projects. The Bank's present practice in seeking the cooperation of other agencies in its missions enlarges the missions and may make them more difficult to operate. The extension of the present practice would increase these difficulties; there would in time be compensating advantages. The other agencies would not need to send out so many separate missions on their own account, so that the total number of missions would be reduced. Officers of the

Bank Group and of the other agencies would become accustomed to working together and would learn from one another. The increased exposure of the other agencies to the problems of selecting, appraising, and supervising projects would strengthen them, making it possible for them gradually to take over from the Bank Group an ever-increasing share of responsibilities within the international aid community.

Aid-coordination groups

Early in 1970, McNamara proposed that the World Bank should take the initiative in seeking to organize, at the earliest appropriate time, coordinating groups for most, if not all, of the thirty developing member countries of the Bank with populations of more than 10 million (embracing over 80 per cent of the total population of developing member countries) and perhaps for some other countries as well. He said that it would, of course, be necessary first to consult with the governments of these and of aid-giving countries wishing to participate in these groups. For some developing countries, he thought that relatively simple and informal coordinating machinery would be sufficient; for others, more formal consultative groups would be needed. As for the nine existing Bank-sponsored coordinating groups, he believed that these could and should be strengthened by meeting regularly and by concerning themselves more than in the past with development strategy and with the coordination of major technical assistance activities. Later, McNamara substantially modified these ambitious proposals. The result was that by the end of the calendar year 1972, the number of aid-coordination groups sponsored by the Bank had increased from nine to only seventeen, and it was expected that only a few more would be established. The seventeen were for Bangladesh, Colombia, East Africa, Ethiopia, Ghana, India, Korea, Morocco, Nigeria, Pakistan, Peru, the Philippines, Sri Lanka, Sudan, Thailand, Tunisia, and Zaire. In addition, the Bank was participating in two other comparable aid-coordination groups, one for Indonesia under the chairmanship of the Netherlands, and one for Turkey under the chairmanship of OECD. The main reasons given by McNamara for not pressing ahead with the more ambitious proposals he had put forward early in 1970 were the arrangements the Bank was making with the CIAP and which it had already made with the European Development Fund, Belgium, and France for the francophone countries of Africa south of the Sahara.

McNamara has not defined what he meant when he said early in 1970 that relatively simple and informal coordinating machinery would be all that would be required for certain countries. Possibly what he had in mind was merely to ask the principal donor countries to send in written comments on the Bank's country economic reports. At the opposite extreme would be formal consortia, such as those established by the Bank in 1958 for India and in 1960 for Pakistan. A formal consortium consists of those members of the Bank which are the principal givers of aid to a country, the aid-receiving country, the UNDP, the appropriate regional bank, the IMF, and DAC. It meets under the chairmanship of the Bank, and at its meetings there is a discussion of the state of the economy of the country, of its plans for development during the next year or so, and of what appear to be its requirements for aid. This discussion is based on the Bank Group's latest economic report on the country, supplemented by memoranda from the country. At the meetings of the consortium, the participating governments and the Bank and IDA are expected to agree, not only on the volume of the net transfer of official development assistance which the country could effectively use in the next financial year, but also on the share of the net transfer it is prepared to provide.[5]

Aid-pledging or burden-sharing preceded by arm-twisting of reluctant donors by the Bank have in the past been the essential features distinguishing consortia from other aid-coordination groups. Since the task of the Bank, as chairman of a consortium, has been to persuade the members to pledge amounts totaling the net transfer of official development assistance which they agree could be effectively used, the Bank has itself had to make pledges in a consortium. It has also, in the process of bargaining at and between meetings, had to be prepared, if necessary, to increase the amount it had previously informed the members of the consortium it would itself provide. If this increase came from the limited IDA funds, it would be at the expense of the other possible beneficiaries of IDA. Similarly, if government members of a consortium devoted more of their limited aid funds to a consortium country than they would have without the pressure resulting from membership in the consortium, this too would be at the expense of other possible beneficiaries of their aid programs. This was the basis of many of the objections Latin American executive directors of the Bank Group made in the early sixties to the operations of the consortia for India and Pakistan. They then contended that the consortia had been used as instruments for giving India and Pakistan preferential treatment. India and Pakistan, they said, had been given fixed allocations of Bank and IDA funds and other countries had not; the Bank Group had taken positive action to find projects and programs sufficient to use up those allocations, but had not done this for other borrowers. These contentions no longer have as much force as in the early sixties. McNamara's decision in his first two years of office to double the volume of Bank Group lending, to improve its quality, and to speed up the pace of the Bank Group's operations forced the Bank Group to draw up confidential five-year country program papers setting forth in detail the projects the Bank and IDA would finance over the next five years in each of its borrowing member countries, together with the size of the Bank or IDA loan for each project. This has of necessity had to be accompanied by earmarking Bank and IDA funds over a five-year period. There still, however, remains a substantial difference between a five-year earmarking in a confidential country program paper circulated only to the staff of the Bank Group and an allocation publicly announced in a press release following a consortium meeting.

The considerations which have led the Bank Group to follow the example of the United States aid agency by making five-year projections for each of its borrowers may well cause the aid agencies of other donor governments, wishing to increase the volume of their aid and improve its quality while at the same time speeding up their operations, to do the same thing. When that happens, perhaps not more than a few years hence, the argument for establishing pledging consortia for all the countries which are relatively large consumers of aid will become very strong. It would therefore seem wise that the Bank Group renew its efforts to persuade its member countries concerned to agree to a gradual increase in the number of pledging consortia which it chairs, and to assist CIAP to establish pledging consortia. Some of the consortia would be not for single countries but for several neighboring ones. The goal might be to have pledging consortia by the late seventies cover about three-quarters of the flow of aid to low-income countries from the Bank Group and its members.

As pointed out above, the central element of a pledging consortium is that the members, including the Bank Group, are expected to agree, as a result of their discussion of the report of the Bank Group's economic survey mission, on the volume and nature of the net transfer of official development assistance which the country could effectively use in its next financial year, and on the share of that net transfer which each is prepared to provide. It is important that these pledges, which should be specific and binding, be made well in advance of the financial year of the recipient country, since this enables it to draw up its annual plans, budgets, and import policies on the basis of precise knowledge about the nature and volume of the external official development assistance it will receive from the members of the consortium. This would enable it to make better use not only of external development assistance but of all the resources available to it from both domestic and external sources. It is highly desirable that pledges cover a period of at least three years, preferably five, even if this means that they may be somewhat lower than they otherwise would be. A smaller quantity of aid guaranteed over a reasonably long period is worth more to an aid-receiving country than a considerably larger quantity of aid which is so uncertain that the aid-receiving country cannot count on receiving it. Here the interests of the aid-receiving countries and those of the taxpayers in the aid-giving countries coincide. The legislatures of aid-giving countries might therefore be prepared to authorize the executive to make pledges covering three to five years.

In all matters relating to the coordination of aid to a country, it is essential to keep constantly in mind that an aid-receiving country will, as one expert from such a country once put it to me, "find aid coordination at the country level bothersome and meaningless unless the total lending program is expanding and the discipline inherent in aid coordination is compensated by rewards in terms of ever-expanding levels of assistance."

Exchanges of staff

Exchanges of staff between the World Bank Group and the other international (and national) agencies concerned with development would help greatly to coordinate and improve aid activities. At present, there is almost no such exchange, even with FAO and Unesco, with which the World Bank has had formal cooperative agreements since the mid-sixties. Thus, in September 1972, the unit in FAO devoted exclusively to the work of the cooperative program between the Bank and FAO consisted of about 60 officers. Of these, only two were on secondment from the World Bank. The agriculture projects department of the Bank had about 150 officers. Not one was on secondment from FAO. About 30 officers of Unesco were working full time on the cooperative program between the Bank and Unesco. There were none on secondment from the Bank. The education projects department of the Bank had about 50 officers, but none from Unesco. This failure to exchange staff casts grave doubt on the protestations of the Bank Group, FAO, and Unesco that they in fact want to work closely together.

Arrangements for extensive exchanges of staff through secondment should be worked out between the Bank and FAO, Unesco, ILO, WHO and UNIDO, UNDP and the regional development banks. Officers who fear that their advancement in the Bank will be jeopardized if they are seconded to other agencies should be assured by the Bank that, if they do well in these assignments, they will be rewarded by advancement as rapid as if they had remained with the Bank. The other agencies must take similar action to insure that their officers do not suffer in their careers from secondment to the Bank. Since the salary scales of the Bank Group are higher than those of the other agencies, arrangements for exchanging staff will have to include provisions under which Bank Group officers seconded to other agencies will receive the pay and benefits they would have received had they remained on the Bank Group staff.

The Bank Group should also intensify its efforts to seek out the right people in other agencies to help it in specific tasks and, in return, be prepared to lend its officers to those agencies for the same purpose.

Research

There are special problems and opportunities relevant to the role of the Bank Group in coordinating research activities. The Bank Group has by far the largest group of experts engaged in research on problems of the economic and social development of middle-income and low-income countries. It can and should provide large sums to finance research by other organizations, either from IDA or from the profits of the Bank. Expert researchers are scarce; the problems they attack are vast, difficult, and urgent. Their scarce skills must not be wasted. The Bank Group should therefore increase its efforts to insure coordination of research activities. One way of doing this would be through exchanges of research staff between the World Bank and the UN, FAO, WHO, ILO, DAC, GATT, UNCTAD, CIAP, the regional banks, and other agencies charged with research on international development, as, for example, the International Development Research Center in Ottawa and the Institute of Development Studies in Sussex.

Another means by which the Bank can promote large, sustained, cooperative programs of research is in supporting the establishment of consultative groups on research on special aspects of development. Thus the Bank was largely instrumental in the establishment in 1971 of the consultative group on international agricultural research, which includes in its membership FAO, the Bank, and UNDP, as well as the Ford, Rockefeller, and Kellogg foundations, the International Development Research Center in Ottawa, and a number of governments, both aid-giving and aid-receiving. The Bank provides the funds to assist activities sponsored by the consultative group and provides the chairman and the secretariat of the group. FAO, UNDP, and the Bank are cosponsors of the technical advisory committee of the group and share its costs. This committee has its headquarters in Rome, and is provided with staff services by FAO; its task is to recommend high-priority research programs to the group; the task of the group is to mobilize the necessary resources.

We are accustomed to inter-governmental organizations such as the specialized agencies. We are accustomed to international associations of voluntary non-governmental organizations, churches, trade unions, learned societies, chambers of commerce, and so on. When governments agreed on the formation of the consultative group on international agricultural research, composed in part of governments and inter-governmental organizations and in part of private foundations, they agreed to the establishment of a new type of creative international organization. This is potentially a most important development in international relations.

Formal cooperative agreements

The Bank Group has concluded formal cooperative agreements with FAO, Unesco, and WHO. Each agreement provides for cooperation by the Bank Group and the agency "in assisting member countries to identify and prepare projects for Bank consideration and in appraising, supervising and, when requested by the country, providing the technical assistance component of such projects. Under the agreement . . . [the agency] has 'primary responsibility' for assisting countries in project identification and preparation."[6] The Bank Group has also made an agreement with UNIDO for the establishment of a unit in that agency, financed jointly by the two agencies, which will: . . . "provide industrial economists and other experts to assist in identifying and preparing industrial projects for financing by the Bank [Group]; make available technical assistance to governments in commissioning and supervising feasibility studies as well as in carrying out industrial projects financed by the Bank [Group]; and participate in industrial sector studies in the developing countries."[7] The Bank should press ahead with negotiations for the conclusion of similar agreements with ILO, the regional development banks, and other international agencies.

The existing agreement between the Bank and WHO covers cooperation only on water supply and sewerage projects. The Bank Group, however, is now active in projects relating to many other fields of direct concern to WHO, such as population planning, the control of endemic diseases affecting productivity, and improvements in nutrition. The Bank Group should, therefore, recommend to WHO that the existing agreement between them be revised to cover all projects relevant to WHO.

Until FAO and Unesco entered into formal cooperative agreements with the World Bank, their officers were not exposed to the difficult and rewarding discipline of having to apply their knowledge to such specific questions as: is one development project more worth financing than another, or, what can be done to increase the economic and social benefits of a project and reduce its costs to make it more worth financing? By exposing their officers to this discipline, the cooperative agreements have strengthened FAO and Unesco. This illustrates how the challenge of increased responsibility can call forth the response of increased capacity. Cooperative agreements with WHO, ILO, UNIDO, the regional development banks, and other international agencies should similarly strengthen these agencies. As these agencies become stronger, they will be able to take over more and more responsibility for identifying, appraising, and supervising Bank Group projects.

International Monetary Fund

Eugene Black is reported to have said at the beginning of the sixties, toward the end of his regime as president of the World Bank, that if the Conference at Bretton Woods had been able to foresee the developments of the succeeding quarter of a century in the Bank and the IMF, it would have created only one institution to do the job, not two. An outright amalgamation of the IMF and the Bank may not now be possible, but there can certainly be moves toward much closer cooperation which would increase efficiency and reduce costs of operation. These moves can be made acceptable both to those who favor amalgamation and those who do not.

Under the McNamara regime, cooperation between the Fund and the Bank has notably improved. The basis for the improved cooperation was laid in a memorandum of February 1970, signed by the heads of the two institutions. It was their intention, they said, "for the Fund and the Bank to complement each other as they work to achieve their common objective, for each to make the fullest use of the expertise and information of the other, to reduce to a minimum the risk of inconsistent policy advice, and to minimize the duplication of requests for information to member governments." In reporting on this to ECOSOC in November 1970, McNamara went on to say: "The staffs of both institutions have been given firm and precise instructions to insure that these aims are achieved. . . . I would . . . like to mention particularly our efforts to coordinate the scheduling of country missions of the two institutions and through more exchange of data, to reduce the number of separate requests made to governments for economic and financial information."[8]

In the light of experience, since the memorandum of February 1970 and of the changing nature of both institutions, it would be helpful if the boards of governors of the Bank and the Fund were to request the president of the Bank and the managing director of the Fund to examine together possibilities of joint action by the two institutions and of a merging of some of their services and departments. They would be invited to submit a report to the executive directors of both institutions. They should consider, among other things, the advantages and disadvantages of merging such administrative services as the secretary's office, the controller's department, and the offices on information and public affairs. They should also consider whether the time has come to combine the economic development institutes and the economics departments or, if not the economics departments as a whole, the statistical sections of the economics departments. Another possibility they could usefully consider is the establishment of a joint IMF-Bank mission to the UN in New York.

It would be best if the executive directors, when they received the report, were to refer to a small joint committee composed of, say, eight directors, four from each agency. The effectiveness of this committee would require that each member consider that he represented the interests of his government or governments in both institutions, not just in the institution of which he was an executive director. The committee, though in form a joint committee of the Fund and the Bank, must, to be successful, act as if it were a committee representing governments. It should therefore be a cross-section of the membership in terms of economic power, stage of development, and geographical location, and should also represent countries possessing a substantial majority of the votes in the governing bodies of the two institutions. It should not consider itself precluded from recommending changes in the international agreements establishing the Fund and the Bank Group, if it concluded that amendments were required to promote effective cooperation, or even from recommending that the two institutions be amalgamated. The rich countries might be represented by the United States, Japan, and a member of the E.E.C., the poorer countries by five states chosen from such countries as Brazil, Egypt, India, Indonesia, Mexico, Nigeria, Senegal, and Zaire.

Regional banks

The regional development banks are the Inter-American Development Bank (1962), the African Development Bank (1964), the Asian Development Bank (1966), the East African Development Bank (1968), and the Caribbean Development Bank (1968). These vary greatly in the scale of their operations. In 1971, the Inter-American bank lent $669 million, and the Asian bank $253 million; the African bank lent only $25 million and the Caribbean and East African banks only $6 million each.[9] In 1970, John White, in his book on regional develoment banks, wrote: "The World Bank's relations with the Inter-American bank are at best uneasy, with the African bank they are crippled by mutual suspicion, while with the Asian bank the problem is one of an excessive harmony of style."[10] Since then, relations between the World Bank Group and the regional banks have improved; but there is room for further improvement. The governments of countries which are members of regional banks should intensify their efforts to strengthen them so as to create a better balance than now exists between their lending activities and those of the Bank Group. On its part, the Bank Group should intensify its efforts to make clear to the regional banks that it would be happy to give them all the help they want in their efforts to become stronger. Both should press ahead with the efforts they are now making to work out the areas of activity on which each should concentrate. A natural area of comparative advantage for regional banks might be the promotion of regional integration. A natural area of comparative advantage for the Bank Group might be large loans (say, of at least $25 million) for large single projects in traditional areas of Bank Group financing, such as power, steel, railways, roads, ports, and telecommunications.

There are other possible areas of cooperation between the Bank Group and the regional banks. The statistical services division of the World Bank already collects and processes data on the external debt of borrowing countries, not only for itself, but also for the regional banks. The banks might wish to consider extending this cooperation to the appraisal and supervision of some of the projects they are considering for financing. If a regional development bank requests the Bank Group to appraise a project for it at its own expense, the Bank Group should conduct the appraisal in precisely the same way as though it were appraising a project to be financed by the Bank, IDA, or IFC. It should also be prepared, at the request of a regional bank, to supervise the execution of a project which the Bank Group had appraised and which the bank had decided, in the light of that appraisal, to finance. In turn, the Bank Group might propose to the banks that they appraise certain types of projects being considered for financing by the Bank Group. These types might be, to begin with, those where it is possible for the Bank Group to establish standard models for appraisal, such as it has already worked out for road projects.

The creation in 1972 of five regional offices at the headquarters of the Bank Group in Washington should facilitate cooperation between the Bank Group and the regional banks. Each regional office of the Bank Group is now in a position to discharge its responsibility for maintaining effective, friendly, and close relations with the regional bank or banks in its area. The model for cooperation could be the cooperation gradually evolved, not without much strain and stress, between the headquarters in Washington of the Bank Group and of the Inter-American Development Bank.

It is not necessary that the Bank Group and the regional banks follow precisely the same development policies. Indeed, some divergencies are desirable. The errors of one lending agency can be corrected by action of another lending agency. But, it is desirable that their policies on such questions as concessional lending should not diverge greatly. It would, for example, be absurd if a regional bank were to provide a relatively wealthy member country with a loan on IDA terms for the foreign exchange costs of building a steel plant when that country was so flush with foreign exchange that its central bank would use the resources provided by the loan to purchase bonds from the World Bank. This kind of extreme situation is not likely to arise. But the Inter-American Bank does make concessional loans at 3 or 4 per cent interest for projects in the relatively less developed regions of all its developing member countries, no matter how wealthy. The justification is that this encourages relatively wealthy member countries, such as Venezuela, to divert more of their development resources to the less developed regions of the country. But development aid on soft terms is so scarce a commodity and the needs of the poorer countries for it are so great that it is doubtful whether this is the best use to make of it. The recommendation of the Peterson task force was that the Inter-American Bank "should reserve its concessional lending for its least developed member nations."[11] Governments which are members of a regional bank and of the World Bank should confer on this question.

At the beginning of the seventies, lending by the regional banks was less than two-fifths of lending by the World Bank Group. (The figure for 1971 was 37 per cent.) A reasonable goal for the next ten years might be that by 1983 lending by the regional banks would be equal to two-thirds of the lending by the Bank Group. This would mean that if Bank Group lending had by 1983 reached a level of about $6,200 million (in 1972 dollars), lending by the regional banks would have to be four times as much in real terms by 1983 as it had been in 1971. (In terms of 1972 dollars, the increase would be from $1,050 million in 1971 to $4,130 million in 1983.) It would be difficult for the regional banks to expand their operations at a faster rate. Perhaps, however, by the end of the eighties the total lending by the regional banks might equal the lending by the Bank Group. It was suggested above (Chapter Sixteen) that if the World Bank was able to work out an arrangement with central banks under which they would hold a certain proportion of their reserves in World Bank bonds, the Bank might re-lend a third to a half of these borrowings to the regional banks. The Bank Group could also usefully explore with regional banks the possibility of their being given a line of credit with the Bank should they have difficulty in raising sufficient financial resources for their non-concessional lending programs. Under such a scheme, the World Bank would, for example, give the African Development Bank a line of credit of, say, $50 million a year; the African Development Bank could draw on this line of credit, without previous approval by the World Bank, for any project it considered desirable, provided that it matched the World Bank's contribution with an equal amount from its own financial resources.

The UNDP

The UNDP is much closer to being a universal institution than the Bank Group. It does not suffer, as does the Bank Group, from being considered by many people in low-income countries as being dominated by wealthy white donor countries. For these reasons the Bank Group must strive to remove any suspicion which still exists, based on the somewhat contemptuous way the Bank Group treated the UNDP in the early sixties, that it is unwilling to treat the UNDP as a partner in matters related to their common concern in pre-investment studies. This common concern stems from the fact that pre-investment studies (also called feasibility studies), the principal function of the UNDP, and investment, the principal function of the Bank Group, are two stages of a single process.

The UNDP resident representatives in developing countries were instructed by the UN General Assembly in 1971 to assist the governments to which they are accredited to formulate country programs of pre-investment surveys and studies, and of technical assistance to be financed by the UNDP.[12] But the UNDP does not have funds to finance all the surveys and studies required. Its funds should therefore be increased; until this is done, some must be financed by the Bank Group. This will cause difficulty unless the Bank Group rigorously adheres to the promise made by McNamara in his address to ECOSOC in 1970 that the Bank Group will finance pre-investment studies "only in those rare instances where the UNDP is for some reason unable to meet a priority need."

Conflict between the two agencies will arise if the Bank Group decides that a pre-investment study, financed by the UNDP, of a project the Bank Group is considering is so unsatisfactory that it has virtually to start from the beginning in making its own investigations. This does not, of course, happen when the Bank Group has, at the request of a member government, been the executing agency for the UNDP in making the pre-investment study. But the Bank Group is not the only executing agency of UNDP, and certainly should not be the only one. The possibility of conflict has been diminished by the agreement of the Bank Group and the UNDP that the technical staff of the Bank Group will review all pre-investment projects being seriously considered by the UNDP. This, as McNamara has put it, enables the Bank Group "to help UNDP and its other Executing Agencies to formulate pre-investment projects so that the results of the studies will provide a sound basis for future investment—even though it may not necessarily be future investment by the World Bank Group."[13] The essence of the problem of establishing and maintaining good relations between the Bank Group and the UNDP is that the Bank Group should not encroach, or even appear to encroach, on the area of activities entrusted to the UNDP by the General Assembly of the UN. The Bank Group must, rather, convince the UNDP by its actions, as well as its words, that its offer of full cooperation to assist it in discharging its responsibilities is made in good faith.

The UNDP already participates in all the aid-coordination groups chaired by the Bank Group. The Bank officer chairing the group should encourage the UNDP representative to participate fully in the group's deliberations. The Bank Group should from time to time remind the UNDP of its desire that the UNDP resident representative also be a full member of every Bank economic mission, of every mission to prepare coordinated programs of pre-investment studies, and of every sectoral mission. In addition to informing the UNDP resident representatives of all Bank Group missions scheduled in the countries of their assignments, the Bank Group should insure that all their visiting missions carry out their instructions to keep in close touch with the UNDP representative. All the Bank Group's resident missions must also carry out their instructions to participate fully in all coordinating committees of local representatives of UN specialized agencies set up under the chairmanship of the UNDP representative.

None of this would detract from the responsibilities entrusted to the UNDP resident representative by the UN General Assembly; rather, it would enable him to discharge them better. As a member of the Bank Group's economic mission or its mission on pre-investment studies, he would submit to the mission a draft of the UNDP country program of pre-investment surveys and studies, and of technical assistance. As a result of examination within the mission and discussions with the authorities of the government, it is to be hoped that agreement would be reached between the government, the UNDP resident representative, and the other members of the Bank Group mission on the inclusion of this program in the mission's analysis of all the pre-investment surveys and technical assistance required by the country. If the necessary agreement could not be reached, the program would be attached as an annex to the report of the Bank Group mission, with an explanation of why they were unable to approve it; the comments of the UNDP resident representative on this explanation would also be attached.

In this way, UNDP resident representatives would be able to keep themselves fully informed of, and to contribute to, the work, the thinking, and the policies of the Bank Group. Under the leadership of the Bank Group and the UNDP, much more effective coordination would be established among aid-giving countries, international aid agencies, and an aid-receiving country in working out, first, an agreed country program of pre-investment surveys and studies; second, an agreed analysis and identification of the principal projects and programs in the country which require financing, and their relative priorities; third, an agreed assessment of domestic and external financing requirements and of the posssibilities of meeting them; and, fourth, an agreed development strategy for the country which would, in McNamara's words, be "both reasonable and worthy of international support."

The adoption of these proposals would involve the risk that the UNDP, because of failure to implement fully the recommendations of the Jackson Report, or for other reasons, would not be able to carry out its responsibilities as a partner, and that the obligation on the Bank Group to treat it as a partner would delay the Bank Group's work. Certainly at the present time, many of the UNDP resident representatives, because of lack of competence, experience, or time, would not be able to make substantial contributions to Bank Group missions and might indeed be a drag on those missions. The risk is real, but the short-run costs of accepting it are offset by the long-run benefits, the main one being that the challenge an offer of partnership would make to the UNDP would increase the pressures on it for reform, pressures coming both from governments and from the top management of the UNDP.

The UN Committee for Development Planning

The UN Committee for Development Planning was instructed by the General Assembly in 1970[14] to prepare for it every two years "an over-all appraisal of the progress in implementing the International Development Strategy" for the second development decade. The Bank Group should establish close relations with this Committee to insure that the Bank's country economic reports and other studies provide the utmost assistance to the Committee in discharging this task. In particular, the Bank Group should find out whether the Committee intends to try to establish a world aid budget, that is a calculation of the domestic and external finances which the middle-income and low-income countries of the world need to sustain a reasonable rate of growth. If it does, and also intends to keep it up to date, the Bank Group should implement promptly the decision announced by McNamara early in 1970 that its periodic country economic reports will contain "an assessment of domestic and external financing requirements and of the possibilities of meeting them." Presumably this assessment would be the kind made in the annual economic reports of the Bank Group on India and Pakistan in 1969 and 1970. That is, the report would state that the government had asked for a net transfer of official development assistance in the next fiscal year of $X million; that the mission had concluded the country could effectively use $Y million provided the aid was of such-and-such a character; and that if aid was continued on the same level as during the current year, there would be a deficit (or surplus) of $Z million. Such an assessment would constitute a national aid budget. To establish a world aid budget, the Committee would have only to add up these national aid budgets and to supplement this sum by similar estimates of the national aid budgets of developing countries not members of the Bank Group.

Bank Group mission to the UN

Since it is important to foster cooperation between the Bank Group and the headquarters of the UN in New York, the Bank should establish in New York a mission to the UN under the direction of a senior member of the Bank Group staff. He would keep in close touch with the secretary-general of the UN, with the under-secretary-general responsible for economic and social affairs, with the administrator of the UNDP and the president of its governing council, and with the UN Committee for Development Planning. The Bank Group now tries to handle its relations with UN headquarters mainly through its own headquarters in Washington. It is not possible to develop on this basis the kind of close relations required.

Aid coordination begins at home

There is much the World Bank Group can do to promote effective coordination among the international aid agencies. But effective aid coordination presupposes coordination by every national government of its own aid policies in the various international agencies, in its own national agency for giving aid or for coordinating the receiving of aid, and in the policies on aid, trade, commodity agreements, the international monetary system, shipping and insurance, science and foreign investment, pursued by its departments of foreign affairs, trade, and finance. Coordination begins at home. Each national government needs machinery at its national capital able to work out for its consideration consistent national policies on these matters. The Peterson task force in 1970 recommended to the President of the United States the establishment in Washington of an international development council whose mission "would be to assure consistency among U.S. development programs, the positions taken in international agencies and forums, and the actions taken on trade and financial issues, relating to developing countries."[15] In other countries, what is required is a cabinet committee supported by an interdepartmental committee of senior officials.

Some inconsistencies in the policies of national governments are intentional, others unintentional. An alert government is never unintentionally inconsistent. International organizations such as the Bank Group can help member governments to realize when they are being unintentionally inconsistent. The Bank Group could, for example, arrange that after every meeting of an aid-coordination group, the Bank officer responsible would report on the meeting to the executive directors of the Bank Group. He might report that, in the light of the conclusions in the Bank Group's recent country economic report, he had stressed at the meeting the importance of bilateral donors agreeing to reschedule the debts of the country; he had endorsed the country's need for program loans and urged the bilateral donors to provide them; he had been pressed hard by the representatives of the governments of countries A, B, and C to agree that the Bank itself should reschedule its loans to the country and should devote a large proportion of its own lending to program loans, but, in accordance with the views of the executive directors, he had refused to agree. The effect of such a statement would be to bring forcefully to the attention of the executive directors as a whole the anomaly of the Bank Group's urging other donors to do what it would not itself do. It might also disclose to the executive directors representing countries A, B, and C that the position they had been taking at meetings of the executive directors of the Bank Group was the opposite of that taken by the representatives of their governments at the aid-coordination group. If so, they would presumably draw this to the attention of their governments; and thus increase pressures in their national capitals to coordinate their national policies on aid.

Coordination among the international aid agencies will be effective only if the government of each member country of the Bank Group (whether rich, middle-income, or low-income) gives careful consideration to the kind of coordination it wants between the Bank Group and the IMF, the Bank Group and the UNDP, the Bank Group and the regional banks, ILO, FAO, WHO, Unesco, UNIDO, and so on. A government should discuss its provisional conclusions with other governments and with the managements of the agencies. It should then instruct its representatives on the governing bodies of the agencies to do their best, in cooperation with like-minded governments, to get the agencies to cooperate with the Bank Group. Thus governments which believe that better and more representative Bank Group missions should result in fewer and smaller missions from other agencies should insist on this in the other international agencies (and in their own national aid agency). Similarly, if the Bank Group does not treat the UNDP, ILO, FAO, WHO, Unesco, and UNIDO as equal to it in status, a government which believes that it should, should instruct its representative to the Bank, in consultation with the representatives of like-minded governments, to do his best to secure the necessary changes in the policy and behavior of the Bank. He would presumably first discuss the matter privately with the president of the Bank. If this was not effective, he would raise it in the board of executive directors. If they did not act, the governments concerned would raise the matter at the annual meeting of the board of governors.

Agencies should realize that member governments may be slow to learn of conflicts between agencies which, if unresolved, will impair effective cooperation between them. They should therefore take the initiative in informing their member governments of such conflicts so that the governments may take the necessary action to insure that the decisions they have approved in one agency are not frustrated by action or inaction in another.

CHAPTER EIGHTEEN

National Aid Agencies

For the aid-receiving countries, multilateral aid from agencies such as the World Bank Group has certain advantages and disadvantages; bilateral aid has different sets of advantages and disadvantages. These vary from one aid-receiving country to another, from one aid-giving country to another. The pattern is not simple. If an aid-giving country grants extensive aid to a country, it may get assurances of effective use of aid from that country stronger than those a multilateral institution like the Bank Group can secure. On the other hand, an aid-giving country may be prepared to provide money to certain countries for second-rate or third-rate projects (which would be rejected out of hand by a multilateral institution as a waste of money) if, in return for its aid, it gets political concessions such as membership in an alliance, or support for its policy on nuclear testing, Vietnam, Quebec, or East Germany. Aid-receiving countries do not consider that a request from an aid-giver for a political *quid pro quo* in return for aid is necessarily a disadvantage, since the *quid pro quo* becomes for them an invisible export. Multilateral aid, being untied, gives the aid-receiving country an opportunity to buy in the cheapest market. Bilateral aid, which is tied, may be worth only 80 cents on the dollar. Bilateral aid from Communist countries has the advantage that these countries accept an obligation to receive exports from the aid-receiver in payment of interest and amortization on the loan. Most bilateral aid-givers other than the Communist countries do not accept the thesis that they share with the borrower an obligation to promote the borrower's exports.

As long as the rich countries have their present preponderance in the bigger multilateral lending agencies, aid-receiving countries do not want the multilateral agencies to control all lending to them. This would give them the feeling of being isolated and cornered. They might even feel that they were being victimized by some great conspiracy of the neo-imperialist rich countries. For the aid-receiving countries, there is safety in numbers. For the aid-giving countries, there is also at present an advantage in giving some aid bilaterally and some multilaterally, even if they do not attempt to get political returns for their aid. Bilateral aid is generally easier to identify; thus, the citizens and taxpayers of the aid-giving country can more easily see the results of their gifts and loans. If the results are good, political support for aid is increased. Because, in countries other than the United States, a national aid bureaucracy is not as large as the bureaucracy of the World Bank Group it can more easily venture into experimental and therefore risky projects, especially in countries where their country has some special interests—political, cultural, economic, or sentimental. Because of all this and because in most aid-giving countries aid to multilateral aid agencies is not likely to increase unless there are also increases in bilateral aid, the Bank Group has a direct interest in doing what it can to help the bilateral aid agencies of its rich member countries to do a good job and so be worthy of public support.

Relations between the Bank Group and the United States aid agency have always been close. This closeness resulted from the special position of the United States in the Bank Group, the size of its aid program (until 1969 larger than that of the Bank Group), the expertise of the United States aid agency, and the fact that the headquarters of the two organizations in Washington are only about a mile apart. Officers of the Bank Group, from the president down, have constantly exchanged information and views with officers of the United States aid agency. Bank Group missions have kept in close touch with United States aid missions in the countries they have visited. Representatives of the United States aid agency have played prominent roles in assisting the Bank Group to organize and operate aid-coordination groups. Some of the most influential officers of the Bank Group were previously senior officers of the United States aid agency. As a result, the United States aid agency has been much closer to the Bank Group and has exerted much more influence on its policies and activities than the United States treasury, which, under the articles of agreement of the Bank, should be the only channel for dealings between the United States government and the Bank.* It is to the credit of the treasury that it has turned a blind eye to this. The Bank Group has been fortunate that its principal contact in the United States government has been the U.S. aid agency, not the U.S. treasury. The aid agency has had more knowledge and understanding of development than the treasury, and more liberal views on the policies and activities of the Bank Group.

Relations between the Bank Group and the aid agencies of other donors have never been as close as those between the Bank Group and the United States aid agency. Since about 1960, the relations have become closer, particularly with the aid agencies of Britain, Canada, Germany, and Sweden. One reason for this has been the formation of aid-coordination groups, at which aid-giving governments are normally represented by officers of their aid agency. There has been more

*The text of this provision in the articles of agreement is given below in Annex Six, page 254.

sharing of information and views between the aid agencies and the Bank Group; together they have worked out procedures under which they cooperate in financing development projects. The development of relations with the agencies of all its member countries as close as those with the United States aid agency would reduce both the appearance and the reality of excessive U.S. influence on the Bank Group.

The costs of administration of the whole group of aid agencies, national and international, have increased greatly since about 1960 and are continuing to increase. The more money that goes into administration, the less there is for the low-income countries from the resources made available for development, and the more vulnerable the aid agencies are to adverse criticism, both from the taxpayers which finance them and from the low-income countries. Every effort should therefore be made to reduce the total costs of aid administration. These costs could be reduced if the agencies would learn from one another how to make their administrations more efficient and economical, and thus profit from one another's successes and failures in administration. In the past they have been slow to learn from one another. Thus, the United States aid administration adopted in the early sixties the reform of preparing every year for its own use a confidential, internal five-year country program paper, setting forth in detail for each of the countries to which it was providing aid the provisional U.S. aid program for the next five years in terms of specific projects, or at least in terms of projects in specific fields, and the probable U.S. contribution to each project. This reform was adopted by the Bank Group only after a lapse of about seven years. To speed the process by which aid agencies learn from the successes or failures of others in administration, the Bank Group could usefully hold every year a discussion on aid administration, to which it would invite the chief administrative officers of national aid agencies and of the regional banks, together with officials from a representative group of aid-receiving countries. Although it is impossible to draw a hard and fast line between policy and administration, every effort should be made to confine the discussion to matters which in pith and substance are administrative. At these meetings it should be possible to agree on simplified common procedures.

As a result of these discussions, it might also be agreed that the Bank Group would provide technical assistance to national aid agencies desiring it, at their expense, just as the Bank Group provides technical assistance to development finance companies in low-income countries. The assistance offered to these companies includes "help with the establishment of new institutions, finding staff, organizational and managerial advice, and staff training (which may involve either secondment of key local personnel to work with the [Bank] Group at its Washington headquarters, or secondment of Bank staff members to work in the offices of the development banks concerned)."[1] The technical assistance the World Bank might give national aid agencies, at their request and at their expense, could include help in establishing new departments or divisions of the agency, finding staff, giving organizational and managerial advice, and staff training, either through secondment of officers of the national aid agency to work with the Bank Group in Washington or through secondment of the Bank Group officers to work in the office of the national aid agency. Thus, when a national aid agency judged that it was weak in a certain sector of its activities, it would ask the Bank Group to second one or more experts in that sector. The task of the expert or experts would be to fill in the gap and to train officers of the agency to take over as their successors. This kind of secondment might be for a year or two or for a few months only.

The Bank Group has had more experience than any national aid agency, with the possible exception of that of the United States, in appraising projects. When a national aid agency has to appraise a project in a field in which it and consulting firms in its country have little or no expertise and the Bank Group has a good deal, the national aid agency should be able to call on the Bank Group to appraise the project, at the agency's expense. A national aid agency might also refer to the Bank Group for appraisal projects which did not appear to it to be of high priority but which it was under considerable pressure to finance, pressure perhaps not only from powerful domestic interests but also from powerful interests in the aid-receiving country. If this practice had been followed in the past, scarce resources might not have been misallocated to such projects as the nuclear power plant in Pakistan, financed by Canada. The Bank Group would appraise projects referred to it by national aid agencies in precisely the same way as it appraises projects which it itself is considering for financing. This would be an extension of the practice the Bank Group had developed by 1971 of stating at the request of an aid-giving government "any reservations it may have about a project, making plain the limitations of its knowledge" and indicating "projects which, in the Bank's judgement, are clearly of low priority, or otherwise not ready for consideration."[2] The Bank Group should be prepared also to supervise the execution of projects which it had appraised for the agency and which the agency had decided to finance. Before asking the Bank Group to appraise or supervise a project, the national agency should get the agreement of the aid-receiving country.

Recently there has been a large increase in the volume of joint and parallel financing by the Bank Group and by national aid agencies. Under joint financing, aid-giving governments finance all or an agreed proportion of the orders awarded to nationals as the result of international competitive bidding on a Bank Group project. Under parallel financing, international competitive bidding is restricted to the Bank Group's share of the project.[3] This kind of financing helps borrowers to obtain the advantages of wide international competitive bidding and, at the same time, to use tied bilateral aid. It enables an aid-giving government, without laborious and expensive investigations of its own, to insure that its aid funds are spent on sound, well-supervised, high-priority projects, so certified by the Bank Group. The Bank Group should press ahead with its efforts to encourage and facilitate joint and parallel financing. It should add to its staff more entrepreneurs who will go out and sell these and other ideas to national aid agencies. One way to encourage joint financing would be for aid-giving governments to make agreements good for periods of, perhaps, three or five years, under which they would undertake to finance one-half of all orders awarded to their nationals as a result of competitive bidding on Bank Group projects, up to a maximum of so many million dollars a year. The terms of the financing of the national aid agency would be identical with the terms on which the Bank Group financed its half of the orders. On these expenditures, the national aid agency would have no costs of administration.

There is, as pointed out above in Chapter Six, the possibility of particularly fruitful cooperation between national aid agencies and the Bank Group in promoting experimental employment-maximizing projects. These projects are bound to be risky; the chances of failure are greater than for the general run of projects. Aid-giving countries have their favorites among aid-receiving countries; the basis for preferred treatment may be a special interest which may elicit support in the legislature and among the taxpayers for expenditures by the national aid agency on well-thought-out but nevertheless risky, experimental employment-maximizing projects. Some of the projects might be undertaken by a national aid agency with the Bank acting as executive agent for the agency in appraising and possibly also in supervising the project. Other projects might be appraised by a mission containing officers from both the Bank Group and a national aid agency; the national agency might then take over full responsibility for the project but might ask the Bank Group to associate one or two of its officers with the project, so that the Bank Group could benefit fully from the experiment.

The closer the cooperation between a national aid agency and the Bank Group, the fewer missions of inquiry a national aid agency will need to send to developing countries. Such missions have often in the past duplicated work being done better by international agencies. They have served little purpose other than publicity for the national aid agency and its officials. They have wasted the scarce time of ministers and officials in the developing countries. Moreover, even if the missions from a national aid agency are serious and not instruments for publicity, there is danger that they will be regarded by aid-receiving governments as inquisitions by another government into their domestic affairs. Inquiries by an international expert institution of which they are members are usually unpalatable to low-income countries. A series of inquiries by bilateral donors can be intolerable.

To facilitate cooperation between the Bank Group and national aid agencies, arrangements should be worked out under which officers of a national aid agency would be seconded to the Bank for two years or so, and officers of the Bank seconded to national agencies for similar periods. The number so exchanged need not be equal. In seconding its own officers to a national aid agency, the Bank would give a preference to nationals of that country, but it would not be limited to these unless so requested by the national aid agency.

These more or less formal ways in which the Bank Group could help national aid agencies to improve the effectiveness of their operations should be supplemented by more informal methods for the exchange of information and for consultation on and coordination of policy. Officers of national agencies should be encouraged to deal directly with officers of the Bank Group by letters, telephone calls, and visits. When a national aid agency finds difficulty in dealing with a specific problem through lack of expertise or experience, it should send one of its officers to Washington to consult with experts there. Similarly, when a national aid agency has greater expertise in dealing with a certain problem than the Bank Group, the Bank Group would send one of its officers to that agency to consult with its experts.

This kind of cooperation would strengthen both the Bank Group and the national aid agencies. The staff of the Bank Group would be enriched by exchanges with these agencies. Because of economies of scale, the undertaking by the Bank Group of work for national aid agencies for which it would be reimbursed would reduce its overhead costs for each million dollars worth of business transacted. The quality of the operations of national aid agencies would be enhanced, and growth in their size and cost would be curbed. This would make them less vulnerable to the criticism that they wasted the taxpayers' money. National aid agencies would to an ever-increasing extent carry out their bilateral aid programs within the framework of an international system. International and national aid agencies and aid-receiving countries would work together to identify projects and to make decisions on aid policy. This would strengthen the hands of ministers and officials in aid-giving countries who do not want the value of their bilateral aid programs reduced as the result of domestic pressures to use these programs to promote national political or trade interests. It would enable them to demonstrate that pet projects favored by groups in their foreign offices or trade departments give a low real return in helping to speed up the development of aid-receiving countries in comparison with other projects.

There is, of course, the danger that closer relations between the Bank Group and the aid agencies of aid-giving countries will be interpreted by aid-receiving countries as a ganging-up of aid-givers against them. The existence of this danger emphasizes the importance of measures to increase the influence of aid-receivers within the Bank Group and to enhance the comprehension by the management and the staff of the Bank Group of the political and psychological problems of aid-receivers as well as their economic and social problems.

CHAPTER NINETEEN

International Political and Security Matters

By ratifying the UN Charter, governments entered into a treaty commitment to impose, without reference to their legislatures, whatever economic sanctions—or, to use the language of the Charter, "measures not involving the use of armed force"—are decreed by the Security Council (Article 41). Governments agreed that they would carry out these decisions of the Security Council "directly and through their action in the appropriate international agencies of which they are members" (Article 48.2). They agreed that, "In the event of a conflict between the obligations of the Members of the United Nations under the present Charter and their obligations under any other international agreement, their obligations under the present Charter shall prevail" (Article 104). They thus agreed that, whatever the articles of agreement of the Bank or IDA or the IFC might say, governments of the UN owning shares in these institutions are under a treaty obligation to vote in favor of resolutions in the governing bodies of the institutions instructing the management of the Bank Group to implement the directives of the Security Council on economic sanctions.[1]

If the UN Charter had worked as it was intended to, the following events would have taken place in the spring of 1971 as a result of the outbreak of wide-spread disorders and killings in East Pakistan and the exodus of millions of East Pakistanis into India. Since it was clear that if the situation continued there was serious danger of war between Pakistan and India, the Security Council would have determined under Article 39 of the Charter that the situation in East Pakistan constituted a "threat to the peace," and that the Council therefore not only had jurisdiction but was also under an obligation to exercise this jurisdiction. As soon as the Council determined that the situation in East Pakistan constituted a threat to the peace, this situation would immediately have become one to which the prohibition against the UN's intervening "in matters which are essentially within the domestic jurisdiction of any state" did not apply (Article 2.7); the Security Council would have had the right under the Charter to intervene by applying "enforcement measures," that is, the economic and military sanctions provided for in Articles 41 and 42.[2] In the exercise of its jurisdiction, the Security Council would first, "in order to prevent an aggravation of the situation," have ordered the governments of Pakistan and India to comply with certain "provisional measures" (Article 40). They might have included the confining of most, if not all, the West Pakistan armed forces in East Pakistan to their barracks, and the withdrawal of Indian armed forces to a certain distance from the frontiers of East Pakistan. Having imposed provisional measures, the Security Council would then have gone on to "decide what measures shall be taken . . . to . . . restore international peace and security" (Article 39). Since it was clear, from the outset of the killings in East Pakistan, that peace could be restored only by giving the elected representatives of East Pakistan the right to decide its future, the Security Council would have decided that this should be done. In the event of failure by Pakistan or India to comply with the provisional measures, or by Pakistan to permit the elected representatives of East Pakistan to decide its future, the Security Council would, under the original concept of its task, have ordered the members of the UN to impose certain economic sanctions against the recalcitrant state or states. These sanctions would probably have included a cessation of Bank Group expenditures on its loans to that state, until its government had complied with the orders of the Council. The Bank Group would have carried out this instruction from the Council.

The failure of the Security Council to act in the Pakistan crisis in the spring of 1971, or, to put it another way, the failure of the great powers to act within the Security Council, accompanied by their failure to take effective action outside the Security Council, created a vacuum into which the Bank Group moved. The Bank Group moved in because it had large investments at stake, and it had power. It had the power to refrain from granting further loans to Pakistan and to cease disbursing on its past loans—and the undisbursed portion of these loans was about $315 million[3]—and to urge the governments which were members of the Pakistan consortium to take similar action. The Bank Group moved in because what was happening in East Pakistan was endangering its investments by weakening Pakistan's capacity to provide its share of the costs of Bank Group projects in Pakistan and to service its debts to the Bank Group, then amounting to about $960 million.[4] An early indication of this was the decision of the Pakistan government in April 1971 to suspend payments in foreign exchange on its debts to the Bank Group. Events in East Pakistan were also endangering the Bank Group's even larger loans to India, amounting to over $2,000 million.[5]

A meeting of the members of the Pakistan consortium was held in Paris at the end of April. The consortium agreed that its chairman, Peter Cargill, then head of the South Asia department of the Bank, should immediately visit Pakistan and do his best to insure that its president was aware of the profound economic effects on the whole of Pakistan, both East and West, of a failure to get normal economic activities in

East Pakistan re-started as rapidly as possible. The president, when they met, assured Cargill that economic activities in East Pakistan were rapidly returning to normal, and invited the Bank to send a mission there to verify this. The mission, composed of officers of both the Bank and the IMF, visited East Pakistan at the beginning of June. The members of the mission were given access to most parts of the province. They were impressed by the evidence they received of the extent of the brutal activities of the Pakistan army. They saw that the transport situation in East Pakistan was desperate, that economic activity was almost at a standstill, and that the general political situation was rapidly getting worse. They reported their findings in some detail to the president of Pakistan and to a group of about fifteen senior government officers in Islamabad. The president, and probably most of the officers, appeared not to know what was happening in East Pakistan, and refused to believe that Cargill was giving an accurate report.

On June 21, Cargill made a full and frank oral report to the Pakistan consortium at a meeting held in Paris. It was against the background of his report on military brutality and on the absence of economic activity that the Bank Group, the Fund, and the member governments of the consortium considered what reply they should make to Pakistan's request for resumption of economic assistance. The lack of decisive action by the government of Pakistan on the foreign exchange and fiscal fronts and the continued disruption of economic activities in East Pakistan led all participants at the meeting to conclude that for the time being there was no basis for further economic assistance to Pakistan. The activities of the Pakistan army in East Pakistan and the possibility, if not certainty, that any economic assistance given to Pakistan at that time would be used to prolong these activities were decisive factors in this decision.

The role of the Bank Group during the crisis in Pakistan in 1971 was clearly important and constructive. The president of Pakistan and most of his advisers in Islamabad were being kept in ignorance of what was happening in East Pakistan and of the reaction in the outside world. The Bank Group put before them the results of a first-hand impartial inquiry into what was happening. The reaction of the governments which were members of the consortium to the results of this inquiry must have helped the Pakistan government to a better comprehension of the reaction in the outside world. The leaking of the Bank Group report to newspapers helped to create a better informed public opinion outside Pakistan. The governments were assisted in obtaining an accurate picture of the situation in East Pakistan. The consortium subjected Pakistan to a form of economic sanctions. In playing this role, the Bank Group was doing a number of the things an effective Security Council would have done, such as sending out a committee of inquiry to East Pakistan, with instructions to inform the government of Pakistan of the results of its inquiry. An effective Security Council would have imposed economic sanctions.

The disturbances in East Pakistan in the spring of 1971 thus thrust the Bank Group into a political role which it did not seek and in which it felt uncomfortable. It felt uncomfortable because it was not well equipped to play this role. It was not well equipped because it did not include the Soviet Union and China, because the United States had a too predominant position in it, and because it had no expertise in dealing with delicate and grave international political and security crises. It is to the great credit of the Bank Group that in spite of these deficiencies, its actions were restrained, intelligent, and positive. The Bank Group came out of the crisis with an enhanced reputation, which is more than can be said of the UN Security Council or General Assembly, or most of the major nations.

What lessons for the future can be drawn from the Bank Group's conduct in this crisis applicable to future international political and security crises in which the Bank Group, because of its investments, may be deeply embroiled? There are three main possibilities. The first is that as a result of the seating of Peking in the Security Council and the improvement in relations between the principal non-Communist and Communist countries, the Security Council will be revived and will assume the duties its founders intended it to discharge. The possibility of its being revived would be enhanced if West Germany and Japan were made permanent members of the Council without the right of veto. A Council so structured would be able to discharge the obligation conferred on it by the UN Charter to compel countries which are not great powers to keep the peace and to accept peaceful change if there is a threat to the peace, and if change is required to restore international peace and security. The second possibility is that the great powers would act together outside the Council to maintain international peace and security. If either of these two developments took place, it would not be either necessary or wise that the Bank Group accept the political functions it assumed in the Pakistan crisis of 1971. The third possible outcome is that the situation in the Council and among the great powers will remain very much what it was during the Pakistan crisis of 1971. In this event the Bank Group may well find itself once again compelled to play the kind of role it played in the Pakistan crisis of 1971.

But, whatever happens, there will be opportunities for the Bank Group to serve as a mediator in helping countries to work out and to make effective explicit and implicit agreements and understandings serving to lessen international tension and to increase productive international cooperation. In the fifties, the Bank Group performed valuable services of this kind in helping India and Pakistan to reach agreement on dividing and developing the waters of the Indus Basin, in helping to clear the Suez Canal after the hostilities of 1956, and in helping to bring about in 1958 the financial settlement between Egypt and the Suez Canal Company after the nationalization of the Canal by Egypt in 1956.

Under the presidency of Eugene Black, the Bank Group had great success in this area of mediation and good offices. His successor, George Woods, discouraged such ventures. It may be that Robert McNamara will accept the challenge. The issues on which the Bank

Group might serve as mediator or offer its good offices include the reconstruction and rehabilitation of Indochina, the most effective use of the waters of the Jordan valley and of the Tigris–Euphrates Basin, the deepening of the Suez Canal and the working out of agreements on its use, and the negotiation of agreements among Afghanistan, Pakistan, Iran, and the Soviet Union to improve access to Afghanistan. All these are issues where the Bank Group has influence because it has the capacity to mobilize resources to help finance an agreed settlement. It should not mediate or offer its good offices when it has no such influence. When it does agree to do either, it should, of course, request the relevant international agencies, in particular the regional banks and the specialized agencies, to join in its efforts. Thus, the reconstruction of Indochina should involve the Asian Bank, WHO, FAO, Unesco, and UNDP. Since the Soviet Union and China are members of almost all these agencies other than the Asian Bank, this would bring these two great powers into the act.

The Bank Group's ability to mediate or to use its good offices to lessen international tension was enhanced in 1973 by the establishment of an external relations office at its headquarters. This office should be placed under the direction of a vice-president. He would be the representative of the president of the Bank in dealing with other international organizations, and would advise the president on international political and security matters of which the Bank Group is seized. The mission which the Bank Group should establish to the UN in New York would report to the president of the Bank through this vice-president and he would, in consultation with the president, issue instructions to the mission. He would also deal with national governments on such questions as the replenishment of IDA. He would direct the Bank Group's activities in these areas subject to the authority of the president, just as the foreign minister of a country conducts the country's foreign affairs subject to the authority of the head of government. He would build up a staff with competence to deal with the Bank Group's external relations. So long as the president of the Bank is a citizen of the United States, this vice-president should be chosen from a member country of the Bank Group other than the United States.

CHAPTER TWENTY

Membership of the Bank Group

The United States, Britain, and the other founding fathers of the Bank and the IMF who met at Bretton Woods in 1944 intended that the Soviet Union, Czechoslovakia, Poland, and China should be original members of the two new organizations. They were all represented at Bretton Woods, and played a part in the drafting of the articles of agreement.

The feeling at the Bretton Woods conference about the importance of Soviet membership in the Bank is indicated by an incident described by Roy Harrod in his life of Maynard Keynes. According to Harrod, when a difficulty over Soviet membership arose during the last days of the Conference, F. M. Vinson, the chief U.S. delegate (later chief justice of the United States), and Keynes, the principal British delegate, "both exerted to the full their very different types of oratorical appeal in urging the Russians to come into line" by accepting a subscription of $1,200 million to the Bank instead of the $900 million they were offering.

At the last meeting of the Commission [*on the Bank*] *the Russians were still obdurate. But at the final Plenary Meeting of all the Bretton Woods delegations, the Russians announced at the outset that they would raise their subscription to the Bank to the full $1,200 million. Delegates jumped to their feet and cheered wildly.*[1]

The Soviet Union, Czechoslovakia, Poland, and China signed the two agreements establishing the Fund and the Bank. The Soviet Union did not ratify the agreements. Czechoslovakia and Poland joined the Bank but subsequently ceased to be members. Romania became a member in 1972. The Fund and the Bank, while calling the representative of Taiwan the representative of China, have in fact treated him in almost all respects as the representative of Taiwan. In consequence, the World Bank is not now a world bank; it is a bank for two-thirds of the world, mostly the non-Communist two-thirds of the world. The question whether the Bank Group would be able to do more for the developing countries if it became a universal, or more nearly universal, organization is extremely difficult. This chapter attempts to clarify some of the issues. The first point to be clear on is the distinction between the possible participation of the Peking government in the Bank Group and the possible membership of the Communist countries which are not now members.

There is no question of the membership of China in the World Bank, IDA, and IFC. "China," so designated in the articles of agreement of the three institutions, is a member of each of them. The question is not whether China should be a member of the Bank Group but what government is entitled to appoint the governor and alternate governor to represent China on the board of governors of the Bank Group, to cast the votes of China in the board of governors, and to vote for an executive director to represent China on the board of directors.

Once the UN General Assembly and the Security Council had decided in 1971 that it was the government in Peking which represents China, there could be only one sensible answer to this question, the government in Peking. The same situation exists in the IMF. Thus, there is no question of China's having to become a member of the IMF in order to become a member of the Bank. China is already a member of the IMF. Presumably, Peking could claim the Chinese seats in the Bank and IDA and not claim the Chinese seats in the IMF and IFC, leaving the representatives of Taiwan in the Chinese seats in those two institutions. This would be illogical, but international relations and national foreign policy are not invariably logical. This would, however, pose some difficult questions. Alternatively, if Peking did not want to be a member of the IMF and IFC, it could withdraw from them. Withdrawal from IFC would be a simple operation. Withdrawal from the IMF would mean, however, that China would, under the articles of agreement of the Bank, "cease after three months to be a member of the Bank unless the Bank by three-fourths of the total voting power has agreed to allow it to remain a member."

As long as the government in Peking does not wish to claim its seat in the World Bank and IDA, the situation will presumably remain as at present: Taiwan will continue to occupy the seat of China; the representatives of Taiwan will continue to be treated as representatives of Taiwan, not of China; the Bank, IDA, and IFC will not make loans or investments in Taiwan. (No such loan, credit, or investment has been made since the fiscal year 1971.)

The government of China is responsible to the Bank and IDA for the Bank and IDA loans which have been granted to China. All these have been, of course, for projects in Taiwan. The outstanding loans from the Bank amounted to $285 million on December 31, 1972, and the loans from IDA to $14 million, a total of about $300 million. If the representatives of Peking were seated in the Bank as representatives of China, the government in Peking would be responsible for meeting the interest and amortization payments on these loans. This would be absurd, since the projects financed by the loans are in Taiwan. But the absurdity would be only temporary, since it can be assumed that an accomodation will eventually be worked out between Peking and Taiwan, under which the jurisdiction of the Peking government will be extended to Taiwan. The

Peking government, once seated in the Bank, could, if it had not by then reached an accommodation with Taiwan, reduce its indebtedness to the Bank and IDA by giving notice to them (under section 6.01 of the general conditions applicable to loan and guarantee agreements) to cancel the undisbursed part of the loans not covered by "special commitments." At the end of December 1972, this would have reduced the debt from $300 million to $180 million, and the payments of interest and amortization on this debt would be about $16 million a year. If this had happened, the government in Taiwan would have had to raise from sources outside the World Bank Group the $120 million necessary to complete the Bank and IDA projects.

The government in Peking might well consider that an annual payment of $16 million a year, or even more, was not an excessive annual fee to pay for participation in the Bank and IDA. In the first place, Peking would eventually control the assets in Taiwan financed by the Bank and IDA loans. Second, participation in the Bank and IDA would make the Peking government eligible to apply for substantial loans from the Bank Group. Third, both because of its size and power and of its experience in development at home and abroad, China could be expected in time to exercise great influence on the molding of Bank Group policy, especially since many of its ideas on development coincide with the ideas of the reformers in the Bank Group: its emphasis on creating employment; on appropriate, rather than on the most advanced, technology; on small-scale light industry; on using local materials as far as practicable; and on low capital input with rapid rates of return.

China, even though it is a very poor country, has since about 1960 been an aid-giving, not an aid-receiving country, and on a grand scale. In the two years 1970 and 1971, China probably committed about $1,600 million, mainly to Tanzania, Zambia, Pakistan, and Romania, almost all of this in the form of grants and interest-free long-term loans. In 1971, disbursements of Chinese aid probably amounted to about $400 million. Because of this, some people believe that the Chinese would consider it beneath their dignity to apply for loans from the Bank and IDA. Moreover, if China were to apply for loans it would, like any other applicant, have to give forthright assistance to Bank Group missions, including both economic and appraisal missions. For China to do this would require a substantial change in Chinese policy and attitudes. But as Nehru once observed to me in the mid-fifties, "The Chinese are a cold-blooded realistic people" (adding, "a little too cold-blooded for my taste"). The Chinese, therefore, in their pragmatic way, might decide that their national interests would be served by getting loans from the Bank and IDA. In estimating the possible volume of the loans they might receive, they would no doubt look at what the Bank and IDA have done for India.

The GNP per capita of China in 1970 was $150* (compared with

* The estimate of $160 in 1970 in the World Bank *Atlas* for 1972 is an error.

$110 in India) and its population in mid-1970 was 836 million (compared with 538 million for India). India, in the four years 1969 to 1972, received almost $300 million a year in loans and credits from the Bank and IDA, or 55 cents a head. About 90 per cent came from IDA. If the Peking government had been representing China in the World Bank and IDA in those years, and if China had received the same amount per head of population as India, China would have received about $450 million a year from the Bank and IDA. Of this, about $400 million would have come from IDA. (This would, of course, have been impossible, since IDA used up all its resources in those years without lending anything to "China.") The decision of the Peking government on whether or not to take over the Chinese seats in the Bank and IDA would not, of course, be based purely on considerations arising directly out of participation in the work of the Bank Group. The government would weigh larger political considerations, such as the effect on its relations with other developing countries, and with the United States, the Soviet Union, Japan, and so on.

The essential point is that in international law the decision on whether Peking takes over the Chinese seats in the World Bank and IDA rests with the Peking government; if the Peking government wants to take over those seats, it has the right under international law to do so, because it is the government of China, so recognized by the UN. It is, moreover, inconceivable in present and foreseeable circumstances that member countries controlling a majority of votes would oppose the seating of Peking. But, if important member states were to believe that the seating of Peking would prevent the Bank Group from raising from the government and capital markets in the United States the funds it needs (and its needs would increase if Peking occupies the Chinese seats), they would do their best to find a means to avoid action which would result in the seating of Peking. Those with good relations with Peking would presumably, for example, urge Peking to postpone sending its representative to Washington to occupy the Chinese seats in the Bank and IDA until opinion in the United States had changed.

It would be unwise, however, to assume that opposition in the United States to Peking's occupation of the Chinese seats in the Bank and IDA would, after United States opinion had had time to adjust to the thought, endanger to any appreciable extent United States financial support for the Bank and IDA. The United States, in what it considers to be its own direct and immediate national interests, has moved toward a *détente* with Peking. Its strategy is apparently to play China, the Soviet Union, and Japan off against one another. The U.S. government might well before long decide that, on balance, the seating of Peking in the Bank and IDA would not prejudicially affect its national interests, and might indeed serve them.

The *Atlas* estimated China's GNP at $121,870 million and its population at 836 million. This means a GNP per capita of $146 or of $150 when rounded to the nearest $10.

It is probable that the timing of a decision by Peking to take over the Chinese seats in the Bank and IDA will depend in part on what the Romanians tell them of their experience. Peking's relations with Romania are friendly; Peking lent Romania $245 million in 1970 for development on generous terms. Romania was admitted to the Bank in December 1972. Romania can be expected to keep Peking fully informed of its experience as an applicant for membership and as a member. It may be that Peking will decide to take over the Chinese seats at the annual meeting of the IMF and the Bank Group in 1974. Perhaps it will wait until 1976 or 1978. (The reason for suggesting even years is that it is in those years that the election of executive directors takes place.)

The possibility of the membership in the Bank of the Soviet Union and of the five East European Communist states not now members raises a different set of considerations than those raised by the possible participation of the Peking government, because they are not members of the Bank, whereas China is. In the first place, this means that the Soviet Union and the Eastern European Communist states must join the IMF in order to join the World Bank. We do not know what kind of IMF will exist in a few years' time. Consequently, we do not know the kind of balance sheet of advantages and disadvantages in membership which the Soviet Union and the Eastern European states would likely draw up, after the IMF has been reconstructed. We do know that special drawing rights will constitute a much larger proportion of the reserves of the central banks of countries which are members of the IMF. Insofar as special drawing rights are a quasi-gift from heaven to central banks, there will be pressure on non-member countries to become members of the IMF in order to share in this manna. Against this must, of course, be set the disadvantages of the obligations of membership, as set forth in the articles of agreement of the Fund, particularly the obligation to furnish information on a wide range of matters, including holdings of gold and foreign exchange, international balance of payments and exchange controls, and the further obligation to receive and give information to annual IMF visiting missions. In practice, however, these obligations would probably prove to be not very onerous.

As for membership in the World Bank, the principal advantage to the Soviet Union and the Eastern European states is that this would make them eligible to apply for loans from the Bank. (None of them would be eligible for IDA credits because none of them is a low-income country.) The Soviet Union, Czechoslovakia, East Germany, and Hungary are rich countries, but their per capita GNPs are lower than that of New Zealand, to which the Bank has been granting loans. They could not, therefore, be judged to be ineligible for Bank loans merely on grounds of their comparative wealth. They could be judged ineligible only if they were able to raise sufficient private capital on reasonable terms on the world's capital markets. Their needs for outside capital are presumably great. Certainly the Soviet Union will not be able, without substantial outside capital, to press ahead rapidly with the development of the vast natural resources of Siberia. Czechoslovakia, East Germany, and Hungary, the other rich members of the Eastern European group, could presumably speed up the pace of their development if they had more outside capital. Bulgaria and Poland are middle-income countries. Their requirements of capital from the Bank may well be greater than the requirements of those middle-income member countries of the Bank which now have about the same per capita GNP's, countries like Argentina, Venezuela, Spain, Singapore, and Panama. A number of the Communist countries would find that another substantial advantage to them of membership in the Bank is that they would secure substantial export business through international competitive bidding on Bank and IDA projects.

Thus, for the Soviet Union and the Eastern European Communist countries, their expectations of loans from the Bank and of increased export business would more than make up for the membership fee in the Bank, which consists of an interest-free paid-in subscription. The Soviet Union was given at Bretton Woods a quota in the Fund, a subscription in the Bank, and a voting power just below that of Britain. The Soviet quota and subscription was $1,200 million, compared with the British $1,300 million. The voting powers bore the same relationship. Presumably the Soviet Union would now wish, if it became a member of the Fund and the Bank, to have a quota, subscription, and voting power somewhere between those of Britain and the United States. If the Soviet Union's subscription to the Bank were halfway between those of Britain and the United States, it would amount to about $4,500 million, of which $450 million would be paid in.

The principal disadvantage to the Soviet Union and the Eastern European Communist countries of applying for loans from the Bank is that they could not receive loans unless they were willing to receive and assist Bank missions. They would no doubt find this distasteful, at least initially.

As with the government in Peking, so with the governments of these countries: their decision on whether or not their national interests would be served by membership in the Bank would be based not just on considerations arising directly from participation in the activities of the Bank. They would also weigh larger political considerations. Their calculations would be profoundly affected by the seating of Peking in the Bank and IDA. It is possible that Romania's membership may be followed in 1974 or 1975 by that of Hungary and Poland. Czechoslovakia, East Germany, and Bulgaria may well not apply for membership until the Soviet Union has also decided to apply.

Faced with clear indications from the Soviet Union or from any one of the Eastern European Communist states of a desire to join the Bank, it seems at present highly unlikely that they would not receive assurances of support from members of the Bank possessing a large majority of the votes in the governing bodies of the Bank, notably the United States, the EEC countries, and Japan, which together possess over 60 per cent of the votes. One thing which is reasonably certain is that because of the importance of this development to the relations between these countries and the Communist countries, the decisions of the principal members of the Bank would be based not so much on an assessment of the direct effects of membership on the capacity of the IMF and the Bank Group to discharge their functions as on larger political considerations. Among these considerations would be the contribution a universal World Bank Group might be able to make to building an international community. A world community is likely to be created only by the slow, patient building up of world-wide institutions, seen by the governments and peoples of the world to serve their interests and in which the governments and peoples of the world learn to work together. A universal World Bank Group with adequate resources and with efficient, effective, and truly international management could become the most important of these world-wide institutions. In the long run, there can be no assurance of world peace without a world community. A nation is a group of people who have done great things together and who intend to do great things together. To build a world community, the nations of the world must do great things together. One of the greatest of these things would be to relieve the misery of the poor two-thirds of mankind. The road to freedom from poverty can become the highway to freedom from war.

A hard-and-fast line cannot be drawn between this central political consideration and considerations relevant to the probable effects of universal membership on the ability of the Bank Group to discharge its functions. Would a universal World Bank Group be able to get the increased financial resources essential to its task? Would it be able to maintain efficient and effective management? What could be done to maximize the advantages of universalization of the Bank Group and to minimize the disadvantages?

As for the first question on financial resources, it would be helpful to hazard an estimate of the size of the increased demands on the Bank and IDA likely to result from universalizing the membership of the Bank Group, even though this estimate is subject to a wide margin of error. To make any such estimate, a number of assumptions have to be made. The first is that the new members would be given treatment no less favorable than that of comparable existing members. The second is that loans to new members would not be at the expense of present members. On these assumptions, the addition of the Soviet Union and the Eastern European Communist states to the group of rich and middle-income countries which borrow from the Bank might increase Bank lending by about $350 million a year (in 1972 dollars). Bank lending to China might, on the same assumptions, be about $200 million a year. The projection (in Chapter Thirteen) of total Bank lending in 1983 was $3,350 million (in 1972 dollars). This would mean an increase to $3,900 million a year. The projection of total IDA lending was $2,750 million a year in 1983, of which $1,100 million would go to India. China's borrowings from IDA might be about $1,000 million a year.[2] This would increase IDA's lending to $3,750 million a year in 1983. Loans to other possible new members—North Korea, North Vietnam, Mongolia, Albania, and Cuba—might increase these totals of Bank and IDA lending to $4,000 million and $3,850 million.

Provided that the governments of rich countries, especially that of the United States, had favored the universalization of the Bank's membership, the financing of the increase in Bank lending from $3,350 million a year to $4,000 million should not cause great difficulty, especially if the Bank had become less dependent on selling its bonds on capital markets. The increase in IDA's resources from $2,750 million to $3,850 million a year would, however, be highly improbable unless IDA were able to get most of its resources by the relatively painless method of the IMF's allocating large quantities of newly created special drawing rights to it or from royalties on the exploitation of the sea bed.

The first question to be discussed was whether it was likely that a universal Bank Group would be able to secure the increased financial resources it would need to carry out its task. The second question was whether it was likely that a universal Bank Group would be able to maintain efficient and effective management. Certainly the difficulties of this would be greatly increased as the Bank Group became more nearly universal. The executive directors of the Bank Group try to reach decisions on important issues not by votes but by consensus. It would be more difficult to reach a consensus in a board of directors which included representatives of the Communist countries. The Bank Group staff has hitherto been relatively homogeneous; almost all its members were educated in universities with a Western European tradition. A staff which included experts from the Communist countries would, at least to begin with, find greater difficulty in working together.

The president of the Bank might also find it difficult to persuade the governments of the new member countries that he was the sole judge of the competence of potential new members of his staff, and that he would not appoint anyone to the staff, no matter what his nationality, who did not meet what he considered to be proper standards of efficiency, competence, and integrity. But he would have to insist on this. At the same time, he would have to try to appoint to the staff at all levels a reasonable number of citizens of the new member countries who did meet the required standards. To do this, with minimum damage to the morale of the existing staff, he would have to be authorized to offer generous immediate pensions to senior members of the staff, so as to open up positions for new staff. Other positions would be created by the expansion in staff required because of increased activities resulting from an extension of membership.

The executive directors, the management, and the professional staff of the Bank Group would need to use great skill and patience in demonstrating to the new executive directors and professional staff that the older members were anxious to help them acquire the influence to which they were entitled in determining and carrying out the policies of the Bank Group. Thus, the Soviet and Eastern European members would have to be encouraged to contribute to the discussion and study of development problems their special experience gained, not only in their aid programs to developing countries, but also in their efforts to assist the more underdeveloped regions of their own countries. None of them, of course, has had to deal, within his own country, with problems of development in underdeveloped areas, such as the Indian subcontinent or Indonesia, with high densities of population. The Chinese, however, have had to deal with these problems and with problems of development in areas of China with low population densities. Their experience and their advice should be immensely valuable. A Bank Group in which the Chinese government and Chinese experts were influential would likely be more effective in helping its poorer member countries work out policies, programs, and projects which maximize both production and employment and which lead to the speedy eradication of the worst forms of poverty than a Bank Group which is not able to make full use of China's experience. Mahbub ul Haq, the Pakistan economist, who had visited China twice in the preceding few years, said in 1971:

It appears that within a period of less than two decades, China has eradicated the worst forms of poverty; it has full employment, universal literacy and adequate health facilities; it suffers from no obvious malnutrition or squalor . . . China has proved that it is a fallacy that poverty can be removed and full employment achieved only at high rates of growth and only over a period of many decades. . . . Is there not a practical illustration here of a selective attack on the problems of poverty, pursuit of a threshold income and minimum consumption standards, merger of production and distribution policies and achievement of full employment with a meagre supply of capital? It is no use insisting that these results must have been achieved at tremendous social and political costs; people in the developing countries are often undergoing these costs without any visible economic results. . . .[3]

The absence from the Bank of the Soviet Union, the Eastern European states, and China, and the predominant position of the United States and of other rich, white, Western capitalist countries, have helped give rise to misgivings about the Bank in a number of important colored low-income countries. These misgivings impede the creation and maintenance of that feeling of mutual confidence between the Bank Group and its low-income borrowers essential to the full success of the Bank Group's operations. The universalization of the Bank's membership would provide the Bank Group with opportunities to allay these misgivings, and these opportunities should be fully exploited. Thus, if the poorer members of the Bank should become convinced, as a result of the universalization of the Bank's membership and of other changes, that there had been a real shift of power within the Bank Group from the rich nations to the poorer nations, and a more profound understanding by the management and staff of their needs, problems, and susceptibilities, they might in time propose that the functions of the UNDP in the pre-investment field be merged with those of the Bank, the UNDP retaining the technical assistance side of its activities. A merger under these conditions should increase greatly the efficiency and effectiveness of the entire international aid effort.

CHAPTER TWENTY-ONE

The Administration of the Bank Group

Even before the great increases, during the first years of McNamara's presidency, in the volume and complexity of Bank Group operations, the general outlines of the kind of changes required to improve the administration of the Bank Group had become clear. Some of the changes could be made by the president of the Bank; others required action by the member governments in the governing bodies of the Bank Group and of other international agencies. More devolution of authority and responsibility was needed at the Bank Group's headquarters and from there to missions in the field. The regional banks had to be strengthened so that they could take over a larger share of development financing. Similarly ILO, FAO, Unesco, WHO, and UNIDO had to be strengthened so that they could take over from the Bank Group a larger share of responsibility for identifying, appraising, and supervising Bank Group projects. Above all, as aid-receiving countries, with the assistance of the Bank Group and other aid agencies, increased their technical and managerial competence in government and in the private sector, and as they built up effective local institutions (planning organizations, development banks, agricultural credit institutions, small industries corporations, consultancy, designing and contracting firms), and acquired experience in working out projects and programs both labor-intensive and yielding a high real rate of economic return, the Bank Group had to play a progressively more limited role in identifying, appraising, and supervising projects and programs; this would demonstrate its confidence in the judgment and the administrative abilities of those countries whose record over many years justified confidence. In return, their confidence in the Bank Group would increase, for confidence begets confidence.

Robert McNamara inherited from George Woods a style of administration which suffered from a fundamental weakness, which made extensive devolution of authority and responsibility impossible. Most senior officers, from the president down, did not consult fully and frankly on all aspects of the framing and implementing of policies with the subordinate officers principally concerned. Most senior officers, from the vice-presidents down, did not believe that they had not only the right to express their views fully and frankly to their superiors, but a duty to do so, especially when they knew that their views would be unwelcome. The style of administration which McNamara inherited was described to me by one officer of the Bank in 1971 as similar to that of an American football team: "The coach makes all the decisions without consulting the players who are meant merely to carry out the strategy, not to help in devising it."

McNamara, as the London *Economist* pointed out shortly after he took office, is a man of extraordinary intelligence and capacity for work; he enjoys power and wants to use power for the public good.[1] This makes him impatient with delay. The result was that during the first four years of his presidency, instead of changing the style of administration which he inherited, he perpetuated it. In the short run, this gave results: he was able to smash his way to his objective of doubling the volume of Bank Group lending. But, in the longer run, this system of administering an organization is wasteful and dangerous. It does not make full use of the talents of the professional staff; it leads to a loss of morale; the organization has difficulty in hiring and keeping able people. Even more important, it can result in the head of the organization being surrounded by advisers who, because they fear him or are devoted to him or are incompetent or lazy or because they want to ingratiate themselves with him, or because they do not think it would do any good, do not point out the weak points in proposals he puts forward, so that he might improve them while they are still fluid. They do not warn him even when they believe he is about to embark on a perilous course. All this can and does insulate the head of an organization from reality.

This happened to Nehru in the last sad years of his prime ministership, when he failed to surround himself with cabinet ministers and officials who would argue with him and to whose arguments he would listen. Neville Maxwell, in his account of the events leading up to India's humiliating defeat by China in 1962, said that many of Nehru's colleagues in the cabinet "were often deeply opposed to Nehru's approach; but they never fought him, being content merely to thwart—just as Nehru himself, it often seemed, was content merely to exhort."[2] The secret accounts now published of the discussions at the meetings of the senior officers of the U.S. administration which took place on December 3, 4, and 6, 1971, immediately after the war between India and Pakistan broke out, demonstrate that they did not give the President the benefit of their advice; instead they took orders from his spokesman, Henry Kissinger.[3] Watergate demonstrated the evils of this style of administration.

McNamara needs to nurture in the Bank Group the best traditions of an efficient national civil service, where senior civil servants argue vigorously with the cabinet minister in charge of their department when they believe his views are mistaken, where a cabinet minister provides his senior civil servants with ample opportunities to argue, and where civil servants, once a decision has been made by the cabinet minister after ample opportunities for argument, carry out that decision as effectively as they can, even if they consider it mistaken, or resign. In an agency cherishing these traditions, there is easy communication within the agency from the top to the bottom and from the bottom to the top at all levels, and, of equal importance, there is easy communication laterally within the agency at all levels. There is mutual confidence between superior and subordinate. They keep each other constantly informed of important developments. Before making a decision on a matter coming within the subordinate's responsibilities, the superior consults him. He gives him ample opportunities to put forward his analysis of a problem and his recommendations on what the decision should be. Throughout the whole agency, a subordinate knows the mind of his superior officers so well that he knows the decision they would make in about nine out of the ten matters which come before him. He can therefore make those decisions himself and consult his superiors on only one out of ten. This implies that superiors explain their view clearly to their subordinates. A subordinate knows that when he makes an occasional error his superiors will protect him, and if it is necessary to correct the error, it will be done in such a way as to save his face. Otherwise, in order to protect himself, he will submit to his superiors not one decision out of ten but three or more, and there is no effective devolution of authority. The obverse of this is that the superior officer is not criticized for the occasional mistakes of his subordinates; otherwise the superior will feel it necessary to go over his subordinate's work line by line; he will spend his time looking at trees rather than forests; his subordinates will stop worrying because they know that whatever comes from their hand will never emerge as their handiwork. In an agency which has developed the best traditions of an efficient national civil service, the subordinate feels that his superiors are trying to bring out his talents and use them to the full, that he will be rewarded by public esteem and by promotion for the good work he does, and that his colleague who is lazy or incompetent or a yes-man will likewise receive his just reward.

In the fifth year of his presidency, McNamara began to move the administration of the Bank and IDA toward greater decentralization of authority at headquarters, clearer lines of authority, and sensible procedures to speed the reconciliation of conflicting views. Previously there had been seven area departments and nine projects departments. Each project department dealt with a sector of the economies of developing countries, such as agriculture, industry, or transportation. The area departments reported to one vice-president; the projects departments, to a different vice-president. McNamara in 1972 combined the five principal projects departments with the seven area departments to form five regional offices at the headquarters of the Bank. The remaining four projects departments, which were too small to be split up, plus a central coordinating advisory staff in the other five sectors, remained in a central projects office, whose task was to guide and assist the regional offices so as to assure uniform sectoral policies. Each of the five regional offices and the central projects office was headed by a vice-president, and these six vice-presidents reported to the same senior vice-president. In announcing this reorganization, McNamara said that within approved policy, the regional offices would be responsible for planning and executing the Bank's lending and technical assistance programs in the member countries.

This was undoubtedly a move in the right direction. How great a move it was depended on how far those put in positions of increased responsibility were ready, willing, and able to assume the responsibility, and on how far they were in fact given the necessary authority. It depended on how far the officers of the Bank Group, from the president down, were prepared to break with the traditional style of Bank Group administration.

The method followed by the management of the Bank Group in 1972 in making the changes in the structure of the administration and in transferring many officers from one post to another did not promise well for the future. Few officers were consulted adequately on the new structure required. Most officers who were moved, including many of the most senior, were simply given notice of their new posting a day or so in advance of the public announcement. The reorganization was carried out so impersonally and abrasively as greatly to lower morale throughout the whole professional staff. The changes in the structure of the administration were, on the whole, wise; the way in which they were made was unfortunate. It did not mark a change in the traditional style of administration but was almost a caricature of it. It underlined the importance of the reforms in the structure being followed by changes in the style of administration. And changes in style are much more difficult to effect than changes in structure.

One of the principal advantages of establishing five regional offices is that this makes it easier to take the next step required to improve the structure of the Bank Group, that is, to devolve authority and responsibility from the headquarters of the Bank Group to offices located in the regions. All that is now required is the transfer of the regional offices from Washington to regional headquarters, and the establishment of a regional council for each regional office in accordance with the provisions of section 10 of article V of the articles of agreement. This section, which has not yet been used, reads as follows:

The Bank may establish regional offices and determine the location of, and the areas to be covered by, each regional office. Each regional office shall be advised by a regional council representative of the entire area and selected in such manner as the Bank may decide.

The core of the staff of each regional office would be the staff of the present regional office in Washington. To this would be added other officers and staff from the economic departments, the legal department, the information department, the administrative departments, and the IFC. The size of the staff at headquarters would probably be reduced by more than half.

The principal advantage of this move would be that the Bank Group staff directly concerned with a region would be living in that region. They would have many opportunities to get to know the people and their culture, and to acquire a better understanding of the special and peculiar problems faced by the politicians, officials, and businessmen of the region in carrying out policies best calculated to promote healthy development. The cost of operating the regional offices and councils would be offset, to some extent at least, by reductions in the Bank Group's expenditures on travel, which amounted in 1972 to $10 million. The wear and tear and loss of efficiency which now plague those members of the staff of the Bank Group who must travel frequently would be reduced. There would be less danger that long journeys would result in short tempers. Above all, the efficiency of operations would improve by reducing the size of the operating units. The Bank Group bureaucracy in Washington is now too large to be efficient.

The most difficult problem to be faced in establishing regional offices and councils is the degree of authority which should be delegated by the president of the Bank Group to the regional offices and by the executive directors to the regional councils. It would be absurd and time-wasting if they had to clear in advance with Washington every step they proposed to take on such matters as the preliminary stages of identifying high-priority projects and examining whether they are likely to be feasible. It would be dangerous is they departed from the general lines of policy laid down by the executive directors without getting approval from both them and the management of the Bank Group. Clearly, on major projects or on those involving a departure from established policy, the officer principally concerned at the regional office would have to come to headquarters in Washington to secure the necessary advice and decisions. The formula for delegating responsibility to regional offices located in the regions might therefore be the same as that used by McNamara in 1972 when he delegated responsibility to the regional offices at the Bank Group's headquarters: within approved policy, the offices in the regions would be responsible for planning and executing the lending and technical assistance programs of the Bank and IDA in individual member countries of the region. They would have responsibility for the whole process of identifying and appraising projects, conducting the loan negotiations, and supervising the projects. Most of this work would be done by members of the regional office, or, if there were a resident Bank mission to the borrowing country, by the members of that mission. Occasionally, when the expertise required was highly specialized, they would be assisted by experts sent from the Bank Group's headquarters.

The more difficult question is the extent to which the executive directors would agree to give regional councils authority to approve loans below a certain amount which conformed with established policy.

Perhaps they might agree that recommendations from regional councils on these loans would be reported to them and, in the absence of objection by an executive director, become effective within a specified short period after the reports had been circulated to them. This procedure would be similar to that followed in Canada with committees of the cabinet, which have "the power not simply to recommend courses of action to the Cabinet, but to take specific decisions." These decisions, however, do not become effective immediately; they are listed in an annex to the agenda of the next meeting of the cabinet. Any cabinet minister not a member of the cabinet committee can notify the secretariat before the meeting that he wishes to have a decision of a committee discussed by the cabinet. If no such notice is given, items on the annex are considered to have been approved by the cabinet and become decisions of the cabinet.[4]

Under this system, regional councils would make recommendations only on loans below a certain amount which do not depart from approved policy. All other proposals for loans would go from the regional office to the president of the Bank, and, if approved by him, would be submitted by him to the executive directors. In a discussion in Washington of proposals submitted by a regional council or a regional office, the regional office would be represented by one or more of its officers. If this kind of devolution of authority worked well, the limit on loans which the regional council might recommend could steadily rise, just as it has risen in the analogous devolution of authority from the Bank Group to national development finance companies.

The willingness of the executive directors to agree to even this kind of limited devolution of authority would, of course, depend on their decisions on the membership and on the voting procedures in the regional councils. A regional council is required by the articles of agreement to be representative of the entire area. The articles of agreement are silent on the representation of countries outside the area. Presumably the executive directors from the rich countries will insist on representation on regional councils. The executive directors might, therefore, arrange for the appointment to each regional council of, perhaps, four persons, each of whom would represent a group of member countries of the Bank outside the area. Each member of the council would cast the number of votes which the government or governments he represents can cast in meetings of the board of governors. A regional council could reject a recommendation from the head of the regional office that a loan be granted, but it could not itself propose a loan, just as the executive directors in Washington can reject a recommendation from the president that a loan be granted but they cannot themselves propose a loan.

The regional offices would be responsible for directing the activities of the Bank Group's resident missions in the region, and would delegate authority and responsibility to these missions. This delegation should not, however, be postponed until the five regional headquarters of the Bank Group have been established. The resident mission in New Delhi, for example, is now the only one regularly responsible for preparing the periodic country economic report; since it was given this responsibility the reports have improved. The responsibility should now be handed over to all resident missions. Some of them would need experts from the headquarters of the Bank to help them prepare the report. The responsibilities of resident missions could also usefully be extended to cover certain kinds of feasibility studies, of appraisals and of project supervision.

The establishment of regional offices within the regions and of more resident missions, the transfer of more authority and responsibility to these missions, and the taking of other steps to delegate authority and responsibility within the Bank Group will improve the morale of the professional staff; improve the quantity and quality of their work; and make it easier to attract able people and to keep them.

Devolution of authority should be accompanied by changes in the personnel policy of the Bank Group to heighten the staff's comprehension of the problems facing the developing countries.

One barrier to a better understanding is that there are so few nationals of developing countries in the senior ranks of the professional staff of the Bank and IDA. The annual reports of the Bank and IDA contain lists of the principal officers. In 1968, 29 officers were listed. Of these, only 4 came from developing countries: one Egyptian, one Indian, one Pakistani, and one Yugoslav. By April 1973, the number of principal officers had gone up from 29 to 80, but the number from developing countries had gone up only from 4 to 12. There had in those five years been almost no increase in the proportion of principal officers coming from developing countries: they formed only 15 per cent. This is certainly not a reasonable proportion for an international development institution. It would therefore be wise to attempt to increase that proportion to at least a third within five years or so. There should also be an increase in the number of officers of other ranks who come from developing countries.

This does not imply that all officers from developing countries have a better comprehension of the problems of developing countries than all officers from rich countries; it implies that normally their chances of having a better understanding are better. Some, especially if they come from the upper classes of a highly stratified society, will have an inferior comprehension to that of most officers from rich countries. The experience of the Bank Group has demonstrated that many officers from developing countries are as insensitive to social aspirations or political problems as colonial old guards—indeed, sometimes more so. Much of the present ruling classes of Latin America, for instance, or of parts of Asia and Africa, are not particularly sensitive to new aspirations. Yet it is from these ruling classes that the Bank Group normally recruits, thus satisfying its conscience about greater diversity without necessarily introducing greater sensitivity.

A senior official in the Indian sub-continent wrote in a personal letter to me in March 1971:

I hope the Bank does not rely for its staff from the developing countries on people who have stayed too long in the Bank. Whether they are Indians or Pakistanis, they soon lose touch with realities in countries of their origin unless they give up the sheltered atmosphere of the Bank and see what it is to work in their own countries. My experience is that people from developing countries who have stayed too long in international agencies are, with a few exceptions, people who have basically lost sympathy with their own countries. At any rate, they have lost touch.

These considerations and the fact that the requirements of governments, banks, businesses, and universities in low-income countries for people who could become valuable members of the Bank Group staff are so great that they cannot be filled suggest that the Bank Group should not encourage many of them to become permanent members of its staff. It should concentrate rather on borrowing experts from low-income countries in their early forties to serve for five-year terms. These younger people could more easily be spared by their countries, since the experience gained from service with the Bank Group would make them much more valuable on their return home. Their employers might therefore be prepared to cooperate with the Bank Group by granting them leave of absence for five years. They would, of course, accept appointment only if given assurances that their stay in the Bank Group would not hinder their careers at home, and that the Bank Group would make full use of their abilities. The two conditions are interdependent. Their fulfilment would require a high degree of flexibility on the part of the management and staff of the Bank Group. By 1978, about one-quarter of the two hundred or so senior posts in the Bank Group service might be held by these experts.

Since it would not be in the interests of the low-income countries that the Bank Group stimulate an excessive brain drain from those countries to its professional staff, even on a five-year basis, the administration of the Bank Group should supplement these measures by others to increase the comprehension of the problems of low-income countries by members of its staff. In recruiting new staff from rich countries, the Bank Group should give preference to those who have lived in low-income countries and have learned from that experience. A special effort should be made to recruit from among former members of overseas youth programs, such as peace corps, who possess the required professional skills. In recruiting staff from both rich and developing countries weight should be given to a background in the humanities and in history. Too many of the officers of the Bank Group forget where today's developed countries stood two centuries ago. Too many of the younger members of the staff, particularly economists, do not value history, nor do they regard development as part of the historical process. They have been trained in universities (such as practically all the universities of the United States) where it is possible to get a Ph.D. in economics without ever having studied economic history. The Bank Group should insure that members of its staff who have not lived in low-income countries should have their horizons widened by postings to regional offices or resident missions and by serving on country economic missions, missions to prepare coordinated programs of pre-investment studies, missions making sectoral studies, and project appraisal missions.

During the four years when I lived in India in the fifties, I was fortunate in having many visitors from home. Whenever possible, I would take them to see two or three average Indian villages, not the best, the show places, not the worst, just the average. Some of these visitors were experts on the economic problems of India. They knew all the statistics about Indian poverty: the per capita GNP; how many calories there were in the diet of the average Indian; how many yards of cloth he used a year; the rate of infant mortality; the average expectation of life. But—and this is a revealing commentary on our inability to communicate with each other—when they saw for the first time with their own eyes their first average Indian village, they were shocked by the depth of its poverty. It was so much worse than anything they had ever dreamed of.

It is particularly important that the economists of the Bank Group should not in practice come to be divided into two groups: those who stay in Washington and those who serve on missions. All economists on the Bank Group's staff should serve on a mission to a low-income country for a period of at least two months every two years or so. Statisticians on such missions could usefully spend a week discovering how statistics are in fact collected in villages. This would reduce the danger of their making sophisticated analyses based on statistics with extremely wide margins of error. They might, for example, discover that normally the person responsible in a town of about two thousand people for collecting statistics on births, deaths, infant mortality, and maternal mortality was an illiterate, ill-paid watchman, and that the internal inconsistencies in the statistics he collected demonstrated their gross inaccuracies.

The level of comprehension by the professional staff of the Bank Group of the problems of the low-income countries would be raised if there were a better balance in the staff between those who have received all or part of their university training in universities in English-speaking countries and those who have received it in other universities. It is probable that 80 or even 90 per cent of the young professional officers recruited by the Bank Group since the young professional program was inaugurated in the early sixties have had all or part of their university education in universities in English-speaking countries. This tends to give them an orientation different from that of the majority of even the most highly educated inhabitants of developing countries.

Greater care should be taken to insure that members of the Bank Group staff possess not only efficiency, competence, and integrity, but also the special qualities appropriate to an international civil servant whose main business is to deal with the problems of low-income countries and with their hard-pressed politicians and civil servants. Foremost among these are respectful sympathy, courtesy, and humility. The Bank Group is fortunate that so many members of its professional staff possess these qualities. But, because the staff is dominated by nationals of rich countries who have not lived in low-income countries, it is likely that the appraisals of the work of members of the staff, on which decisions on promotion are based, do not attach sufficient weight to the degree to which they possess these qualities. It would therefore be useful to instruct the heads of Bank resident missions to send confidential assessments to the Bank Group's vice-president in charge of the personnel department on the degree to which members of visiting missions have demonstrated possession of them. The assessment of the head of mission would be based in part on discreet soundings of officials and others in the country. If there are resident bank missions in countries responsible for about two-thirds of Bank Group lending, and if a high proportion of the staff is sent on a visiting mission at least once every two years, the Bank Group's evaluation of its officers would before long be greatly influenced by their skill in the art of development diplomacy. It would be the responsibility of the Bank Group's vice-president in charge of the personnel department to see to it that officers were told of criticisms made of them on this as on other aspects of their work.

The officers of the Bank Group hold well-paid, secure jobs, and live in one of the wealthiest areas of the wealthiest country in the world. The Bank Group bureaucracy is highly expert, large, and dominated by people from rich countries. It is difficult for people working for long in such a bureaucracy, whether they come from rich or low-income countries, to remain sensitive to the political, social, and administrative problems facing hard-pressed politicians, businessmen, and civil servants in low-income countries. Therefore, while the core of the staff should be officers making their careers in the Bank service, a quarter to a third of the officers serving at any one time in Bank headquarters, whether they come from rich or developing countries, should be appointed for terms of about five years. The president of the Bank Group would have to be alert to insure that international patronage, from which the Bank Group has been free, did not slip in through this door. He would have to insist that merit be the sole criterion for appointment. In addition, the Bank Group might establish a corps of reserve officers. These would be persons who had agreed, with the approval of their employers, to be available to work for the Bank Group for periods of a few months or a few years, as the Bank Group needed them.

The concept of the Bank Group as a partnership between rich, middle-income, and low-income nations would be further strengthened if greater care were taken to insure that members of the Bank Group staff attach sufficient weight, in their assessments of the problems of low-income countries and the advice they give, to the political and social factors inhibiting governments from following what seem to outsiders the obviously wise courses of action. The greater the influence in the Bank Group of officers who have served in senior positions in national governments, the less the danger that the staff would overlook these factors. As a senior official of a low-income country expressed it in a personal letter to me, officials in national governments "understand what it is to live in a complex world where there is always more than one side to every issue . . . [whereas] most of the Bank staff who have had little experience of work in national governments tend to assume that other people also live in a sheltered environment where there is no such thing as accountability or having to reconcile a number of conflicting objectives or indeed to maintain a degree of harmony amidst all kinds of passions."

A special effort should be made to insure that the reduction in the proportion of all ranks of professional officers in the Bank Group who come from rich countries results in a more than proportionate reduction in the number and influence of officers who are citizens of the United States. In its early years, it was inevitable that the Bank would be dominated by the United States. It was founded at Bretton Woods in 1944, when Western Europe was in eclipse and when about three-fifths of the present low-income members of the Bank did not yet exist as independent nations. In its early years, when Europe was still struggling toward post-war recovery, the only place where it could borrow was Wall Street. The headquarters of the Bank therefore had to be in the United States, its president had to be a citizen of the United States appointed, in fact though not in form, by the president of the United States, the senior ranks of management and of the professional staff had to contain a high proportion of United States citizens, and the United States government had to have a predominant voice in determining Bank policy.

The heavy preponderance of United States citizens in the senior staff of the Bank Group persisted long after the United States had ceased to be the source of almost all its funds. Thus, when I joined the staff, in mid-1962, eighteen years after the Bretton Woods Conference, 11 out of the 21 principal officers (those listed in the annual report of the Bank and IDA) were United States citizens.[5] (Of the others, five were from Britain, two were Dutch, two were French, and one was Canadian.) Under the presidency of George Woods, the proportion of the principal officers of the Bank and IDA who were citizens of the United States fell from 52 to 40 per cent. Unfortunately, during the first four years of McNamara's presidency, this desirable trend was reversed. This was one of McNamara's principal failures as president. Of the 80 senior officers listed in the organization chart published in *Bank Notes* in April 1973, 36 (or 45 per cent) were United States citizens.

Clearly, over the next five years or so, a more appropriate balance should be achieved at all levels of the professional staff, from the vice-presidents down, among citizens of the United States, citizens of other rich countries, and citizens of middle-income and low-income countries while at the same time maintaining high standards of efficiency, competence, and integrity in the new appointments and leaving plenty of room for promoting present members of the staff on merit, regardless of nationality. It would be impossible to do this were it not for the fact that, even if the professional staff increases by only about a third between mid-1973 and mid-1978 (from about 1,800 to about 2,400), compared with the 125 per cent increase in the preceding five years, at least 1,200 new appointments will have to be made between mid-1973 and mid-1978.

By the end of the seventies the Soviet Union, and all the East European Communist states, may have become members of the Bank and IDA, and the government in Peking may have taken over the representation of China. The membership of the Communist countries would presumably be accompanied by the membership of the other countries not now members, so that by the end of the seventies the World Bank and IDA may have become universal institutions. The wider their membership, the larger the proportion of their financial resources coming from countries other than the United States, the stronger will be the arguments for moving the headquarters of the Bank Group from Washington to a city more appropriate to an international institution.

An independent city-state of a reunited Berlin might be a desirable site for the new headquarters. The time for such a move may come by the early eighties, if by then the Soviet Union and the Eastern European Communist states have joined that Bank, and if a relaxation of tension between the Soviet Union and the United States and between the Soviet Union and the European Economic Community has proceeded apace. This relaxation might make the question of the reunification of Berlin practical politics. Any scheme for the reunification of Berlin with any chance of success would have to be based on the independence of a united Berlin from both East and West Germany. Berlin would become an independent city-state with close economic ties with the other two Germanies. The transfer of the headquarters of the World Bank Group to an independent city-state of a united Berlin would have many advantages for the Bank Group. With the proceeds from the sale of its valuable properties in Washington, the Group could construct much more efficient, less costly, and more commodious buildings at or near the blighted area of the Berlin wall. The transfer would be symbolic of the waning influence of the United States on the Bank Group. A move to Berlin would make it easier for the Bank Group to recruit able officers for its headquarters staff, since many qualified candidates would be more attracted by the prospect of living in a united Berlin rather than in Washington. It would also be easier for the Bank Group to establish close and productive relations with the European Economic Community, with the Soviet Union and the states associated with it. If governments were to decide on this move, it is desirable that they agree also to move to Berlin the headquarters of the IMF.

It can be assumed that McNamara will wish to resign as president before he reaches the age of sixty-five in 1981. He may wish to give up the presidency in 1978, after ten years in office. It seems likely that well before 1978 he will have transformed the three Bank Group institutions into much more powerful instruments for economic and social growth in the low-income countries than they were when he became president. By 1978, the United States would have held the presidency of the Bank for the entire thirty-two years of its existence. It would seem wise and appropriate that McNamara's successor, the sixth president of the Bank, should come from a country other than the United States.

All this would help to transform the Bank Group into a truly international partnership, in which all partners, large or small, rich or poor, North American or South American, European, Asian, African, or Australasian, socialist or capitalist, would consider the Bank to be their bank. Today, too many influential people in too many member countries of the Bank think that it is somebody else's bank. Too many British still think of it as an American bank, that is, a United States bank. Too many Western Europeans still think of it as an Anglo-American bank. Too many people in low-income countries still think of it as a bank run by the rich aid-giving countries. The more truly international the partnership within the World Bank Group becomes, the more readily can it assume increased responsibilities.

CHAPTER TWENTY-TWO

The Executive Directors

The executive directors of the Bank Group who form the board of directors are appointed or elected by the shareholders who are the member governments. The relationships of the directors to the governments which appointed or elected them differ. Some represent only one government; some a group of governments, in which no one government controls half the votes which went toward their election; others also a group of governments, one of which does control more than half those votes. Each of the five largest shareholders (the United States, Britain, Germany, France, and Japan) appoints a director. He is subject to instruction from the government which appointed him and can be removed from office at any time. The other fifteen directors are elected by the other 117 shareholders. In this election each shareholder casts a number of votes, which is the same as the number of shares his government owns plus 250, and the number of shares depends on the economic strength of the country. As the result of arrangements made before the election, which takes place at every second annual meeting of the board of governors, countries form themselves into groups so that the total vote of each group is sufficient to elect one director. The actual balloting is then a formality.

Each of seven of the fifteen elected directors represents a group of countries in which no one country possesses more than half the votes which counted toward his election. One of these directors represents five countries; the others, nine to eighteen. Each of these directors attempts to reflect the views of the countries which elected him. He is, no doubt, especially influenced by the views of the government of the country of which he is a national, particularly if his future career is dependent on the good will of that government, but the fact that he is elected by a large number of countries of more or less equal importance would make it unlikely that his government would want him to support policies those governments would not also support. Each of these seven directors is assisted by an alternate director, who is appointed, in fact though not in form, by one of the countries in the group which elected the director. He never comes from the same country as the director.

The other eight of the fifteen elected directors occupy an intermediate position between the five appointed directors and the seven who are elected by a group of countries in which no one country possesses a majority of the votes. Each of these eight directors represents from three to five governments, one of which possesses more than half the votes which counted toward his election. In the election of the director representing India, Bangladesh, and Sri Lanka, the votes of India constituted 80 per cent of the total votes. Similarly, the votes of Canada constituted 80 per cent of the votes which counted toward the election of the director representing Canada, Guyana, Ireland, and Jamaica. These directors are normally appointed, in fact though not in form, by the government of the country which controls more than half the votes counting toward their election. These countries are Argentina, Australia, Belgium, Brazil, Canada, India, Italy and the Netherlands. One of the other countries in the group will appoint the alternate director. Australia, Brazil, and Italy have on occasion agreed that the director respresenting their group should be appointed by a minority shareholder in the group. Thus, in the elections of 1972, a New Zealander replaced the Australian and a Colombian the Brazilian. In a previous election, a Spaniard took the place of the Italian. But the other five countries (Argentina, Belgium, Canada, India, and the Netherlands) are unlikely ever to agree that a minority shareholder appoint the director: they are virtually permanent non-permanent members of the board of directors. They cannot dismiss their executive director during his two-year term of office. If, however, he is an officer in their public service, they could recall him from Washington and he would cease to be an executive director. This has happened. If this was not possible, they could let the president of the Bank know that the director no longer possessed their confidence; he would then cease to exercise influence at the Bank, though he would continue to cast votes. They are therefore in a position to control the votes of their director. These five governments must, however, pay due regard to the views of the "minority shareholders," since, if their views are consistently disregarded, they may at the next biennial election join a group whose representative on the board of directors is more likely to reflect their views.

These five governments and the governments of the five principal shareholders are in a position to exercise complete, or almost complete, control over one director. Of these ten countries, eight are rich: Belgium, Britain, Canada, France, Germany, Japan, the Netherlands, and the United States. They cast 61 per cent of the total number of votes at meetings of the board of directors of the Bank and 63 per cent at meetings of the board of directors of IDA.[1] Of the other two countries, Argentina is one of the wealthiest middle-income countries, and India is a very poor country.

The degree to which each of the ten governments does in fact exercise control over its executive director depends on many factors:

the pattern of behavior which has been established in each country during the Bank's existence; the degree of interest in the senior ranks of the bureaucracy in each country in the problems and activities of the Bank Group; the personal position of the executive director in the hierarchy of power at home; and the traditions of government at home. Thus, the British executive director will probably receive from London firm instructions on such major issues of Bank Group policy as local cost financing, program lending, the volume of the Bank's lending operations, and the proportion of the resources of IDA which should go to the Indian sub-continent. On other issues, he will be expected to use his own judgment and to know when he should ask for guidance or instructions from the authorities in London. The Canadian executive director has been given even wider discretion by the Canadian government. The United States director receives instructions from an interdepartmental committee in Washington on most issues coming before the board. A strong United States director will insure that he receives the instructions he wants to receive, or he will get them reversed by higher authority.

There is relatively little formal voting at meetings of the board. The normal procedure is that after the board has discussed a proposal, the chairman of the board, who is the president of the Bank, will say that the consensus is clearly in favor of the proposal, and that the proposal is therefore adopted. After he has made this announcement, directors may ask that certain member governments which they represent be recorded as abstaining or as opposing the decision. But, even if formal voting took place more often, the influence of an executive director cannot be measured by the number of votes he can cast at meetings of the board. His influence depends on his knowledge of the problems of the Bank Group, his understanding of these problems, his interest in them, his relations with the president of the Bank, the senior members of the Bank bureaucracy, and his fellow directors, and on his influence on the policies of the government or governments he represents. An executive director who possesses the confidence of the president of the Bank, particularly if he represents a government which in general is in sympathy with the president's ideas, will be asked by the president for advice; and the president will try out new ideas on him.

Executive directors have responsibilities other than assisting in determining the policy of the Bank Group. Directors representing borrowing countries will try discreetly to get more loans for the countries they represent, and with as little delay as possible. Directors representing rich aid-giving countries may spend a good deal of time in trying to establish closer relations between their national aid agency and the Bank Group. They will help to work out proposals for better exchange of information and experience, and for cooperation on specific loan projects through joint or parallel financing by the Bank Group and the aid agency of their country. They will take up on behalf of companies in the countries they represent complaints that these companies have been discriminated against in the award of contracts financed from

Bank Group loans. They will do their best to insure that the appropriate authorities of their governments receive information at least as early as the authorities of any other government about contracts for goods and services likely to be awarded during the next few years, so that their governments may in turn inform the firms that might be interested; those firms can then get in touch with the borrowing countries, for it is these countries which award the contracts.

The total value of the contracts financed by Bank Group loans amounts to a very large sum. Bank Group lending in the five years beginning in mid-1973 may total about $20,000 million (in 1972 dollars). If two-thirds of this is put out to international competitive bidding, the value of the contracts awarded under this bidding will be about $2,700 million a year. This is an important source of business. Therefore, the ten executive directors appointed by rich industrial countries will be expected by their governments to do what they properly can to insure that nationals of their countries have at least as good an opportunity as those of any other country to make successful bids on projects financed by the Bank and IDA. The longer the advance notice which a company is given of a project likely to be financed by the Bank Group, the better are its chances of being able to submit a successful bid.

All executive directors, whether they represent borrowing or rich countries, become expert in clothing an appeal to the board on behalf of the countries they represent in terms, not of the special interests of those countries, but of the general interest. The two may, of course, coincide. Thus, a director who represents a rich country which is a traditional supplier of goods to a certain borrowing country will warmly support program lending to that country and local cost financing there.

The representative of a borrowing country on the board does not by convention participate in a board discussion of a proposed loan to that country. If that loan is criticized by other directors on the ground, for example, that it has too great a program content, or that the proportion of local costs financed is too high, or the preference to local suppliers excessive, he does not reply; the staff does. But, the next time a loan to some other country, which could be subjected to the same sort of criticism, comes before the board, he will, without mentioning his own country, strongly rebut that criticism.

Emphasis has been laid in this book on the influence the rich countries exercise in determining the policies of the Bank Group on issues they consider to affect their special national interests. But, within the limits imposed by this influence on these issues, the Bank Group is an institution dominated by its management, not by its directors. In this, it differs from the IMF, which is dominated by its executive directors. The board of directors of the Bank Group, even though it consists almost entirely of full-time directors, is closer in its nature to the board of directors of a great United States bank than it is to the board of the IMF.

Some of the sources of weakness in the Bank Group's board are irremediable. An executive director who represents borrowing countries represents clients of the Bank Group. If, at meetings of the directors or in private discussions with the management and the staff, he is so forthright in his criticisms of the policies of the management and the staff that he offends them, he runs the risk, human nature being what it is, that loans to his clients will proceed at an unusually slow pace, that especially onerous conditions will be proposed, and that the management and staff will be particularly intransigent in resisting modifications in traditional Bank Group policies. He will be imprudent if he runs this risk. He will not cease to be concerned with trying to assist the Bank Group to become a more effective institution, but he will be careful to avoid deep probing into areas where it is clear that the management and staff are especially sensitive to criticism. This caution diminishes the effectiveness of the Bank Group's board of directors. It has been further diminished by the fact that some directors representing rich countries have been more interested in seeing to it that nationals of their countries get contracts under Bank Group loans than that the Bank Group become a more effective institution for promoting the development of its poorer member countries. These directors have served rather as commercial counselors of their embassies in Washington than as directors of the Bank Group.

The board would be more effective if more of its members served for longer terms. On November 1, 1972, when the new directors took office, only seven of the twenty had been members of the board for two years or more. Perhaps the convention might be established that members normally serve for four or six years. The first two years' service could be as alternate executive directors. This might indeed be the rule when a director represents a number of countries and the post of executive director is rotated among the principal countries represented. This would mean that only somewhere between a third and a half of the members of the board would retire every two years.

The board would be more effective also if more of the directors had the very considerable knowledge, understanding, and interest in the problems of development which many of their colleagues possess. Too many directors are still of the type which tended to dominate the board in its earlier years; they are more interested in, and have more experience in, the financial side of the Bank's operations than in its lending activities; they are more interested in such issues as the terms on which the Bank borrows and the appropriate degree of liquidity than in McNamara's new gospel of development. Too great a proportion of them come from central banks and departments of finance. Directors from aid-giving countries should normally come from the national aid agencies. Directors from aid-receiving countries should normally have had experience in agencies of their government directly concerned with problems of development. The board of directors of the Bank Group should not be "a paradise for bankers, economists and bureaucrats with narrow specializations and preoccupations." They should be people "with a wide vision, social consciousness and a sense of history."[2]

Since McNamara began to preach his new gospel of development in 1969, the number of directors with these qualities has increased. Indeed, by 1971 most of the directors were supporters of his new gospel, though not all of them realized the extent of the changes which would have to be made in the operations of the Bank Group, and in the policies of its member governments, if this gospel were to be put into practice. An indication of their growing support was that, increasingly from 1970 on, they would, at meetings of the board, criticize projects brought before them for approval on the ground that they would help not the poorer half of the population in the borrowing countries but the larger landowners or the bigger industrialists, or would result in substituting machinery for labor.

The answer of the management and staff of the Bank Group to this kind of criticism was that the question of how far the Bank Group was in fact applying the new concepts of development to its lending to a particular country could be judged by examining not single loan projects but rather the whole strategy of Bank Group lending to that country. This answer was scarcely likely to convince the critics, since they were not given copies of the confidential documents setting forth Bank Group lending strategy country by country. Moreover, some of the directors who most strongly supported McNamara's new concept of development believed that a number of the most influential members of the senior staff did not support these concepts and that they were doing their best to slow down the application of them to the actual lending operations of the Bank Group, as no doubt some of them were. By the beginning of 1973, the problems of finding a more useful role for the directors and of speeding up the process of translating McNamara's concepts of development into actual Bank Group operations were converging.

Under McNamara's presidency, the management of the Bank Group has provided the directors with greatly increased opportunities to discuss the policies of the Bank Group. Thus, in 1970, the board discussed in turn each of the principal recommendations which the Pearson Commission had made to the Bank Group. In 1972, it discussed each of the ten sector papers which subsequently became chapters in the volume entitled *World Bank Operations*, published in the autumn of that year. In 1971 and 1972, it discussed program lending, local cost financing, and preferences to local suppliers; and it began a series of discussions on the development problems of individual countries, starting with Brazil, India, Nigeria, and Yugoslavia. The report submitted by the president to the board on each loan for which he asked the board's approval was expanded to include statements on the development program of the borrowing country, the external financial assistance it was receiving from the Bank Group and other sources, and how the loan fitted into the program.

All this was an advance on the procedures of the fifties and sixties. But the advance stopped short of the point where the management of the Bank Group would share with the directors information about the Bank Group's strategy of lending to each borrowing country, set forth in the five-year country program paper introduced into Bank Group practice by McNamara. This paper, which was confidential and circulated only within the staff of the Bank Group, contained a franker appraisal of social, political, and economic developments in the borrowing country than it was possible to include in the economic report on the country circulated to the executive directors and, through them, to all the member governments. It set forth the volume of lending by the Bank and IDA which the Bank Group contemplated during the five-year period covered by the paper. It discussed, sector by sector, the strategy of lending by the Bank Group during this period. It listed the projects which the Bank Group intended to process during the period and described how these projects fitted into the Bank Group's lending strategy, how far, for example, they would promote more employment and a better distribution of income.

It would clearly be unwise if this paper in an unexpurgated form were circulated to the directors and through them to all the member governments. The immediate effect would be a toning down of the frank evaluations in them, so that neither the Bank Group nor the government concerned would be embarrassed if the paper were published as the result of a leak. It would likewise be unwise to include in a paper circulated to directors the tentative forecasts of volume of lending for a country for the next five years. Once its government became officially aware of this figure, it would be inclined to consider that the Bank Group was committed to lending in that volume. Arguments might break out in the board on whether the volume proposed for one country was equitable compared with that for other countries. There might be logrolling; a group of directors might privately agree to press for an increase of lending to countries A, B, and C, if the directors representing those countries in return pressed for an increase in lending to countries X, Y, and Z.

But, by the spring of 1973, it was becoming clear that it would be wise to circulate to the directors some sort of outline of the strategy which the Bank Group was following in its lending to each of its borrowers. This outline might form the concluding section of the periodic Bank Group economic report on each country. It would give the directors an opportunity to discover how far the doctrines of the president of the Bank Group were reflected in these lending strategies. The board would then be better able to appraise the merits of projects submitted to it for its approval. In time it might be possible for the president to ask the executive directors not just to examine but also to approve papers setting forth the strategies of lending, country by country. Experience might, indeed, indicate that the executive directors would be prepared to agree that their approval of a five-year program of lending to a country would carry with it approval for loans during each of the five years for projects of not more than so many million dollars each, and amounting over each year to not more than so many million dollars. This, especially if accompanied by the establishment of regional councils (see pages 184 to 187), would enable the board of directors to avoid being so swamped by a large volume of projects that it would not have time to consider broad questions of Bank Group policy.

The danger that this might happen was real. In the three years immediately before IDA began to lend money—1958, 1959, and 1960—the directors approved an average of 44 loans and investments a year. By 1968 the number had gone up to 70. In the three years 1970, 1971, and 1972, it averaged 152 a year. By 1978, the number of loans will probably have increased to about 250 a year. The burden imposed on the directors by the large number of projects coming before them for approval is increased because projects are bunched in June, the final month of the Bank Group's financial year. In June of 1972, the directors approved 40 loans and investments. This was one-quarter of the total for the entire year, and almost as many as were approved in a year at the end of the fifties. The value of these loans and investments was also almost equal in real terms to the lending in a year at the end of the fifties.

* * *

The administration of the World Bank Group has been able to influence the development policies of its poorer member countries; it has had little influence on the development policies of its rich member countries. One of the most important problems facing the president of the Bank is what steps he can take to increase his influence on the policies of the rich countries on issues affecting the development of the poorer countries.

The president and the staff bring their influence to bear on the governments which borrow from the Bank Group in many ways. They have discussions in the country with ministers and officials of the government on specific projects, on sectors of the economy of the country, and on the country's general development strategy, and with ministers and officials in Washington when these visit Washington for negotiations on loans. They have discussions during the annual meetings of the Bank Group. They talk to the director or alternate director representing the country, and to its ambassador in Washington. They have, of course, many channels of communication with the government of the United States, and through these influence flows in both directions. Officers of the Bank Group discuss matters with officers in the United States aid agency, the state department, and the treasury, and with the United States ambassadors in the borrowing countries. The president of the Bank attempts to influence United States policy in the Bank by talking, not only to the director representing the United States, but also to the secretary of the treasury, the secretary of state, the head of the United States aid agency, and leading senators and congressmen. On very important matters he talks to the president of the United States. The channels the Bank Group uses to influence its other principal aid-giving members are fewer; most often, it is the director or alternate director who represents the country concerned. The degree of influence the Bank Group can exercise on the governments of these countries largely depends, therefore, on the quality of these representatives. In this context, quality means a capacity both to understand the problems of the Bank Group and interpret them to his government, and to influence his government. His value to the Bank Group depends to a great extent on his influence at home.

Some presidents of the Bank Group before McNamara were inclined to like weak directors, who would not be a nuisance to them but who would be happy to draw a generous salary in return for being not much more than rubber stamps. If this was ever a sensible policy, it has ceased to be. When McNamara, during his first five years of office, doubled the volume of lending by the Bank Group and announced that there would be a further increase of about 50 per cent during his second five years of office, he made the Bank Group into an institution the ten principal rich member governments would consider to be too serious to be entrusted to the president of the Bank or even to the president and the directors acting without instructions from their governments on main policy issues. The day of the executive director representing one of the principal rich member governments who acted on his own, in the light of his concepts of the long-run interests of the Bank Group, is passing, if it has not already passed. From now on, because of the expansion of the Bank Group's activities and because of the dependence of IDA on increasingly large gifts from governments, the governments of the principal rich member countries will take more interest in the activities of the Bank Group and will try to exert greater influence on its policies. On important issues, the statements their executive directors make at meetings of the directors, like the statements of their colleagues in the North Atlantic Council or the UN Security Council, will be prepared in their national capitals.

This does not mean that they will not influence their government's policy. An able ambassador can have great influence. So can an able director. Nor does it mean that there will not be wide differences between the role of these executive directors and that of an ambassador. Unlike ambassadors to a country, directors of the Bank Group meet constantly as a body to make decisions on important issues; they have offices near one another in the same building; they usually have lunch with one or more of their colleagues. They thus develop a sense of belonging to a community and a feeling of loyalty to the institution they are directing. They try hard to get their instructions changed if in their view these are inimical to the interests of the Bank Group. Within the interstices of their instructions, they do their best to serve what they consider to be the long-run interests of the Bank Group. On some important issues, they will deliberately refrain from consulting their governments in advance, knowing that a government is more likely to acquiesce in some decisions than to approve them in advance.

Because directors possess power and influence, a wise president of the Bank will consider that one of his most important tasks is to try to sell his ideas to the directors representing the major financial contributors. He will encourage them to call on him whenever some issue of Bank Group policy arises which they would like to discuss with him. He will take the initiative in asking them to give their views to him orally and in writing. He will ask them from time to time to arrange for him to be invited to their capitals, and he will seek their advice on the principal issues he should discuss on those visits.

A wise president will not, however, be content with discussing his problems with representatives of the governments of the main financial supporters of the Bank Group, no matter how able they may be. He will want to have discussions also with the governments themselves. He will therefore pay unhurried visits, perhaps once a year, perhaps once every eighteen months, to the capitals of the ten countries responsible, together with the United States, for providing seven-eighths of the contributions from governments to IDA, and probably about the same proportion of the Bank's resources. These countries are, in order of their contributions to IDA, Britain, Germany, Canada, France, Japan, Sweden, Italy, the Netherlands, Australia, and Belgium. On these visits he will have discussions with the heads of government, the governors of the Bank Group, the alternate governors, and the heads of the national aid agencies. The purpose of these visits will be to persuade these ten countries to give him increased support in making the Bank Group a more effective agency for helping the poorer nations of the world improve the living conditions of their peoples, particularly the poorer half.

Such visits will complement those which a wise president will make every year to the capitals of the dozen or so chief borrowers from the Bank Group.

Since increasingly from now on the executive directors representing rich countries will be acting on important issues on instructions from their governments, it is important that these instructions be prepared by officials in the national capital with experience, knowledge, and understanding of the problems of development of the poorer countries of the world. In rich countries, this normally means officials in the national agency responsible for the country's bilateral aid program. Because it is essential that national policies expressed in bilateral aid, multilateral aid, trade policy, and international financial and monetary policy be coordinated, the national aid agency will on important issues clear instructions to the executive director with the other departments and agencies of government principally responsible—the ministries of finance, trade, and foreign affairs, and the central bank—which would be represented on an interdepartmental committee or council on international development policy. On borrowings by the Bank, especially on borrowings from the local capital market and the local central bank, the views of the ministry of finance and the local central bank will prevail unless overruled by the head of government.

The articles of agreement of the Bank stipulate that "each member shall deal with the Bank through its Treasury, central bank, stabilization fund or other similar fiscal agency, and the Bank shall deal with members only by or through the same agencies." As the nature of the Bank Group has changed, this provision has become anachronistic, and is being disregarded. It should be amended. It certainly should no longer be a factor in the choice by the government of a rich country of its governor and alternate governor on the Bank Group's board of governors. From now on, these should normally be the cabinet ministers or senior officials with responsibility for the country's bilateral aid program, rather than the ministers of finance or the governors of the central bank. The interdepartmental committee or council on international development policy at the national capital and the executive director in Washington would report to the governor and the alternate governor.[3]

CHAPTER TWENTY-THREE

Weighted Voting in the Bank and IDA

As noted earlier, it seems highly probable that within the next ten years or so, most of the low-income countries will be more and more insistent on what they call their right to run their own affairs in their own way. It is possible that many of them may even decide that to give up foreign aid is for them a lesser evil than to accept foreign aid at the price of constant outside interference in their affairs. It is therefore vital that the rich member countries of the Bank Group make it easier for the low-income member countries to distinguish sharply between "foreign aid" and aid from the Bank Group, and between "outside interference" and the Bank Group's contribution to a dialogue between partners. A principal obstacle to their making this distinction is the great preponderance of votes held by the rich countries in the governing bodies of the Bank Group. This preponderance exists because the number of votes held by a country is determined by its relative economic strength. The voting power possessed by the rich members of the Bank Group is so great as to make it difficult for the poorer countries to believe that the Bank Group is in any real sense a partnership between the rich countries and themselves.

The preponderant power of the rich countries in the Bank Group is, of course, derived only in part from the system of weighted voting in the governing bodies of the two organizations. The other main source of their power is the dependence of the Bank Group on the governments of rich countries and their capital markets for almost all its financial resources. Chapter Fifteen discussed what might be done to reduce the importance of the second cause of dependence. This chapter deals with what might be done to reduce the importance of the first cause. The two are related. The less the Bank Group is dependent for its funds on the governments and the capital markets of rich countries, the less a change in the weighting of voting in its governing bodies (in the interests of the poorer members) would seriously affect its ability to raise the funds to carry out its tasks.

Y. B. Chavan, the finance minister of India, put neatly the issue of the relative powers of the richer and poorer countries in the government of the Bank Group in his opening address in December 1971 to a seminar in New Delhi on world partnership in the second development decade, an address already cited in Chapter Three:

If there is to be a genuine World Partnership [*in international institutions such as the World Bank and the International Monetary Fund*], *it has to be reflected first and foremost in a greater willingness* [*of the big powers*] *to share in the process of taking decisions regarding how this partnership is to be actually brought about in practice. Without that, the words 'World Partnership' will ring a little hollow in millions of ears.*[1]

In the late sixties and early seventies, there was an improvement in the balance between rich countries and low-income countries on the board of directors of the Bank and IDA through the addition of three executive directors from Africa, all from low-income countries. By 1972, seven of the executive directors came from low-income, two from middle-income, and eleven from rich countries. But there has been almost no change in the ratio between the votes of rich countries and those of the low-income countries on the board of directors and the board of governors.* The rich countries hold 64 per cent of the votes in the Bank and 65 per cent in IDA, the low-income countries 25 per cent in the Bank and 29 per cent in IDA. The population of the rich countries comprises 26 per cent of the total population of all Bank members, the population of the low-income countries 64 per cent. The rich countries, with about a quarter of the population of the Bank Group, possess almost two-thirds of the votes. The low-income countries, with almost two-thirds of the population of the Bank Group, possess a quarter of the votes in the Bank and about three-tenths in IDA. In the Bank Group, 1 million people in the rich countries have about as many votes as 6 million people in the low-income countries.

A simple substitution of the one-state one-vote formula for the present system of weighted voting in the Bank and IDA is out of the question. The rich countries would not turn over 3,000 million dollars a year to an organization in which the low-income countries (providing virtually none of the money) would control more than 60 per cent of the votes (76 out of 122 in the Bank, 74 out of 112 in IDA). They would not be alone in rejecting out of hand a proposal that every member state should have only one vote in the governing bodies of the Bank Group. The more populous of the low-income countries would also reject it. The 58 least populous of the low-income member countries of IDA have a total population of 350 million. Under the one-state one-vote system, these countries would be able to cast a majority of the votes in IDA, which has a membership of 112. The six most populous low-income countries with more than two and a half times the population of the 58 countries would have one-tenth of their votes. One million people in the

*The votes of member countries in the Bank and IDA and the votes under the revision proposed in this chapter are given in Table Four, pages 238 to 244.

58 least populous low-income countries would have the voting power of 25 million people in the 6 most populous low-income countries. In an agency charged with the responsibility of allocating scarce financial resources among a host of hungry claimants, this would not only be absurd; it would result in a grossly inequitable distribution of the scarce resources of IDA. Even now the most populous low-income countries get much less aid per capita from all sources than do the small low-income countries. If the small low-income countries controlled the allocation of aid from IDA, the discrimination against the big low-income countries would be magnified many times, since it would be naive to expect that the smaller low-income countries would not be corrupted by their absolute power over IDA.

If the regional banks had a system of voting less heavily weighted on the side of wealth than that of the Bank Group, a solution to the problem posed by the very heavy weighting in the Bank Group could be found in a transfer of power from the Bank Group to the regional banks. But, while in most of the regional banks the low-income countries have relatively more voting power than they have in the Bank Group, this is not true of the Asian bank, and about two-thirds of the population of all the low-income members of the Bank Group live in the region covered by the Asian bank. In the Asian bank, the rich member countries possess 65 per cent of the votes, almost exactly the same proportion they posses in the Bank Group.

It is obvious that there must be some kind of weighted voting in the Bank Group in favor of the rich countries which provide the funds. What is not obvious is that the weighting need be so heavy as it is today. Certainly the rich countries do not need to hold 64 per cent of the votes to veto loans they do not approve; they need only 50.1 per cent, since decisions to approve loans are made by a majority of the votes cast. They do not need to hold even a majority of the votes to veto loans they are unanimous in disapproving, since rich and powerful countries are able in international organizations to exert a strong influence on the voting behavior of less rich and less powerful countries. They certainly do not need 64 per cent of the votes to block amendments to the articles of agreement, since amendments require either unanimity or 80 per cent of the total voting power.

Is it necessary, wise, or reasonable that the United States possess 23 per cent of the votes in the Bank and 26 per cent in IDA? It needs only 20.1 per cent of the votes to block amendments to the articles of agreement. Since it is inconceivable that an amendment opposed by the United States would not also be opposed by a substantial number of other member countries, it needs, in fact, a good deal less than 20.1 per cent. To block a loan, the United States now has to rally to its side countries possessing 35 per cent of the rest of the votes. If the United States were to agree that its voting power be reduced to 20 per cent of the total votes, it would have to rally 38 per cent of the remaining votes to block a loan. The difference is not substantial.

A move to transfer some of the voting power in the governing bodies of the Bank Group from the rich countries to the poorer countries has, of course, to be made with great caution, since it will arouse fears and suspicions among some groups in the legislatures of rich countries whose consent is required for the amendments to the articles of agreement of the Bank and IDA. A small initial move might be more productive in the longer run than an attempt to take a big first step. A big first step might be blocked by the veto of one or two legislative bodies. A short first step might be given grudging acquiescence; then, when it was found that the governing bodies of the Bank Group continued to act responsibly in spite of (or perhaps because of) the increased voting strength of the poorer countries, it might well be possible to make further progress.

A modest reduction in the votes of the rich countries and a correspondingly modest increase in the votes of the poorer countries in the governing bodies of the Bank and IDA would have a symbolic value, even though it did not threaten the control of the rich countries over the policies of the Bank Group on issues on which they were substantially united. It would therefore seem wise for the rich countries, as a demonstration of the importance they attach to emphasizing that the Bank Group is a partnership between rich, low-income, and middle-income nations, to propose amendments to the articles of agreement of the Bank and IDA to reduce their present excessive preponderance in voting strength.

One way to accomplish this would be to give to each member country 30 additional votes in the governing bodies of the Bank and 90 additional votes in IDA for every 1 million of its population. (The reason for the difference between the formula for the Bank and that for IDA is that the total number of votes in IDA is now about three times the total number in the Bank.) The effect of this amendment would be to transfer 8 per cent of the votes in the governing bodies from the rich countries to the low-income countries. The rich countries would still have 56 per cent of the votes in the Bank and 57 per cent in IDA. The six principal rich countries (Britain, Canada, France, Germany, Japan, and the United States) would have to obtain only about a twelfth of the votes of all the other members, rich, middle-income, and low-income, to have a majority. A step would, however, have been taken in the right direction. The voting strength of the middle-income countries as a group would remain unchanged; they, with 10 per cent of the total population of member countries, would continue to hold 10 per cent of the votes in the Bank and 6 per cent in IDA. The low-income countries, with 64 per cent of the population of all Bank countries, would have 33 per cent of the votes in the Bank, instead of their present 25 per cent, and 37 per cent in IDA, instead of 29 per cent. The effect on the United States would be to reduce its votes in the Bank and IDA from 23 per cent in the Bank and 26 per cent in IDA to 20 per cent and 22 per cent respectively.

Since the Soviet Union, Czechoslovakia, and East Germany are rich countries, and Bulgaria, Hungary, and Poland are middle-income countries, their entry into the Bank would reduce the proportion of votes held by low-income countries. But, if Peking takes over the Chinese seats in the Bank and IDA, the balance would be restored, since the vote of a China represented by Peking would increase greatly through the proposed amendment. The following table gives the percentage distribution of the votes in the Bank at present, the distribution among existing members under the proposed amendment, and what the distribution would likely be if the amendment were passed, and if the Soviet Union and the five Eastern European Communist states not now members were admitted to membership and if Peking took over the Chinese seats.[2]

Countries	*1972*	*Under proposed amendment*	*Under amendment plus universalization*
Rich			
United States	23	20	15
Others	41	36	42
Total	64	56	57
Middle-income	10	10	10
Low-income	25	33	33

The rich countries, with one-quarter of the population of the world, would have almost three-fifths of the votes. The low-income countries, with two-thirds of the population of the world, would have one-third of the votes. Great weight would still be given to the possession of economic power, but the weight would not be so great as at present. The distribution of voting power between rich and low-income countries would be less inappropriate for an agency which was trying to become a genuine partnership between the two.

If it should prove impossible at present to make this change in the weighting of votes in the governing bodies of the Bank Group, two other possibilities could usefully be considered. Seven of the executive directors now come from low-income countries, two from middle-income, and eleven from rich countries, giving the rich countries a majority of 11 to 9 over the developing countries. The appearance, though not the reality, of the predominant position of the rich countries would be diminished—and this in itself would be salutary—if the majority of executive directors came from developing countries. This could be done by adding three more executive directors from developing countries, preferably from the low-income developing countries. This would not require an amendment of the articles of agreement of any of the three Bank Group institutions. It would, however, require a four-fifths majority of the total voting power in the board of governors of the Bank Group. The other possibility would be to amend the articles of agreement of each of the three Bank Group institutions to require that matters now decided by a majority of the votes cast could be decided only if the majority of the votes cast included the votes of an agreed proportion of the member countries having an agreed proportion of the total population of the member countries. The requirement might be one-third of the member countries and one-half of the total population. A simpler formula would be that decisions should require not only a majority of the votes cast but also a two-thirds majority of the executive directors present and voting.

CHAPTER TWENTY-FOUR

Partnership

One central theme running through this book has been that the rich member countries of the Bank Group should give the poorer member countries a greater share of power in the processes by which the Bank Group makes decisions and carries them out, so that the Bank Group will become a less unequal partnership between the rich and the poorer nations. This, it has been contended, would enable the Bank Group to do more to help its poorer member countries provide the mass of their people with more food, better clothes, better shelter, better protection against disease, more jobs, and more social justice. Two reasons have been advanced to support this contention. The first is that the policies, the programs, the projects, and the advice of the Bank Group would be sounder if the preponderance of power of the rich countries were lessened. The second is that unless lessened, the influence of the Bank Group will decline as more and more of the poorer countries become more and more unwilling to accept advice from outsiders, and, if the relative power of the rich countries within the Bank Group is not substantially diminished, the poorer countries will regard the management and staff of the Bank Group as outsiders. This chapter discusses some of the implications of an effort to hasten the evolution of the Bank Group into a less unequal partnership between the rich and the poorer countries.

* * *

One of the principal reforms advocated in this book is that the aid-receiving poorer countries be given an opportunity, either within the Bank Group or in an international agency such as DAC, to examine the performance by each rich country of the obligations it has voluntarily assumed to assist the poorer countries by aid and by trade, just as the rich countries are able through the operations of the Bank Group to examine the performance by each of the poorer countries which has borrowed or wishes to borrow from it of the obligations it voluntarily assumed when it borrowed or applied for a loan. It would be easier to surmount the obstacles in the way of this reform if the legislatures and taxpayers of the rich countries would envision an international impartial, expert audit of their aid performance, in which aid-receivers and aid-givers would participate, as a reinforcement of the audit systems which they themselves have established to insure that funds voted by their legislatures are spent efficiently on the purposes for which the funds were voted. This is, in fact, what an international impartial, expert examination of the performance of an aid-giving country's aid would do. It would make it more difficult for the aid authorities of a rich country to waste the funds voted by the legislature.

The difficulty, of course, is in defining the term "waste." The representatives of aid-receiving governments on international audit committees on aid would consider that aid money was wasted if it was not used as efficiently as possible to help aid-receiving countries hasten their economic and social growth. The representatives of the aid-receiving governments would presumably try to quantify the extent of the waste as thus defined; they would estimate as best they could the extent to which the real value of the aid to the recipients had shrunk because the aid-giving government whose aid program was being audited had tried to combine assistance to the development of the poorer countries with such objectives as greater employment at home, greater export trade, and better protection for their investors in the poorer countries.

When the Bank Group is auditing the performance of an aid-receiving country, it should not be content to draw the attention of the country to the slow-down in the rate of its healthy economic growth stemming from its pursuit of objectives other than such growth. It should suggest how that country might attempt to reconcile these objectives with those of healthy economic growth. Similarly, when an international committee, consisting of givers and receivers of aid, audits the aid performance of a rich country, it should not be content with drawing the attention of the country to the shrinkage in the real value of its aid to the recipients resulting from its pursuing objectives in its aid program other than the rapid development of the recipient countries. Rather, it should suggest how that country might attempt to reconcile these objectives. Thus, an expert outside audit might be able to demonstrate fairly conclusively to a country with an aid program of $500 million a year that to spend $50 million a year to help domestic export industries improve their productivity would do more in the long run to increase its exports than using aid to stimulate exports directly at the cost of reducing by 10 per cent the real value of the aid to the recipients. If this were so, the aid-giving country would be better-off if it reduced its annual aid appropriation by $50 million and used this saving to help domestic export industries and sectors to improve their productivity. The aid-receiving countries would be as well off with $450 million spent solely to promote development than with $500 million spent partly to promote development and partly to promote exports; they would indeed be better off if the aid came as loans, since they would not be incurring so heavy a burden of debt.

* * *

As the Bank Group moves toward becoming a real partnership, it should be easier for all its members to realize the full implications of partnership.

One important implication is that an aid-receiving country should consider a request from the Bank Group for its cooperation not in the context just of the direct effects on its relations with the Bank Group if it accepts or rejects the request, but also of whether or not acceptance is likely to strengthen the Bank Group's ability to help other aid-receiving countries who are its partners. Thus, one aid-receiving country may have acquired so much experience in areas (such as large-scale programs of rural development works or of small-scale industries) in which the Bank Group has had little experience, that it believes it would not benefit by accepting suggestions from the Bank Group that it ask the Bank Group for loans for these programs, but rather that the Bank Group's descent upon these politically difficult areas would be distasteful and perhaps even embarrassing. Before turning down the Bank Group's suggestions, it should, however, as a partner, weigh carefully the importance of the Bank Group's acquiring experience in these areas of lending, so that it could help other developing countries with little or no experience in these areas to work out excellent projects on rural development works and small-scale industries for submission to the Bank Group.

Another, and the most important, implication of an approach to real partnership is that each partner should consider itself under an obligation to do what it can to make it easier for the other partners to carry out their obligations.

These obligations are onerous. A government does not get much, if any, domestic political capital from fulfilling them. Indeed, in many countries more votes might be gained, in the short run at least, by welching on the obligations than by fulfilling them. The main obligation of the poorer countries is to mobilize domestic resources for development, even though this means restraining consumption of almost all goods and services other than those essential to the maintenance of a national minimum standard of living. Poorer countries must also use all their resources effectively for development, whether these resources come from domestic or foreign sources, and they must submit to searching examinations of their policies by outsiders. The main obligation of the rich countries is to make generous transfers of real resources to help the poorer countries speed up the pace of their economic and social development, even though this means slowing down the rate at which their own citizens get wealthier. Rich countries must also encourage the entry into their markets of goods from the poorer countries, even though this means that some of their own industries will close down.

The rich countries can make it easier for the poorer countries to carry out their obligations within the World Bank Group the more they do to turn the Bank Group into a real partnership between the rich and the poorer nations. The poorer countries can make it easier for the rich nations to carry out their obligations within the Bank Group the better the assurances they give of better use of aid. This means assurances that the specific projects and programs which aid helps to finance are soundly conceived, soundly constructed, and soundly managed, and that the aid-receiving country is making a reasonable effort to mobilize its own resources for development and to use them effectively. It also means that the aid-receiving country is making a reasonable effort, not only to speed up its pace of economic growth, but also to insure that the benefits of this growth are equitably distributed among all groups of its population. For, what induces taxpayers in rich countries to support or acquiesce in appropriations for aid and in concessions to the trade of the poorer countries is that they believe the present disparities of wealth between the rich countries and the poorer countries are morally wrong, in a world in which the poorer countries are so poor and the rich countries are so rich and getting so much richer. They also believe that the great disparities of wealth which exist within the poorer countries are morally wrong. If the aid appropriations and the trade concessions approved by the legislatures of the rich countries can be seen to be helping to raise the standards of living of the poorer two-fifths of the people in the poorer two-thirds of the world, these appropriations and concessions are likely to get more support in the rich countries. If the wealthier people in the poorer two-thirds of the world support policies and programs designed to help the poorer two-fifths of their own fellow citizens, aid is likely to get more support in the rich countries.

The poorer peoples of the world and the poorer countries of the world demand, not only a more equitable sharing of goods, but also a more equitable sharing of power, within nations and in international agencies such as the World Bank Group. A more equitable distribution of the benefits of economic growth within the poorer countries, and the evolution of the Bank Group into a less unequal partnership between the rich countries and the poorer countries, would constitute a recognition by the rich countries and the rich peoples of the world that the poorer countries and the poorer peoples of the world have a right to a reasonable say in running the affairs of the world. The rich must share with the poor not only their goods but also their power.

Many of the suggestions and proposals put forward in this book for making the World Bank Group into a less unequal partnership between the rich countries and the poorer countries will be distasteful to powerful groups in the rich countries. If the carrying out of these suggestions and proposals would result in a moderate shrinkage in the financial resources which the Bank Group would otherwise have acquired, this would be a reasonable price to pay for turning the Bank Group into a less unequal and therefore a more effective partnership. If the carrying out of the suggestions and proposals would result in a severe shrinkage of financial resources, then they would have to be modified or temporarily withdrawn. But it is to be hoped that in the rich countries "statesmen with a wide vision, social consciousness and a sense of history"[1] will accept the responsibility of persuading voters and legislatures to agree to the necessary changes in the World Bank Group of institutions. Great enterprises and little minds go ill together.

I end this book with the concluding sentences of the first report on the Colombo Plan for the development of south and southeast Asia. What was said there in 1950 applies to the developing world in general:

> *Stress has been laid . . . on the poverty of the peoples in the area. In economic terms that is the cardinal fact which must be held in mind. In another sense, however, these countries are rich. They are rich in the dignity of peasants, tilling the soil, and in the wisdom of teachers and scholars. They also possess incalculable capital in the form of the traditions of civilisations which are older than history itself—traditions which have produced treasures of art and learning and which still mould the minds and spirits of their peoples. The worst effect of poverty has been to cloud and circumscribe those human aspects. They must be liberated so that they can contribute toward the self-realisation of individuals, towards the fulfilment of national aspirations, and towards the enhancement of the lives of other peoples throughout the world.*[2]

Acknowledgements

I am very grateful to officers of the World Bank Group and of other agencies who have talked frankly to me off the record about the Bank Group and who have sent me their personal and confidential comments on drafts of chapters of this book. Not one of them will approve of everything I say in this book. I hope, however, that most of them will approve of most of the things I say. They are not responsible for the errors in this book. They are responsible for the book's not containing more errors. The book expresses only my own views.

When I asked officers of the Bank Group and of other agencies to talk to me about the Bank Group or to write to me about it, I told them that I would treat their comments as personal and confidential. I am, therefore, not able to mention by name those who have been especially helpful to me. I can, however, mention by name a number of others to whom I owe a great debt of gratitude. The name of one appears a dozen times in the text or in footnotes. This is I. G. Patei, for many years the senior public servant in the Indian department of economic affairs. But the references to him by name in the text do not exhaust his influence on what I have written. Another is Geoffrey Wilson, at one time a vice-president of the World Bank, and later head of the British international development agency. Edward S. Mason and Robert E. Asher have been generous in their advice. I owe much to Archibald Day of Kingston, Ontario, and I am particularly grateful to the Adlai Stevenson Institute, the publisher of this book, of which I was a Fellow during a part of its preparation, and to its editor, Susan Philipson. The Institute, devoted to study and action on the problems of poverty, pollution, population pressure, and peace-seeking, is a particularly congenial place for constructive work aimed at solving our most desperate problems.

I am grateful to the Canada Council for a grant toward my expenses in writing this book. I am also grateful to Queen's University in Kingston, Ontario, where I was Skelton-Clark fellow in the year 1972-73. In the stimulating yet peaceful atmosphere of Queen's University, I completed the writing of this book.

Some of the material in chapters 5, 6, 7, 15, 21 and 23 appeared in *Foreign Affairs* for July 1973.

E.R.

ANNEX ONE
SUMMARY OF PRINCIPAL PROPOSALS

Partnership

1. The votes of the low-income countries in the governing bodies of the Bank and IDA should be increased from the present ratio of 25 per cent in the Bank and 29 per cent in IDA to 33 per cent and 37 per cent by amending the articles of agreement of those bodies to give member countries thirty additional votes in the Bank and ninety in IDA for every one million of their population.

2. The proportion of influential posts in the management and professional staff of the Bank Group held by nationals of developing countries should be substantially increased.

3. The rich countries which are members of the Bank Group and of the Development Assistance Committee of OECD should insure the participation of representatives of developing countries in discussions in DAC regarding the assistance they are receiving from the members of that Committee.

4. At the periodic meetings between the president (or a member of the management or senior professional staff) of the Bank Group and representatives of a developing country, there should be discussions not only of the developing country's development strategy, but also of the strategy, tactics, and organization of the Bank Group.

5. The Bank Group should pay greater attention in recruiting, training, and promoting professional staff to their capacity both to comprehend the economic, political and social problems of developing countries and to become skillful development diplomats.

Jobs and Justice

6. The Bank Group should increase substantially the help it now gives to its developing member countries to work out and implement development strategies and projects leading to a high rate of increase in the production of essential goods and services, and to a high level of employment on productive work at proper pay.

7. To encourage and assist its developing member countries to pursue the objectives of more jobs and greater social justice, the Bank and IDA should increase greatly the proportion of their loans used to finance local costs. Further, the Bank Group should, in association with the other agencies concerned, establish a fund to bear the costs of failures in experimental, employment-maximizing projects; it should contribute $100 million a year to this fund for five years, the money to be spent over a period of ten years. Any amendments to the articles of agreement which may be required in this endeavour should be agreed to by the member countries.

8. The Bank Group should devote generous financial and intellectual resources to assisting its developing—especially its very poor—member countries to work out and finance employment-maximizing programs and projects in construction, small industries, rural development works, tourism, and retirement villages, with a high real rate of economic return.

Management Skills and Technology

9. The Bank Group should do more to help its developing member countries surmount or avoid the obstacles to their economic growth created by the scarcity in these countries of management ability, administrative resources, and entrepreneurial energy, and by the difficulty of adapting the capital-intensive technologies of the rich countries to the needs of the poorer countries where capital is scarce and labor abundant. To this end, the Bank Group should provide adequate financial assistance toward the establishment and effective operation of national and regional institutes in the developing countries for training in management and business administration, and for conducting practical research on problems of management and business administration and on technological adaptation and innovation.

10. To build up the competence of local suppliers and contractors, to launch them into international competition, and to expand the size of their potential market, the Bank Group should, in selected countries over defined periods of years, increase the preference of 15 per cent now given to local suppliers and contractors over foreign firms so that they will receive a fair proportion of Bank Group contracts.

11. The Bank Group should give special training to selected members of its professional staff in helping borrowing countries to work out techniques and technologies appropriate to developing countries where capital is scarce and labor is abundant.

Trade

12. The Bank Group should, in each of its periodic country economic reports, note (on the basis of information furnished it by GATT) difficulties faced by the country in gaining access to markets in certain named rich countries.

13. The Bank Group should do more to help its developing member countries participate more effectively in international commodity arrangements under which the producers would secure stable and remunerative prices for primary products, especially tea, coffee, and cocoa.

14. The rich member countries of the Bank Group should agree to move progressively over a certain fixed period, perhaps ten years, toward the abolition of all tariff and non-tariff barriers to all imports from low-income countries (those with less than $440 GNP per capita).

Terms of Lending by the Bank

15. Countries which can raise some but not all of the capital they need on reasonable terms in the world's private capital markets (market-

eligible countries) should be charged a rate of interest on Bank loans 1½ percentage points above the current cost of Bank borrowing.

16. When the current cost of Bank borrowing falls below 6¾ per cent, all other countries which borrow from the Bank should be charged a rate of interest on Bank loans ½ of 1 percentage point above the current cost of Bank borrowing.

17. Bank loans to market-eligible countries should have maturities of 10 to 15 years and grace periods of 1 to 5 years. Bank loans to middle-income countries, which are not market-eligible, should have maturities of 20 to 25 years and grace periods of 1 to 10 years. Bank loans to low-income countries, which are not market-eligible, should have maturities of 30 years with grace periods of 10 years. The grace periods on loans to market-eligible countries and middle-income countries should be related to the gestation period of the project financed by the loan.

18. About one eighth of IDA's resources should be used to pay to the Bank the present value of the interest for the first ten years on Bank loans to low-income countries which are eligible for loans from IDA, which do not at present qualify for substantial loans from the Bank because of low credit-worthiness, but which in ten years' time are likely to be able to service substantial loans from the Bank.

Terms of Lending by IDA

19. IDA credits should have a maturity of 30, not 50, years, and should be renegotiable in the twentieth year at the request of the borrower. If at that time the borrower's credit-worthiness is still low, the credit should be extended for another 10 to 20 years, making its total length 40 or 50 years. The annual amortization payments in the second decade of the credit should be increased from 1 per cent to 2½ per cent. For subsequent periods, the annual amortization payments should be 7½ per cent on 30-year credits, 3¾ per cent on 40-year credits, and 2½ on 50-year credits.

Sources of Bank Funds

20. To provide the Bank with an additional $2,200 million of interest-free capital, the capital of the Bank should be doubled, and 10 per cent of the new capital paid in.

21. To reduce the dependence of the Bank on private capital markets in rich countries, all the members of the Bank (and Switzerland) should agree that their central banks hold 5 per cent of their reserves in special World Bank bonds. Whenever a central bank's holdings of those Bank bonds rises above 5 per cent of its reserves, the Bank should buy the surplus back from the central bank. This would not affect the right of central banks to hold other issues of World Bank bonds in addition to these special bonds.

Sources of IDA Funds

22. The members of the Bank in their capacity as members of the

International Monetary Fund should agree that a part of the special drawing rights created by the IMF should be made available to IDA without interest. Perhaps, beginning in 1975, an average of about $1,000 million a year (in 1972 dollars) might be made available to IDA (and $500 million to the regional banks). By 1983, the allocation might be $1,500 million to IDA (and $1,500 million to the regional banks).

23. The members of the Bank should agree to an international treaty providing that royalties on the exploitation of the sea-bed outside national jurisdiction be paid over to IDA, UNDP, and the regional banks.

Sources of IFC Funds

24. The members of IFC should agree to an increase in the paid-in capital from $110 million to $400 million.

25. The members of the Bank should agree to an amendment of the articles of agreement of the Bank permitting IFC to use the proceeds of Bank loans both for equity investment and for loans.

Volume of Lending by the Bank Group

26. The volume of lending by the Bank Group (which doubled in real terms from 1968 to 1972) should double again in real terms from 1972 to 1983. The rate of increase in IDA lending should be greater than in Bank lending; lending by the Bank might go up from the level of $2,000 million in 1972 to about $3,350 million in 1983 (in 1972 dollars), and lending by IDA from the level of $1,000 million in 1972 to about $2,750 million in 1983. (There should be substantial further increases if the government in Peking takes over the Chinese seats in the Bank and IDA, and if the Soviet Union, the Eastern European Communist states, and other countries not now members of the Bank and IDA join the Bank Group.)

Administration

27. The five regional offices of the Bank and IDA now located at the headquarters of the Bank in Washington should be moved to their regions and strengthened by the addition of staff from the economic departments, the legal department, the information department, the administraive department, and the IFC. These regional offices would continue to bear their present responsibility for planning and executing, within approved policy, the lending and technical assistance programs of the Bank and IDA in the member countries in the region.

28. Each regional office should be advised by a regional council containing representatives of member countries both in the region and outside. Regional councils should be given authority to make recommendations on loans below a certain amount which conform to approved Bank Group policy. Such recommendations would be circulated to the executive directors in Washington and, in the absence of objection by an executive director, would become effective within a specified short period after circulation.

29. Whether or not regional offices and councils are established at

regional headquarters, the administration of the Bank Group should be decentralized by both establishing more resident missions and granting them greater authority. Resident missions should be established in each of the dozen or so principal borrowers from the Bank Group. A resident mission should prepare the periodic country economic report as well as feasibility studies and appraisal reports on smaller and more routine projects; conduct the loan negotiations on these projects; and assume responsibility for supervising all projects. If regional offices are established at regional headquarters, they should delegate some of their responsibilities to resident missions, which in turn should report to them.

Other International Agencies

30. The members of the Bank Group which are members of the United Nations should press within the UN for the adoption of such measures as the following so that the Economic and Social Council may become the leader of the international aid community: the establishment by ECOSOC of an executive committee of twelve countries; the appointment by the governments of these countries of full-time, able representatives on this committee; the participation of this committee in an advisory committee of the UN General Assembly, together with the executive heads of the ten principal UN organs and agencies responsible for economic and social matters; and the strengthening of the staff of the economic and social department of the UN.

31. The Bank Group should establish a council to advise it on matters of general policy. This council, whose establishment is mandatory under the articles of agreement of the Bank, would consist of the president of the Bank as chairman and eight members serving in their personal capacities as experts, but selected by the board of governors in agreement with the relevant international agency: FAO, GATT, ILO, IMF, UNCTAD, Unesco, UNIDO, and WHO.

32. The Bank Group should negotiate a formal agreement with ILO (similar to those already concluded with FAO, Unesco, and UNIDO), providing for cooperation by the Bank Group and ILO in assisting member countries to identify and prepare projects for Bank Group consideration, in appraising and supervising these projects, and in providing their technical assistance component. The Bank Group should inform WHO that it wishes to extend the present cooperative agreement, which covers only water supply and sewerage projects, to all projects suitable for Bank Group financing which are of concern to WHO.

33. The Bank Group should do its best to have effective pledging consortia established by 1980 covering about three quarters of the flow of aid to low-income countries from the Bank Group and its member countries.

34. The boards of governors of the IMF and the Bank should request the managing director of the IMF and the president of the Bank to submit a joint report to their boards of directors on measures to increase the effectiveness of the two institutions (including the merging of depart-

ments and services); this report should be referred by the boards of directors to a small joint committee for study and report back to the boards of governors.

National Aid Agencies

35. The Bank Group should be prepared, at the request and at the expense of the aid agency of an aid-giving member country, to appraise projects and to supervise the execution of those the national aid agency decides to finance, provided the request of the agency is concurred in by the aid-receiving country.

36. To increase the efficiency of its own administration, and to help other international aid agencies increase theirs (by such measures as agreeing on common simplified procedures), the Bank Group should hold a discussion on aid administration each year, to which it would invite representatives of the aid administrations of aid-giving and aid-receiving governments, and of international agencies dealing with aid.

Amendments to the Articles of Agreement
(in addition to those recommended in paragraphs 1, 7 and 25 above)

37. So that the Bank and IDA may increase greatly program lending and lending for projects with a large program content, the articles of agreement should be so amended that instead of reading, as they now do, that loans should, except in special circumstances, be for specific projects, the articles should provide that most of the total lending commitments should be for specific projects.

38. To give member governments the same freedom to designate the authority to deal with the Bank as they have for IDA and IFC, the present provision in the Bank's articles of agreement requiring that the Bank and its members should deal with each other through a member's treasury, central bank, stabilization fund, or other similar fiscal agency should be amended to read that each member would designate an appropriate authority with which the Bank would communicate.

ANNEX TWO
STATISTICAL MATERIAL

Table 1. The evolution of the Bank Group, 1960-73.

Table 2. Gross national product and population in 1970 and average growth rate in GNP per capita and in population in the sixties by countries and categories of countries.

Table 3. Bank loans and IDA credits and net transfer for the four fiscal years 1969 to 1972 by categories of countries.

Table 4. Votes in the Bank, IDA, and IMF.

Table 5. Loans and grants by multilateral aid agencies: 1971 and 1972.

TABLE 1

THE EVOLUTION OF THE BANK GROUP 1960-1973[1]

	1960	*1961*	*1962*	*1963*	*1964*	*1965*	*1966*	*1967*	*1968*	*1969*	*1970*	*1971*	*1972*	*1973*
Volume of Operations (current dollars) $ million														
Bank	659	610	882	449	810	1023	839	777[2]	847	1399	1580[2]	1921[3]	1966[2]	2051
IDA	—	101	134	260	283	309	284	353	107	385	606	584	1000	1357
IFC	22	6	21	18	21	26	36	49	51	93	112	101	116	147
Total	681	717	1037	727	1114	1358	1158	1179	1005	1877	2298	2606	3082	3555
Deflator[4]	74	76	76	77	78	79	81	83	84	85	87	91	100	106
Volume of Operations (constant fiscal year 1972 dollars) $ million														
Bank	891	803	1161	583	1038	1295	1036	936	1008	1646	1816	2111	1966	1935
IDA	—	133	176	338	363	391	351	425	127	453	697	642	1000	1280
IFC	30	8	28	23	27	33	43	59	60	109	129	111	116	139
Total	920	943	1364	944	1428	1719	1430	1420	1195	2208	2641	2864	3082	3354
Net transfer to developing countries[5] (current dollars) $ million	NA	NA	121	239	261	369	401	485	458	387	304	497	674	767[12]
Net transfer (constant fiscal year 1972 dollars) $ million	NA	NA	159	310	335	467	495	584	545	455	349	546	674	724
Number of operations[6]														
Bank	31	27	29	28	37	39	37	46	44	82	69	78	72	73
IDA	—	2	16	17	17	18	12	17	16	29	50	51	68	75
IFC[7]	13	10	9	11	18	16	19	11	10	20	26	23	19	25
Total	44	39	54	56	72	73	68	74	70	131	145	152	159	173

TABLE 1
THE EVOLUTION OF THE BANK GROUP 1960-1973[1]

	1960	1961	1962	1963	1964	1965	1966	1967	1968	1969	1970	1971	1972	1973
Administrative Expenses (current dollars) $ million														
Bank	10	12	13	16	19	22	30	31	34	41	45	56	66	79
IDA	—	1	1	2	3	3	3	4	4	4	16	19	27	31
IFC	2	2	2	2	3	3	3	3	4	4	5	7	7	8
Total	12	15	16	20	25	28	36	38	42	49	67	83	100	118
Administrative expenses as percentage of total volume of operating in current dollars	1.8	2.1	1.5	2.8	2.2	2.1	3.1	3.2	4.2	2.6	2.9	3.2	3.2	3.3
Member countries[8]														
Bank	68	68	75	85	102	102	103	106	107	110	113	116	117	122
IDA	—	51	62	76	93	94	96	97	98	102	105	107	108	112
IFC	59	59	63	73	78	78	81	83	86	91	94	96	96	98
Staff[8]														
Bank and IDA														
Professional	316	320	363	429	463	532	667	734	767	961	1170	1348	1516	1711
Non-professional	368	447	509	559	613	668	797	878	950	1046	1202	1402	1611	1752
Total	684	767	872	988	1076	1200	1464	1612	1717	2007	2372	2750	3127	3463
IFC														
Professional	38	42	38	44	47	44	57	56	56	69	81	96	99	108
Non-professional	37	41	38	44	44	46	50	57	56	59	56	71	76	78
Total	75	83	76	88	91	90	107	113	112	128	137	167	175	186
Professional	354	362	401	473	510	576	724	790	823	1030	1251	1444	1615	1819
Non-professional	405	488	547	603	657	714	847	935	1006	1105	1258	1473	1687	1830
Total	759	850	948	1076	1167	1290	1571	1725	1829	2135	2509	2917	3302	3649

Average cost of current Bank borrowing[9]	4.97	4.14	4.54	4.18	4.00	4.69	5.26	5.49	6.34	6.53	7.54	8.03	7.38	6.92
Interest rate on Bank loans[10]	6.06	5.75	5.75	5.54	5.50	5.50	5.75	6.00	6.15	6.48	6.95	7.23	7.25	7.25
Spread between cost of current Bank borrowing and interest rate	1.09	1.61	1.21	1.36	1.50	.81	.49	.51	−.19	−.05	−.59	−.80	−.13	.33
Funded debt of Bank[11] $ million	2073	2228	2521	2519	2492	2724	2806	3075	3290	4081	4569	5424	6951	8882
Reserves of Bank[8] $ million	506	602	699	813	846	895	954	1023	1160	1254	1329	1444	1597	1750

Notes

1. Fiscal year ending June 30. The fiscal year 1972 means the year ending June 30, 1972. The unit of account is the U.S. dollar.

2. Omitting loan to IFC.

3. Beginning in 1971 this figure includes loans approved by the Board of Directors by June 30 but not signed whereas previously loans which had not been signed by June 30 were excluded.

4. The deflator for the years 1960 to 1970 is based on the UN unit value index for machinery exported from developed to developing countries. This index, while not entirely satisfactory, seems to be the best indicator now available of the deterioration of the purchasing power of Bank Group loans. Data for 1960-70 are taken from the UN Monthly Bulletin of Statistics, November 1971. The estimates for 1971-73 are based on the unit value index for all manufactured goods exports from eleven industrial countries. (UN Monthly Bulletin of Statistics, June 1973).

5. Net transfer to developing countries resulting from Bank and IDA loans.

6. IBRD/IDA number of operations excludes loans to IFC and treats operations involving more than one loan agreement or both an IBRD loan and an IDA credit as simply one IBRD operation.

7. Excludes minor investments.

8. On June 30.

9. Weighted by amount and maturity.

10. Weighted by amount only.

11. On June 30. Excludes delayed deliveries.

12. Estimated.

TABLE 2

GROSS NATIONAL PRODUCT AND POPULATION IN 1970 AND AVERAGE ANNUAL GROWTH RATES IN GNP PER CAPITA AND IN POPULATION IN THE SIXTIES BY COUNTRIES AND CATEGORIES OF COUNTRIES

Country Name	Gross National Product			Population	
	Per capita 1970 ($)	Total 1970 ($ billion)	Avg. annual growth rate per capita 1960-70	Total mid-1970 (million)	Avg. annual growth rate 1960-70
RICH COUNTRIES					
United States	4760	975	3.2	205	1.2
Sweden	4040	33	3.8	8	0.7
Kuwait	3760	3	−3.5	1	9.7
Canada	3700	79	3.6	21	1.8
Bermuda	3540	0	7.4	0	2.0
Switzerland*	3320	21	2.5	6	1.5
Denmark	3190	16	3.7	5	0.7
France	3100	157	4.6	51	1.0
Virgin Islands (U.S.)	3050	0	6.4	0	8.8
Germany, West	2930	180	3.5	62	1.0
Luxembourg	2890	1	2.5	0	0.8
Norway	2860	11	4.1	4	0.8
Guam	2840	0	6.1	0	2.7
Australia	2820	35	3.1	13	2.0
Belgium	2720	26	4.0	10	0.6
New Zealand	2700	8	2.1	3	1.7
Canal Zone	2500	0	7.0	0	4.0
Germany (East)*	2490	43	4.2	17	0.0
Netherlands	2430	32	3.9	13	1.3
New Caledonia	2430	0	3.3	0	3.2
Finland	2390	11	3.9	5	0.6
United Arab Emirates	2390	1	18.5	0	9.3

Country Name	Gross National Product			Population	
	Per capita 1970 ($)	Total 1970 ($ billion)	Avg. annual growth rate per capita 1960-70	Total mid-1970 (million)	Avg. annual growth rate 1960-70
Bahama Islands	2300	0	3.4	0	4.1
United Kingdom	2270	127	2.2	56	0.6
Czechoslovakia*	2230	32	3.8	14	0.6
Iceland	2150	0	3.1	0	1.6
Austria	2010	15	3.9	7	0.5
Faeroe Islands	2000	0	4.9	0	1.0
Israel	1960	6	4.7	3	3.2
Japan	1920	199	9.6	103	1.0
French Polynesia	1890	0	8.3	0	3.1
Channel Islands	1810	0	6.9	0	1.2
USSR*	1790	435	5.8	243	1.2
Libya	1770	3	20.4	2	3.7
Italy	1760	95	4.6	54	0.8
Greenland	1730	0	2.1	0	3.9
Qatar	1730	0	0.5	0	9.1
Puerto Rico	1650	5	5.8	3	1.8
Hungary*	1600	16	5.4	10	0.3
Members	3210	2019	4.1	629	1.1
Non-Members	1880	547	5.4	291	1.1
Total	2790	2567	4.4	920	1.1
MIDDLE-INCOME COUNTRIES					
Poland*	1400	46	5.2	33	1.0
Isle of Man	1390	0	1.7	0	1.2
Netherlands Antilles	1380	0	−1.3	0	1.5

Ireland	1360	4	3.6	3	0.4
Brunei	1220	0	−0.4	0	3.6
Argentina	1160	27	2.5	23	1.5
Greece	1090	10	6.6	9	0.7
Gibraltar	1090	0	0.5	0	1.1
Ryukyu Islands	1050	1	10.6	1	0.7
Spain	1020	34	6.1	34	1.1
Venezuela	980	10	2.3	10	3.5
Hong Kong	970	4	8.4	4	2.5
Cyprus	950	1	5.3	1	1.1
French Guiana	940	0	8.4	0	3.7
Romania*	930	19	7.7	20	0.9
Singapore	920	2	5.2	2	2.4
Martinique	910	0	10.0	0	1.7
Trinidad and Tobago	860	1	1.9	1	2.1
Uruguay	820	2	−0.4	3	1.3
Malta	810	0	5.8	0	0.0
Reunion	800	0	4.6	0	2.9
American Samoa	780	0	10.0	0	1.3
Bulgaria*	760	6	7.4	8	0.8
Guadeloupe	760	0	8.4	0	1.8
South Africa	760	17	3.0	22	3.0
Panama	730	1	4.2	1	3.3
Chile	720	7	1.6	10	2.3
Mexico	670	34	3.7	51	3.5
Jamaica	670	1	3.5	2	1.6
French Ter. of Afars and Issas.	670	0	5.3	0	1.6
Portugal	660	6	5.3	10	0.9
Yugoslavia	650	13	4.3	21	1.1
Gabon	630	0	5.1	0	1.0

Country Name	Gross National Product			Population	
	Per capita 1970 ($)	Total 1970 ($ billion)	Avg. annual growth rate per capita 1960-70	Total mid-1970 (million)	Avg. annual growth rate 1960-70
Albania*	600	1	4.8	2	2.9
Lebanon	590	2	0.5	3	2.5
British Honduras	590	0	1.9	0	2.8
Barbados	570	0	3.4	0	1.1
Costa Rica	560	1	3.2	2	3.3
Bahrain	550	0	2.8	0	3.5
Cuba*	530	4	−0.6	8	2.1
Surinam	530	0	5.2	0	3.4
Mongolia*	460	1	0.0	1	3.0
Peru	450	6	1.4	14	3.1
Saudi Arabia	440	3	8.0	7	1.7
Members	810	190	4.1	236	2.2
Non-Members*	1060	78	5.6	73	1.2
Total	870	268	4.5	309	2.0
POOR COUNTRIES					
Nicaragua	430	1	2.8	2	3.5
Fiji Islands	430	0	2.5	1	2.8
New Hebrides	430	0	4.9	0	2.4
Brazil	420	38	2.4	93	2.9
Zambia	400	2	7.1	4	2.5
Gilbert and Ellice Is.	390	0	−1.5	0	2.0
Sao Tome and Principe	390	0	2.4	0	0.0
Taiwan	390	5	7.1	14	2.9
Iran	380	11	5.4	29	2.9
Malaysia	380	4	3.1	11	3.1

Antigua	370	0	5.2	0	1.5
Guyana	370	0	1.1	1	2.8
Guatemala	360	2	2.0	5	3.1
Trust Ter. of the Pacific Is.	360	0	3.4	0	2.8
Oman	350	0	17.1	1	2.0
Dominican Rep.	350	1	0.5	4	3.0
St. Lucia	340	0	8.1	0	2.7
Colombia	340	7	1.7	22	3.2
Korea (North)*	330	5	5.1	14	2.7
Ceuta And Melilla	330	0	3.7	0	−1.3
Iraq	320	3	2.5	10	3.5
St. Kitts-Nevis-Anguilla	320	0	4.9	0	0.2
Turkey	310	11	3.9	35	2.5
Ghana	310	3	−0.4	9	2.6
Ivory Coast	310	2	4.5	5	3.0
El Salvador	300	1	1.7	4	3.7
Grenada	300	0	5.6	0	1.5
Papua New Guinea	300	1	4.5	2	2.3
Algeria	300	4	1.7	14	3.1
Angola	300	2	3.2	6	1.3
Congo	300	0	4.8	1	1.5
Syria	290	2	3.4	6	2.9
Ecuador	290	2	1.7	6	3.4
Tonga	290	0	−2.9	0	3.3
Honduras	280	1	1.8	3	3.3
Dominica	280	0	3.7	0	2.2
Rhodesia	280	1	0.4	5	3.3
Spanish Sahara	270	0	4.4	0	1.8
Paraguay	260	1	1.3	2	3.1
Korea (South)	250	8	6.8	32	2.6

Country Name	Gross National Product			Population	
	Per capita 1970 ($)	Total 1970 ($ billion)	Avg. annual growth rate per capita 1960-70	Total mid-1970 (million)	Avg. annual growth rate 1960-70
Tunisia	250	1	0.5	5	3.0
Portugese Guinea	250	0	4.9	1	0.7
Jordan	250	1	2.9	2	3.5
St. Vincent	240	0	3.4	0	1.9
Mozambique	240	2	3.4	8	1.9
Liberia	240	0	0.9	2	3.0
Mauritius	240	0	−0.7	1	2.4
Morocco	230	4	1.0	15	2.9
Senegal	230	1	0.0	4	2.1
Philippines	210	8	2.9	37	3.0
Egypt	210	7	1.7	33	2.5
Equatorial Guinea	210	0	3.6	0	1.8
Thailand	200	7	4.9	36	3.1
Vietnam (South)	200	4	1.0	18	2.6
Sierra Leone	190	0	4.7	3	1.4
Bolivia	180	1	2.5	5	2.6
British Solomon Islands	180	0	−0.8	0	2.7
Cameroon	180	1	3.8	6	2.1
Swaziland	180	0	5.2	0	2.9
Cape Verde Islands	160	0	1.0	0	2.4
Members	300	150	3.2	502	2.8
Non-Members*	330	5	5.1	14	2.7
Total	300	155	3.2	516	2.8
VERY POOR COUNTRIES					
China*	150	122	2.1	836	2.0

Macao	150	0	−4.3	0	6.2
Kenya	150	2	3.6	11	3.1
Western Samoa	140	0	−1.1	0	2.6
Togo	140	0	1.2	2	2.9
Central African Rep.	140	0	0.2	2	2.6
Mauritania	140	0	4.5	1	1.9
Comoro Islands	140	0	3.5	0	2.3
Khmer	130	1	0.1	7	3.2
Uganda	130	1	2.4	10	2.7
Malagasy Rep.	130	1	1.2	7	2.6
Pakistan	120	7	3.1	58	2.6
Laos	120	0	1.9	3	2.4
Yemen (South)	120	0	−5.0	1	2.3
Nigeria	120	7	0.1	55	2.9
Sudan	120	2	1.0	16	2.9
Guinea	120	0	2.7	4	2.6
Gambia	120	0	1.1	0	2.0
India	110	57	1.2	538	2.3
Sri Lanka	110	1	1.5	13	2.4
Haiti	110	1	−0.9	5	2.0
Portuguese Timor	110	0	1.3	1	1.5
Botswana	110	0	1.4	1	2.0
Vietnam (North)*	100	2	3.2	21	2.8
Maldive Islands	100	0	1.2	0	1.6
Tanzania	100	1	3.6	13	2.5
Zaire	90	2	2.7	19	2.8
Niger	90	0	−2.0	4	2.9
Dahomey	90	0	0.1	3	2.9
Lesctho	90	0	0.0	1	2.0
Yemen (North)	80	0	2.0	6	2.2

Country Name	Gross National Product			Population	
	Per capita 1970 ($)	Total 1970 ($ billion)	Avg. annual growth rate per capita 1960-70	Total mid-1970 (million)	Avg. annual growth rate 1960-70
Sikkim	80	0	0.0	0	2.1
Bangladesh	80	6	1.5	72	2.8
Indonesia	80	9	1.0	116	2.0
Ethiopia	80	2	2.8	25	2.2
Malawi	80	0	2.1	4	2.6
Chad	80	0	0.4	4	1.8
Burma	80	2	0.6	28	2.1
Afghanistan	80	1	0.5	14	2.0
Nepal	80	1	0.5	11	1.8
Bhutan	70	0	0.2	1	1.7
Mali	70	0	4.4	5	2.1
Somalia	70	0	−1.1	3	2.4
Seychelles Islands	70	0	−0.4	0	2.2
Upper Volta	60	0	−0.6	5	2.1
Rwanda	60	0	1.5	4	3.0
Burundi	60	0	0.8	4	2.0
Members	100	108	1.3	1076	2.4
Non-Members*	140	124	2.1	857	2.0
Total	120	232	1.8	1933	2.2

SUMMARY

	Gross National Product			Population	
	Per Cap 1970 ($)	Total 1970 ($ billion)	Avg. annual growth rate per capita 1960–70	Total mid-1970 (million)	Avg. annual growth rate 1960–70
Rich					
Members	3,210	2,019	4.1	629	1.1
Non-members	1,880	547	5.4	291	1.1
Total	2,790	2,567	4.4	920	1.1
Middle					
Members	810	190	4.1	236	2.2
Non-members	1,060	78	5.6	73	1.2
Total	870	268	4.5	309	2.0
Poor					
Members	300	150	3.2	502	2.8
Non-members	330	5	5.1	14	2.7
Total	300	155	3.2	516	2.8
Very Poor					
Members	100	108	1.3	1,076	2.4
Non-members	140	124	2.1	857	2.0
Total	120	232	1.8	1,933	2.2
Total					
Members	1,010	2,468	3.9	2,442	2.1
Non-members	610	754	4.9	1,236	1.8
Total	880	3,222	4.1	3,678	2.0

FOOTNOTES TO TABLE 2

The estimates for each country are from the *World Bank Atlas* for 1972. The *Atlas* contains the following statements about these estimates. The estimates of GNP are calculated at market prices; they include indirect taxes net of subsidies; they thus relate more closely to the value of goods and services as they are sold in the marketplace than estimates of GNP at factor cost. The conversion of GNP from national currencies to U.S. dollars is essentially on the basis of official exchange rates; in several cases, however, the rates have been adjusted to correspond more closely to realistic market rates and levels of economic activity. The base period for the conversion of national currencies to dollars is the period 1965–71. In view of the usual errors inherent in this type of data and to avoid a misleading impression of accuracy, the figures for GNP per capita have been rounded to the nearest $10. The estimates for Communist countries of GNP per capita and its growth rate have a wide margin of error mainly because of problems in deriving the GNP at market prices from net material product and in converting the GNP estimate into U.S. dollars. The estimates of GNP per capita and its growth rate in Jordan, Mauritania, Togo, Laos, Guinea, and in countries with GNP's per capita of under $100 are tentative. Some estimates of under $100 are based on data that have a large margin of error, and are thus likely to be less reliable than estimates of over $100. The growth rate for GNP per capita for Algeria is for the period 1963–70, not 1960–70.

The *World Bank Atlas* for 1972 gives the following information for "Pakistan and Bangladesh": population 130 million; annual growth rate in population 2.7 per cent; GNP $12,820 million; annual growth rate in GNP per capita 2.4 per cent. This has been changed to:

Pakistan: population, 58 million; annual growth rate in population 2.6 per cent; GNP $7,000 million; annual growth rate in GNP per capita 3.1 per cent; GNP per capita $120.

Bangladesh: population, 72 million; annual growth rate in population 2.8 per cent; GNP $5,800 million; annual growth rate in GNP per capita 1.5 per cent; GNP per capita $80.

The *World Bank Atlas* for 1972 estimates the GNP per capita of China as $160. This is an error; it should be $150, since the total GNP of $121,870 million divided by the population of 836 million gives a GNP per capita of $146. China is therefore shown in this table with a GNP per capita of $150.

Gross national product is given to the nearest billion (1,000 million); this means that countries with a GNP of less than $500 million are shown as having a zero GNP. Population is given to the nearest million; this means that countries with populations of less than 500,000 are shown as having a zero population.

An asterisk denotes countries which are not members of the World Bank. "China" is shown as a non-member and "Taiwan" as a member, but this is short-hand for saying that in 1970 the member state China was represented in the World Bank by persons appointed by the government in Taiwan, not by persons appointed by the government in Peking. Romania, which became a member of the Bank in December 1972, is shown as a non-member in this table. Countries which are not fully self-governing are shown as members if the country in control of their foreign relations is a member.

The names of eleven countries as given in the *World Bank Atlas* have been shortened or simplified. Thus, "Korea, Rep. of" is referred to as "Korea (South)" and "Egypt, Arab Rep. of" is referred to as "Egypt."

TABLE 3
BANK LOANS AND IDA CREDITS AND NET TRANSFER
Fiscal Years 1969, 1970, 1971, 1972.

		LOANS						
		Annual average 1969, 1970, 1971				1972		
	Popn. (1970	Bank	IDA ($ million)	Total	per cap. ($)	Bank	IDA ($ million)	Total
Rich	629	40	—	40	.06	38	—	38
Middle-income	236	488	—	488	2.07	574	—	574
Poor	502	845	93	938	1.87	1,127	225	1,352
Very poor								
India	538	27	208	235	.44	60	412	472
Others	538	234	224	458	.85	167	362	530
Total	1,076	261	432	693	.65	227	775	1,002
Total	2,443	1,633	525	2,158	.90	1,966	1,000	2,966

		NET TRANSFER						
		Annual average 1969, 1970, 1971				1972		
	Popn. (1970	Bank	IDA ($ million)	Total	per cap. ($)	Bank	IDA ($ million)	Total
Rich	629	−184	—	−184	−.30	−210	—	−210
Middle-income	236	77	—	77	.33	98	—	97
Poor	502	121	41	161	.32	275	50	327
Very poor								
India	538	−37	77	40	.07	−35	79	44
Others	538	27	82	109	.20	92	109	201
Total	1,076	−10	159	148	.14	57	188	245
Total	2,443	4	199	203	.08	222	237	460

TABLE 4
VOTES IN THE BANK, IDA AND IMF

RICH COUNTRIES	GNP per capita 1970 ($)	Popn. mid-1970 (million)	Votes in Bank Dec. 31, 1972	Votes in IDA Dec. 11, 1972	Revised votes in Bank (1)	Revised votes in IDA (2)	Votes in IMF Nov. 11, 1972
United States	4760	205	63,750	210,927	69,900	229,377	67,250
Sweden	4040	8	3,023	22,538	3,263	23,258	3,500
Kuwait	3760	1	917	4,089	947	4,179	900
Canada	3700	21	9,668	32,464	10,298	34,354	11,250
Denmark	3190	5	2,461	8,922	2,611	9,372	2,850
France	3100	51	13,042	38,284	14,572	42,874	15,250
Germany (West)	2930	62	13,903	49,874	15,763	55,454	16,250
Luxembourg	2890	0	450	2,010	465	2,055	450
Norway	2860	4	1,850	6,739	1,970	7,099	2,650
Australia	2820	13	5,580	13,079	5,970	14,249	6,900
Belgium	2720	10	5,795	9,597	6,095	10,497	6,750
New Zealand	2700	3	1,966		2,056		2,270
Netherlands	2430	13	6,173	15,989	6,563	17,159	7,250
Finland	2390	5	1,871	4,037	2,021	4,492	2,150
United Arab Emirates	2390	0	378		393		400
United Kingdom	2270	56	26,250	71,857	27,930	76,897	28,250
Iceland	2150	0	434	1,806	449	1,851	480
Austria	2010	7	2,554	5,232	2,764	5,862	2,950
Israel	1960	3	1,209	836	1,299	1,106	1,550
Japan	1920	103	10,480	30,541	13,570	39,811	12,250
Libya	1770	2	450	702	510	882	490
Italy	1760	54	6,910	4,132	8,530	8,992	10,250
Qatar	1730	0	421		436		450
Total		626	179,535	533,655	198,375	589,820	202,740

(1) Thirty additional votes for every one million of population. Fifteen additional votes for countries with populations of less than 500,000.

(2) Ninety additional votes for every one million population. Forty-five additional votes for countries with populations of less than 500,000.

MIDDLE-INCOME COUNTRIES	GNP per cap. 1970 ($)	Popn. mid-1970 (million)	Votes in Bank Dec. 31, 1972	Votes in IDA Dec. 11, 1972	Revised votes in Bank	Revised votes in IDA	Votes in IMF Nov. 11, 1972
Ireland	1360	3	1,282	3,825	1,372	4,095	1,460
Argentina	1160	23	3,983	14,661	4,673	16,731	4,650
Greece	1090	9	917	1,004	1,187	1,814	1,630
Spain	1020	34	2,917	8,673	3,937	11,733	4,200
Venezuela	980	10	2,222		2,522		3,550
Cyprus	950	1	472	652	502	742	510
Romania	930	20	1,871		2,471		2,150
Singapore	920	2	570		630		620
Trinidad & Tobago	860	1	717		747		880
Uruguay	820	3	661		751		940
Malta	810	0					410
South Africa	760	22	2,383	3,777	3,043	5,757	3,450
Panama	730	1	426	504	456	594	610
Chile	720	10	1,183	1,206	1,483	2,106	1,830
Mexico	670	51	2,530	2,248	4,060	6,838	3,950
Jamaica	670	2	696		756		780
Portugal	660	10	1,050		1,350		1,420
Yugoslavia	650	21	1,317	4,525	1,947	6,415	2,320
Gabon	630	0	350	600	365	645	400
Lebanon	590	3	340	590	430	860	340
Barbados	570	0					380

	GNP per cap. 1970($)	Popn. mid-1970 (million)	Votes in Bank Dec. 31, 1972	Votes in IDA Dec. 11, 1972	Revised votes in Bank	Revised votes in IDA	Votes in IMF Nov. 11, 1972
Costa Rica	560	2	357	1,892	417	2,072	570
Bahrain	550	0	335		350		350
Peru	450	14	885	854	1,305	2,114	1,480
Saudi Arabia	440	7	1,393	1,240	1,603	1,870	1,590
Total		249	28,857	46,251	36,357	64,386	40,470
POOR COUNTRIES							
Nicaragua	430	2	330	560	390	740	520
Fiji	430	1	361		391		380
Brazil	420	93	3,983	14,661	6,773	23,031	4,650
Zambia	400	4	783	1,038	903	1,398	1,010
Taiwan	390	14	7,750	22,503	8,170	23,763	5,750
Iran	380	29	1,830	1,408	2,700	4,018	2,170
Malaysia	380	11	1,583	3,480	1,913	4,470	2,110
Guyana	370	1	410	2,308	440	2,398	450
Guatemala	360	5	373	2,022	523	2,472	610
Oman	350	1	310		340		320
Dominican Republic	350	4	393	2,022	513	2,382	680
Colombia	340	22	1,183	4,168	1,843	6,148	1,820
Iraq	320	10	890	2,273	1,190	3,173	1,340
Turkey	310	35	1,400	5,733	2,450	8,883	1,760
Ghana	310	9	984	3,372	1,254	4,182	1,120
Ivory Coast	310	5	450	2,437	600	2,887	770
El Salvador	300	4	370	560	490	920	600
Algeria	300	14	1,050	1,306	1,470	2,566	1,550

Congo	300	1	350	600	380	690	380
Syria	290	6	650	2,400	830	2,940	750
Ecuador	290	6	421	2,200	601	2,740	580
Honduras	280	3	330	560	420	830	500
Paraguay	260	2	310	1,951	370	2,131	440
Korea (South)	250	32	932	2,615	1,892	5,495	1,050
Tunisia	250	5	623	2,793	773	3,243	730
Jordan	250	2	412	560	473	740	480
Liberia	240	2	463	2,273	523	2,453	540
Mauritius	240	1	438	2,344	468	2,434	470
Morocco	230	15	1,210	4,168	1,660	5,518	1,380
Senegal	230	4	583	836	703	1,196	590
Philippines	210	37	1,572	5,211	2,682	8,541	1,800
Egypt	210	33	1,671	5,231	2,661	8,201	2,130
Equatorial Guinea	210	0	314	1,967	329	2,012	330
Thailand	200	36	1,393	3,825	2,473	7,055	1,590
Vietnam (South)	200	18	677	2,793	1,217	4,413	870
Sierra Leone	190	3	400	652	490	922	500
Bolivia	180	5	460	2,473	610	2,923	620
Cameroon	180	6	450	702	630	1,242	600
Swaziland	180	0	314	1,968	329	2,013	330
Total		481	38,407	117,973	52,867	161,163	44,270
VERY POOR COUNTRIES							
Kenya	150	11	583	2,904	913	3,894	730
Togo	140	2	400	2,273	460	2,453	400
Western Samoa	140	0					270

	GNP per cap. 1970($)	Popn. mid-1970 (million)	Votes in Bank Dec. 31, 1972	Votes in IDA Dec. 11, 1972	Revised votes in Bank	Revised votes in IDA	Votes in IMF Nov. 11, 1972
Central African Republic	140	2	350	600	410	780	380
Mauritania	140	1	350	2,093	380	2,183	380
Khmer Republic	130	7	453	2,452	663	3,082	500
Uganda	130	10	583	2,904	883	3,804	650
Malagasy Republic	130	7	469	702	679	1,332	510
Pakistan	120	58	2,250	8,673	3,990	13,893	2,600
Laos	120	3	350	2,093	440	2,363	380
Yemen (South)	120	1	485	2,561	515	2,651	540
Nigeria	120	55	1,317	4,057	2,967	9,007	1,600
Sudan	120	16	850	2,437	1,330	3,877	970
Guinea	120	4	450	2,437	570	2,797	490
Gambia	120	0	303	1,931	318	1,976	320
India	110	538	9,250	29,426	25,390	77,846	9,650
Sri Lanka	110	13	1,077	3,825	1,467	4,995	1,230
Haiti	110	5	400	652	550	1,102	440
Botswana	110	1	282	1,859	312	1,949	300
Tanzania	100	13	583	2,904	973	4,074	670
Zaire	90	19	1,210	3,823	1,780	5,533	1,380
Niger	90	4	350	600	470	960	380
Dahomey	90	3	350	600	440	870	380
Lesotho	90	1	282	1,859	312	1,949	300
Yemen (North)	80	6	335	2,041	515	2,581	350
Bangladesh	80	72	1,317	5,444	3,477	11,924	1,500
Indonesia	80	116	2,450	9,360	5,930	19,800	2,850
Ethiopia	80	25	364	2,093	1,114	4,343	520
Malawi	80	4	400	2,273	520	2,633	400

Chad	80	4	350	2,093	470	2,453	380
Burma	80	28	757	3,138	1,597	5,658	850
Afghanistan	80	14	550	2,437	970	3,697	620
Nepal	80	11	362	2,093	692	3,083	366
Mali	70	5	423	674	573	1,124	470
Somalia	70	3	400	652	490	922	440
Upper Volta	60	5	350	600	500	1,050	380
Rwanda	60	4	400	652	520	1,012	440
Burundi	60	4	400	2,273	520	2,633	440
Total		1,075	31,835	119,488	64,100	216,283	35,456
Total of Totals— All Countries		2,431	278,634	817,367	351,699	1,031,652	322,936

SUMMARY OF VOTES

	Popn.* mid-1970 (million)	Votes in Bank Dec. 31, 1972	Votes in IDA Dec. 11, 1972	Revised votes in Bank	Revised votes in IDA	Votes in IMF Nov. 11, 1972
Rich Countries	626	179,535	533,655	198,375	589,820	202,740
Middle-Income Countries	249	28,857	46,251	36,357	64,386	40,470
Poor Countries	481	38,407	117,973	52,867	161,163	44,270
Very Poor Countries	1,075	31,835	119,488	64,100	216,283	35,456
Total	2,431	278,634	817,367	351,699	1,031,652	322,936

VOTES IN PERCENTAGES

Rich Countries	26	64	65	56	57	63
Middle-Income Countries	10	10	6	10	6	13
Poor Countries	20	14	14	15	16	14
Very Poor Countries	44	11	15	18	21	11
Total	100	100	100	100	100	100

*These population figures are not the same as the population figures in Tables 2 and 3, which are: rich countries, 629 million; middle-income countries, 236 million; poor countries, 502 million; and very poor countries, 1,078 million. One reason for the difference is that Tables 2 and 3 include as members of the Bank Group non-self-governing territories, such as Hong Kong, Angola, Rhodesia, and Mozambique, which are not separate members of the Bank, IDA, or IMF. Another reason for the difference is that Romania, which became a member in December 1972, is not included as a member in Tables 2 and 3 but is included as a member in Table 4.

TABLE 5
LOANS AND GRANTS BY MULTILATERAL AID AGENCIES

	$ million			
	Ordinary	Special	Other	Total
Regional Banks				
African	25	—	—	25
Asian	202	51	—	253
Caribbean	2	2	1	6
East African	6	—	—	6
Inter-American	238	400	31	669
Total	473	453	32	959
Other Agencies				
European Development Fund	227	21	—	248
UNDP (omitting administrative budget of $56 million)	—	224	—	224
Total	227	245	—	472
Total	700	698	32	1,431
BANK GROUP				
Bank	1,966	—	—	1,966
IDA	—	1,000	—	1,000
IFC	116	—	—	116
Total Bank Group	2,082	1,000	—	3,082

NOTE: The figures for the World Bank Group are for the fiscal year ending June 30, 1972. The figures for the other agencies are for the calendar year 1971. Ordinary lending is on terms equivalent to lending by the World Bank. Special lending is on concessionary terms.

ANNEX THREE

NOTE ON THE LIMITATIONS ON THE USEFULNESS OF ESTIMATES OF GROSS NATIONAL PRODUCT PER CAPITA

The first set of difficulties in estimating the GNP of a country lies in defining what goods and services are to be included in it, in applying the definitions, and in choosing index numbers. These difficulties are discussed in Appendix 1, "Reliability of national accounts data," of the OECD publication of December 1970, "The Growth of Output 1960-80." Then there is the problem of the reliability of the statistical observations of the volume of those goods and services which it has been decided should be included in the GNP. Here the margins of error are likely to be larger the less developed or the poorer the country. The volume of goods and services has to be valued in terms of local currency; here further errors are inevitable.

Estimates of GNP in local currency must be translated into a common unit of measurement if they are to be usable as tools in calculations or analysis relative to countries with different currencies. The U.S. dollar is normally the unit of measurement. The *World Bank Atlas* for 1972 summarized the difficulties in converting from local currencies to the U.S. dollar:

> For purposes of international comparison, GNP estimates in US dollar equivalents should be derived, ideally, on the basis of purchasing power parities or through direct real product comparisons. To date, however, only a limited number of countries have been covered by such studies.

Therefore, the conversion from estimates of GNP in local currency to estimates in terms of U.S. dollars are made "essentially on the basis of official exchange rates," and this can lead to distorted results. More important, "exchange rates equate at best the prices of internationally traded goods and services only. They may bear little relationship to the goods and services not entering international trade, which, in most developing countries, form the bulk of the national product. Agricultural products and services in particular are generally priced lower in relation to industrial output in developing than in industrialized countries—and agriculture typically accounts for much the largest share of total product in the developing countries. The result is that the currency conversion method used tends to exaggerate the real income differences between less developed and more developed countries." The *World Bank Atlas* in 1972 estimated Japan's GNP per capita in 1970 as $1,920 and South Korea's as $250, but it is hardly likely that the real average income in Japan in 1970 was almost eight times that in South Korea.

But, in spite of all this, per capita GNP works reasonably well as a short-hand device for expressing a country's relative poverty. This is demonstrated by an examination of the list of the twenty-five "least-developed" countries, prepared by the UN Committee on Development Planning and approved by the UN General Assembly on November 18, 1971.[1] A simple decision that the two criteria for inclusion in this category were a per capita GNP of not more than $120 and a population of not more than 16 million would have resulted in much the same list. Under these two criteria, Uganda and Western Samoa would not have been included in the category of "least developed," because their per capita GNP's are over $120. Ethiopia would not have been included because it has a population of 25 million. South Yemen and Sri Lanka would have been included.

On the value of estimates of growth in GNP per capita, the UN Committee for Development Planning has said:

> Although the rate of growth of gross product per head is by no means an adequate indicator of economic and social progress—since it does not fully reflect such major conditions of development as income redistribution or structural change—it is the one aggregative indicator which comes closest to providing some quantitative impression of the underlying change. And it is in this spirit that a norm for the growth of the per capita gross product of developing countries should be viewed.

Notes

1. General Assembly Resolution of November 18, 1971. 2768 (XXVI).
2. CDP. paragraph 16, p. 6.

ANNEX FOUR
SUPPLEMENTARY NOTE ON THE INCIDENCE OF WORLD POVERTY

Any boundary between categories of countries based on their GNP's per capita is arbitrary. Therefore, the wider the gap between the categories and the smaller the population of countries on the borderline, the better.

The border between rich countries and middle-income countries is placed between Hungary, with a per capita GNP of $1,600 in 1970, and Poland, with a per capita GNP of $1,400. This not only places exactly 25 per cent of the population of the world in the category of rich countries; it sets the border at a point where the gap between the two categories is $200. The other point where the border might have been put, where there is a gap of at least $200 between countries of more than a few million people, is between Poland, with a GNP of $1,400, and Argentina, with a GNP of $1,160. This would have placed Poland and Ireland in the category of rich countries, and would have brought the population of the rich countries to 956 million, 26 per cent of the total world population.

The border between middle-income and poor countries is placed between Saudi Arabia, with a per capita GNP of $440, and Nicaragua, with a per capita GNP of $430. This places exactly two-thirds of the population of the world in the group of low-income countries (poor plus very poor). The gap is narrow, but the number of people in the borderland between Peru, with a per capita GNP of $450, and Brazil, with $420, is only 10 million.

The border between the poor countries and the very poor countries is set between Cameroon, with a per capita GNP of $180 (disregarding the two territories of Swaziland and the Cape Verde islands, with a total population of less than a million), and China, with a per capita GNP of $150. This places 52.6 per cent of the population of the world in the category of very poor countries. If China and Kenya (which also has a GNP per capita of $150) were moved to the category of poor countries, this would leave less than 30 per cent of the population of the world in the category of very poor countries.

The following are some of the principal differences between the categories as defined in this book and the categories used by international agencies. (In the discussion which follows, countries with populations of less than 1 million are disregarded.)

Developing countries are defined in this book to include the middle-income, the poor, and the very poor countries—that is, all countries with not more than $1,400 GNP per capita in 1970. Their populations amount to three-quarters of the population of the world.

The group of countries which the World Bank usually calls "developing" is the same, except that the Bank includes Israel in its list of developing countries. Israel has a per capita GNP of $1,960, higher than that of Japan, the U.S.S.R. and Italy.

The UN, in its *Monthly Bulletin of Statistics,* includes Kuweit and Libya, as well as Israel, in its category of "less-developed regions." The definition used in this book excludes all three, because they have GNP's per capita of $1,600 or more. The UN *Bulletin* does not include in its category of "less-developed regions" nine of the ten European countries with per capita GNP's of $1,400 or less; these countries, in descending order of GNP per capita, are Poland, Ireland, Greece, Spain, Romania, Bulgaria, Portugal, Yugoslavia, and Albania. The *Bulletin* does include Turkey as a less-developed region. The definition used in this book includes in the category of developing countries all ten European countries with per capita GNP's of $1,400 or less.

The Development Assistance Committee of OECD published in its annual report for 1971 (pages 154-5) a table listing "all developing countries." This list included Libya and Israel but did not include Poland, Ireland, Romania, Bulgaria, Portugal, and Albania; Kuweit was included as a developing country in a subsequent table (page 187). In his annual report for 1972 (page 15), the chairman of DAC suggested that the time had come to remove Libya, Israel, and Kuweit from the category of developing countries.

The UN list of the least developed of the developing countries comprises the following twenty-five countries: Afghanistan, Botswana, Bhutan, Burundi, Chad, Dahomey, Ethiopia, Guinea, Haiti, Laos, Lesotho, Malawi, Maldives, Mali, Nepal, Niger, Rwanda, Sikkim, Somalia, Sudan, Tanzania, Uganda, Upper Volta, Western Samoa, and North Yemen. These have a total population of 145 million. All come within the category of very poor countries used in this book; this category includes the following additional countries with populations of more than a million: Bangladesh, Burma, Central African Republic, China, India, Indonesia, Kenya, Khmer, Malagasy, Mauritania, Nigeria, North Vietnam, Pakistan, South Yemen, Sri Lanka, Togo, and Zaire. These have a population of 1,788 million.

The category of very poor countries used in this book is very much the same as the group of "the poorer developing countries" referred to in the DAC annual report for 1972 (page 78). In this report these poorer developing countries were defined as countries "with under $150 per capita income" in 1969.

The category of rich members of the Bank and the category of members of the OECD, often called 'the rich countries' club," are similar but not identical. The OECD does not include in its membership four rich member countries of the Bank: Israel, Kuweit, Libya, and New Zealand. It does include four middle-income members of the Bank (Greece, Ireland, Portugal, and Spain) and one poor member (Turkey), as well as one rich non-member of the Bank, Switzerland.

ANNEX FIVE

PROJECTIONS OF POPULATION AND OF GROSS NATIONAL PRODUCT BY THE MIDDLE EIGHTIES AND BY THE END OF THE CENTURY

The volume entitled *World Bank Operations,* published in 1972, contains an annex on pages 329-42 entitled "Population Projections, 1970-2100." There are two alternative projections. The lower level "can be attained only if considerable effort is applied to changing present attitudes towards high fertility among peoples of less developed countries." The upper level "is considered likely to occur if efforts for fertility control continue at the present level." The population of the People's Republic of China in 1970 is given as 750-950 million. If the alternative projections for the years 1985 and 2000 are averaged and rounded to the nearest 10 million, the result is as follows:

	1970	1985	2000
Developed	1,122	1,270	1,410
India	534	750	1,020
China	750 to 950		
Other		2,950	3,870
developing	1,246 to 1,046		
TOTAL	3,652	4,970	6,300

Since the population of the rich countries of the world in 1970 as defined in this book is 920 million, the category of "developed" used in this World Bank projection must include 202 million people of middle-income developing countries. The *World Bank Atlas* for 1972 estimated that the population of China in 1970 was 836 million, the population of India 538 million, and the total population of the world 3,678 million. With these changes, the column for 1970 would read in millions:

Rich countries	920
India	538
China	836
Other developing	1,384
TOTAL	3,678

The estimate for India in the column for 1985 appears somewhat high, since it assumes that the population of India will increase from 1970 to 1985 at the rate of increase in the sixties (2.3 per cent a year). This might therefore be reduced to 740, and the projection for India to 1,000 for the year 2000.

The average annual growth rate in the population of China in the sixties was 2.0 per cent, compared with 2.3 per cent for India. It is reasonable, therefore, to assume that the population of China is not likely to increase so rapidly as that of India. It is also reasonable to assume that by the year 2000 Taiwan will be part of China. The estimate for Taiwan is a population of 25 million in 2000.

With these factors taken into account, the population projections for 1985 and 2000 might be something like this:

	1970	1985	2000
Rich countries	920	1,050	1,100
Developing			
India	538	740	1,000
China	836	1,100	1,300
Others	1,384	1,985	2,900
Total	2,758	3,825	5,200
Total	3,678	4,875	6,300

The estimates of population and GNP in 1970 and of growth rates from 1960 to 1970 in Table 2, pages 227 to 236, which were derived from the *World Bank Atlas* for 1972, are:

	Popn. 1970 (million)	Popn. avg. annual growth rate 1960-70 percentage	GNP 1970 ($1,000 million)	Per cap. GNP 1970 ($)	Per cap. GNP avg. annual growth rate 1960-70 percentage
Rich countries					
Members	629	1.1	2019	3210	4.1
Non-members	291	1.1	547	1880	5.4
Total	920	1.1	2567	2790	4.4
Middle-income countries					
Members	236	2.2	1902	806	4.1
Non-members	73	1.2	78	1060	5.6
Total	309	2.0	2683	870	4.5
Poor countries					
Members	502	2.8	150	300	3.2
Non-members	14	2.7	5	330	5.1
Total	516	2.8	155	300	3.2
Very poor countries other than China and India					
Members	538	2.5	51	90	1.4
Non-members	21	2.8	2	100	3.2
Total	559	2.5	53	90	1.4
India (member)	538	2.3	57	110	1.2
China (non-member)	836	2.0	122	150	2.1
Total					
Members	2,443	2.1	2467	1009	3.9
Non-members	1,235	1.8	754	610	4.9
Total	3,678	2.0	3222	876	4.1

When these growth rates are taken into account, the population projections by categories might be somewhat as follows:

	1970	1985	2000
Middle-income			
Members	236	325	400
Non-members	73	85	100
Total	309	410	500
Poor countries			
Members	502	745	1,095
Non-members	14	20	30
Total	516	765	1,125
Very poor countries other than China and India			
Members	538	780	1,225
Non-members	21	30	50
Total	559	810	1,275
India (member)	538	740	1,000
China (non-member)	836	1,100	1,300
Total developing countries	2,758	3,825	5,200
(Rich countries)	920	1,050	1,100
(Total all countries)	3,678	4,875	6,300

The rich countries

The OECD study *The Growth of Output 1960-80,* published in December 1970, stated: "There is a strong presumption that the gross domestic product of the OECD area may again double in the next decade and a half," that is, by 1985 (page 100), and that "Governments need to frame their policies on the assumption . . . that potential GDP for the OECD area might quadruple between now and the end of the century" (page 106). The rich member countries of the Bank and the countries of the OECD area are not identical, but the correspondence is so close that the OECD forecasts of the rate of growth of the GDP of the OECD area can be taken as forecasts of the rate of growth of the GNP of the rich member countries of the Bank.

The category of rich countries not members of the Bank comprises the U.S.S.R., East Germany, Czechoslovakia, Hungary, and Switzerland. Since Switzerland has only 2 per cent of the population of this category of countries and only 4 per cent of the GNP, the category is substantially that of the four rich Communist countries. The category of rich non-members of the Bank had a higher average annual growth rate in per capita GNP in the sixties than the rich member countries of the Bank—5.4 per cent, compared with 4.1 per cent. For purposes of this forecast, it is therefore reasonable to assume that their total GNP's will more than double from 1970 to 1985. We might assume a growth rate of 125 per cent, compared with 100 per cent for the rich member countries. From 1985 to the year 2000, we might assume that the rate of growth would be the same for the two groups of rich countries, 100 per cent.

This results in the following projections of GNP and GNP per capita for rich countries:

	Members	Non-Members	Total
1970			
Population (million)	629	291	920
GNP ($1,000 million)	2,019	547	2,567
GNP per cap. ($)	3,210	1,880	2,790
1985			
Population (million)	720	330	1,050
GNP ($1,000 million)	4,040	1,225	5,265
GNP per cap. ($) (rounded)	5,600	3,700	5,000
2000			
Population (million)	750	350	1,100
GNP ($1,000 million)	8,080	2,450	10,530
GNP per cap. ($) (rounded)	10,800	7,000	9,570

Richard Jolly has estimated that the average per capita domestic product for the non-Communist developed countries would be $7,450 in the year 2000 in U.S. dollars at 1960 prices (WG, p. 284). The OECD study *The Growth of Output 1960-80* (page 105) estimated that price increases in the OECD area between 1958 and 1968 averaged about 2.7 per cent a year. If this was the average for the sixties, Jolly's estimate would be equivalent to $9,685 in 1970 dollars, which is close to the estimate of $10,800 given above.

Projection of GNP per capita of India

The alternative projections of India's population in the annex to *World Bank Operations* were 948 million and 1,100 million. According to this study, the projection of 948 million was the minimum, that is to say, the most optimistic, forecast possible; it would result in a population of 1,365 million in the year 2050 and 1,400 million in the year 2075; from the year 2075 on, the population would be stationary. The *World Bank Atlas* for 1972 estimated that India had in 1970 a GNP of $57.3 billion. Increases in GNP at 5, 6, and 7 per cent a year for thirty years give the following results for the year 2000, compared with the per capita GNP of $110 for 1970:

Annual percentage increase in GNP	GNP ($ billion)	Population (million)	GNP per cap. ($)
5	248	950	260
		1,000	250
		1,100	225
6	329	950	345
		1,000	330
		1,100	300
7	436	950	460
		1,000	435
		1,100	400

ANNEX SIX
AMENDMENT OF THE ARTICLES OF AGREEMENT

The international agreement which established the Bank, called the articles of agreement, was drawn up at the Bretton Woods Conference in 1944, at which the international agreement establishing the International Monetary Fund was also concluded. The Bank and the IMF were, as Harrod puts it, "the product of English and American brains, with valuable assistance from the Canadians."[1] In the framing of the international agreements, Germany and Japan, which are now two of the Bank's most important aid-giving members, played no part, since they were then enemy powers. France, Italy, the Netherlands, Belgium, and the Scandinavian countries were in eclipse. Of the six most populous of the low-income members of the Bank (Bangladesh, Brazil, India, Indonesia, Nigera, and Pakistan), only Brazil was, at the time of the Conference, an independent country. Indeed, over half the present members of the Bank did not exist as independent countries at that time (64 out of 122).

The members of the Bank underrepresented or not represented at the Conference might long ago have insisted that the articles of agreement of the Bank be amended—and the articles of IDA also, since they were modeled on those of the Bank—if the articles had not been substantially modified by practice, convention, and interpretation. An extremely broad interpretation has been made possible by the fact that under the articles of agreement of the Bank and IDA, questions of interpretation are submitted not to a judicial tribunal but to political bodies: first to the executive directors and then, on appeal, to the board of governors, whose decision is final.

But, it has become increasingly clear that the possibilities of broad interpretation may soon be just about exhausted, and that, unless some articles are formally amended, they will be obstacles to the pursuit by the Bank Group of wise policies. Amendments are desirable to establish clearly the ability of the Bank and IDA to increase greatly the proportion of their lending which goes to finance program loans or loans with a substantial program content and loans with a substantial local cost component. One amendment is required so that IFC will not have to put excessive emphasis on loans and not enough on equity investments. Others are required to redistribute voting strength in the governing bodies of the Bank and IDA; to give member governments the same freedom to designate the agency in their government responsible for dealings with the Bank as they have for dealings with IDA and IFC; and to give member governments freedom to move the headquarters of the Bank Group from Washington.

It is not surprising, therefore, that a demand for revision of the articles of agreement is emerging and is likely to grow. Swaran Singh, the foreign minister of India, in his speech in the opening debate at the UN General Assembly in the autumn of 1971, said:

> The world today is facing a major economic crisis comparable to the one when sterling went off the gold standard and new trade barriers began to disrupt world trade. Something similar is threatening the system of international trade and payments which had been built up after World War II. The G.A.T.T., the International Monetary Fund and the World Bank have not between them been able to provide the kind of orderly and balanced growth in the world economy which was hoped for. The developing countries who had little say at the time of their formation have long cherished the feeling that a new look at the articles of these three bodies is called for if the widening gap between the rich nations and the poor nations is not to grow wider each year as it has been in the last two decades. In the crisis that now confronts them some of the most developed nations also have begun to feel that the Charters of these institutions do not provide adequate answers to the emerging problems.

In the light of these considerations and of the analysis of the Bank Group's problems as set forth in this book, the following proposals are made for the amendment of the articles of agreement of the Bank and IDA.

Program lending

Article III, section 4 (vii) of the Bank's articles of agreement provides that:

> Loans made or guaranteed by the Bank shall, except in special circumstances, be for the purpose of specific projects of reconstruction or development.

Article V, section 1(b) of IDA's articles of agreement contains a similar provision.

So that the Bank should not be inhibited from proceeding with much more program lending and much more lending for projects with a large program content, the article should be amended to read:

> Most of the total lending commitments of the Bank shall be for the purpose of specific projects of reconstruction or development.

A similar amendment should be made in IDA's articles of agreement.

Local cost financing

Article IV, section 3, sub-sections b and c of the Bank's articles of agreement provides that:

> The Bank may, in exceptional circumstances when local currency required for the purposes of the loan cannot be raised by the borrower on reasonable terms, provide the borrower as part of the loan with an appropriate amount of that currency.
>
> The Bank, if the project gives rise indirectly to an increased need for foreign exchange by the member in whose territories the project is located, may in exceptional circumstances provide the borrower as part of the loan with an appropriate amount of gold or foreign exchange not in excess of the borrower's local expenditure in connection with the purposes of the loan.

Article V, section 2(e) of IDA's articles of agreement provides that:

> The Association in special cases may make foreign exchange available for local expenditures.

In order that the Bank and IDA should not be inhibited from proceeding with much more local cost financing, these provisions should be struck out and the following substituted:

> The Bank (Association) may make foreign exchange available for local expenditures on a project or program if in its opinion this would better advance the development of the borrowing country than the provision of foreign exchange for other projects or programs.

The International Finance Corporation

Article III, section 6(a) of the Bank's articles of agreement provides that:

> The Bank may make, participate in, or guarantee loans to the International Finance Corporation, an affiliate of the Bank, for use in its lending operations.

The use of the term "lending operations" means that the proceeds of Bank loans to IFC can be used only for loans by IFC and not for equity investment. The restriction does not seem to be wise or necessary. The article of agreement should therefore be amended by striking out the word "lending" before "operations."

Voting in the Bank and IDA

The arguments for reducing the great preponderance of votes held by the rich countries in the governing bodies of the Bank and IDA have been set forth in the chapter on weighted voting in the Bank and IDA.

Article V, section 3(a) of the articles of agreement of the Bank provides that:

> Each member shall have two hundred fifty votes plus one additional vote for each share of stock held.

To make the desired change, the following sentences should be added:

> Each member with a population of 500,000 or more shall also have thirty additional votes for every one million population. Each member with a population of less than 500,000 shall also have fifteen additional votes.

The voting provisions in the articles of agreement of IDA are complicated. In essence, however, they link voting power with subscriptions to IDA's resources. To make the same sort of change in voting power in IDA as would be made by the proposed amendment to the articles of agreement of the Bank, the following sentence should be inserted at the beginning of article VI, section 3(a) of the articles of agreement of IDA:

> Each member with a population of 500,000 or more shall have ninety votes for every one million of population. Each member with a population of less than 500,000 shall have forty-five votes.

Dealings between members and the Bank

Article III, section 2 of the articles of agreement of the Bank provides that:

> Each member shall deal with the Bank only through its Treasury, central bank, stabilization fund or other similar fiscal agency, and the Bank shall deal with members only by or through the same agencies.

Article VI, section 10 of the articles of agreement of IDA and Article IV, section 10 of the articles of agreement of IFC provides that:

> Each member shall designate an appropriate authority with which the Association [Corporation] may communicate in connection with any matter arising under this Agreement.

In order that member governments may have the same freedom to designate the authority in their government which deals with the Bank as they have for IDA and IFC, the Bank article should be amended to read as the IDA and IFC article, substituting "Bank" for "Association" or "Corporation."

Headquarters of the Bank

Article V, section 9 (a) of the articles of agreement of the Bank provides that:

> The principal office of the Bank shall be located in the territory of the member holding the greatest number of shares.

Article VI, section 8 of the articles of agreement of IDA provides that:

> The principal office of the Association shall be the principal office of the Bank.

Article IV, section 8 of the articles of agreement of IFC provides that:

> The principal office of the Corporation shall be in the same locality as the principal office of the Bank.

So that member governments may have freedom to move the headquarters of the Bank Group, the Bank article should be amended to read:

> The Board of Governors may by a two-thirds majority vote change the location of the principal office of the Bank.

Notes

1. H.K., p. 579.

ANNEX SEVEN
BANK GROUP PUBLICATIONS

This is a selected list of Bank Group publications. The publications which are marked with an asterisk are free. The free publications, other than the *Finance and Development,* can be obtained by writing to the World Bank Group, 1818 H Street, N.W., Washington D.C. 20433 U.S.A. A subscription to *Finance and Development* can be obtained by writing to Finance and Development, International Monetary Fund Building, 19th & H Streets, N.W. Washington, D.C. 20431 U.S.A. The publications which are not marked with an asterisk are published by the Johns Hopkins University Press.

The best introductions to the work of the Bank Group are *Policies and Operations, The World Bank, IDA and IFC,** a 79-page pamphlet published in June 1971, *World Bank and IDA: Questions and Answers,** a 97-page pamphlet published in September 1971, and *World Bank Operations: Sectoral Programs and Policies,* a 526-page book published in September 1973.

In order to keep in touch with developments in the work of the Bank Group, it is necessary to read the *Annual Reports* of the Group* (one report covers the Bank and IDA, the other, IFC) and the reports of the annual meetings of the board of governors of the three institutions, called *Summary Proceedings of Annual Meetings.**

Other useful documents which are issued from time to time are *Speeches and Articles** and *Press Releases—Bank-IFC-IDA.**

The Bank Group and IMF publish the quarterly, *Finance and Development.** Each issue contains articles by members of the staffs of the two institutions, a note on the recent activity of IMF, a similar note on the Bank Group, and book reviews.

The Bank Group publishes a *World Bank Atlas** every year, which is about 14 pages long. This gives the following information for each country and territory in the world: population; average annual growth rates in population; total GNP; GNP per capita and average annual growth rates in GNP per capita. The Bank Group also publishes every year a chart book of about 62 pages, entitled *Trends in Developing Countries*;* this contains charts and tables on population, socio-economic indicators, economic growth, international capital flow, and external debt and international trade.

The Bank Group began in 1972 a new series of publications, entitled *Country Economic Reports:* The first to be published is *Economic Growth of Colombia: Problems and Prospects,* a book of about 600 pages.

The basic constitutional documents of the Bank Group are the articles of agreement of the Bank, IDA, and IFC,* the by-laws of each institution*, the *General Conditions Applicable to Loans and Guarantee*

*Agreements** of the Bank, and the *General Conditions Applicable to Development Credit Agreements** of IDA.

The Bank Group publishes annually the *World Bank Catalog: Studies, Reports, Statistics, References.*

There is no up-to-date history of the Bank Group published by the Bank Group or on behalf of the Bank Group. An authoritative and comprehensive analytical history of the Bank Group by Edward S. Mason and Robert E. Asher was published in 1973 by the Brookings Institution under the title *The World Bank Since Bretton Woods.*

A collection of Robert McNamara's speeches was published by Praeger in 1973 under the title *One Hundred Countries, Two Billion People—The Dimensions of Development.*

ANNEX EIGHT
SOME ACRONYMS AND ABBREVIATIONS

CIAP	Inter-American Committee for the Alliance for Progress
DAC	Development Assistance Committee of the Organization for Economic Cooperation and Development
ECOSOC	Economic and Social Council of the United Nations
FAO	Food and Agriculture Organization
GATT	General Agreement on Tariffs and Trade
IADB	Inter-American Development Bank
IBRD	International Bank for Reconstruction and Development, commonly called the World Bank
IDA	International Development Association
IFC	International Finance Corporation
ILO	International Labor Organization
IMF	International Monetary Fund
OECD	Organization for Economic Cooperation and Development
WHO	World Health Organization
UN	United Nations
UNCTAD	United Nations Conference on Trade and Development
UNDP	United Nations Development Program
Unesco	United Nations Educational, Scientific, and Cultural Organization
UNIDO	United Nations Industrial Development Organization
USAID	United States Agency for International Development
WB	World Bank (the International Bank for Reconstruction and Development)
WBG	World Bank Group (IBRD, IDA, and IFC)

ANNEX NINE
DEFINITIONS

Better-off developing countries
The countries which contain 22½ per cent of the population of the world and which lie between the rich countries and the very poor countries on a scale listing countries in order of GNP per capita in 1970; the better-off developing countries thus include the middle-income and the poor countries. These countries had in 1970 GNP's per capita of $160 to $1,400 inclusive.

Developing countries
The countries at the bottom of a scale listing countries in descending order of GNP per capita in 1970 whose populations add up to three-quarters of the population of the world; the developing countries thus include the middle-income and the low-income countries. These countries had in 1970 GNP's per capita of $60 to $1,400 inclusive.

Gross national product (GNP)
The value at market prices of all the goods and services produced within the nation during a year, less net income payments abroad, such as income on foreign investments.

Leverage
The practice of linking development loans with requirements for changes in the policies of the borrower.

Low-income countries or the poorer countries
The countries at the bottom of a scale listing countries in descending order of GNP per capita in 1970 whose populations add up to two-thirds of the population of the world; the low-income countries include the poor and the very poor countries. These countries had in 1970 GNP's per capita of $60 to $430 inclusive.

Middle-income countries
The countries which contain one-twelfth of the population of the world and which lie between the rich countries and the low-income countries on a scale listing countries in order of GNP per capita in 1970. These countries had in 1970 GNP's per capita of $440 to $1,400 inclusive.

Net economic benefit of a project to the community
The present value of the true economic benefits of a project to the community during its whole life less the present value of the true economic costs of the project to the community during its whole life; costs and benefits include indirect as well as direct costs and benefits; the present

value is a discounted value; at a discount rate of 10 per cent, a cost or benefit of a million dollars seven years from now has a present value of half a million dollars. In estimating the net economic benefit to the community, a social discount rate is used. This discount rate basically reflects the relative weights the society attaches to the levels of consumption expected to occur at future dates. Under normal circumstances, the marginal private return on investment would not automatically equal this rate, especially when, as in developing countries, the savings rate is below the socially desired rate.

Net flow
Gross disbursements minus repayment of principal and redemptions.

Net transfer
Gross disbursements minus repayment of principal, redemptions, dividends, interest, and charges.

Official development assistance
"All flows to less-developed countries and multilateral institutions provided by official agencies, including state and local governments, or by their executive agencies, which meet the following tests: (a) They are administered with the promotion of the economic development and welfare of developing countries as their main objective; and (b) Their financial terms are intended to be concessional in character." (World Bank *Annual Report,* 1972, p. 80.)

Opportunity Costs
See shadow prices.

Poor countries
The countries which contain one-seventh of the population of the world and which lie between the very poor countries and the middle-income countries on a scale listing countries in order of GNP per capita in 1970. These countries had in 1970 GNP's per capita of $160 to $430 inclusive.

Poorer countries
See low-income countries.

Rich countries
The countries at the top of a scale listing countries in descending order of GNP per capita in 1970 whose populations add up to a quarter of the population of the world. These countries had in 1970 GNP's per capita of $1,600 to $4,760 inclusive.

Shadow prices or opportunity costs or true economic costs
The shadow prices which the Bank Group uses in evaluating projects are designed to measure the opportunity cost of the resources used in

a project in terms of the economic and social objectives of the country concerned. As the economic and social objectives change, so do the shadow prices. Shadow prices normally differ from market prices, since market prices seldom reflect accurately the costs and benefits of a project from the point of view of the country's economic and social objectives. The shadow price of a resource absorbed by a project, whether labor, equipment, or raw material, is the benefits foregone by using the resource on that particular project, rather than on its best alternative use, from the point of view of attaining the country's economic and social objectives. Thus, to obtain the shadow wage rate for labor, the Bank Group estimates the sacrifice of economic welfare entailed in withdrawing the labor from alternative uses. The shadow wage rate for labor may differ widely from the market wage rate, especially when there is involuntary employment in the area. Similarly, because of import restrictions, a piece of equipment may be produced at home at twice the cost of importing it (c.i.f. plus domestic transport); the true cost to the economy is the import price, not the cost of production at home. The price of an imported good is measured by using the shadow price of foreign exchange, not the officially maintained rate. If there are widespread import restrictions (quotas, duties, licensing, etc.), the value of a unit of foreign exchange at the margin, its shadow price, may exceed the officially maintained rate.

SDRs
Special drawing rights of the International Monetary Fund.

True economic costs
See shadow prices.

Very poor countries
The countries at the bottom of a scale listing countries in descending order of GNP per capita in 1970 whose populations add up to 52½ per cent of the population of the world. These countries had in 1970 GNP's per capita of $60 to $150 inclusive.

An Explanation to the Notes

Any publication which is referred to three times or more in the Notes is given an abbreviated title and is referred to in the Notes by this title, which is printed in capitals. The following is a list of these titles:

BN	*Bank Notes* (Washington, World Bank).
CDP	*Committee for Development Planning: Report on the Sixth Session. 5-15 January 1970* (ECOSOC).
DACR	*Development Assistance: Efforts and Policies of the Members of the Development Assistance Committee: Report by the Chairman of the Development Assistance Committee.* (Paris, Organization for Economic Cooperation and Development.)
FD	*Finance and Development* (Washington, IMF and World Bank Group).
HK	R. F. Harrod, *The Life of John Maynard Keynes* (New York: Harcourt Brace; 1951).
IFCAR	International Finance Corporation *Annual Report* (Washington, IFC).
JR	*A study of the Capacity of the United Nations Development System* [the Jackson Report] (Geneva: United Nations; 1969).
JJ	*International Development: Development Targets for the 70's: Jobs and Justice* (Dobb's Ferry: Oceana Publications; 1972).
McN	Robert S. McNamara, *Address* (Washington, World Bank).
PR	Lester B. Pearson, *et al., Partners in Development: Report of the Commission on International Development* (New York: Praeger; 1969).
PS	I. G. Patel, *Foreign Aid, Lal Bahadur Shastri Memorial Lectures* (Bombay: Allied Publishers Private Ltd.; 1968).
PETR	*U.S. Foreign Assistance in the 1970's: A New Approach.* Report to the President from the [Peterson] task force on international development, March 4, 1970. (Washington: U.S. Government Printing Office; 1970.)
SCE	Dudley Seers, *Matching Employment Opportunities and Expectations.* Report of a program of action for Ceylon, prepared by an Inter-Agency Team organized by the International Labor Office (Geneva: International Labor Office; 1971).
SCO	Dudley Seers, *Towards Full Employment.* Report of a program for Colombia prepared by an Inter-Agency Team organized by the International Labor Office (Geneva: International Labor Office; 1970).

SWP — *Seminar on World Partnership in the Second Development Decade, 3-4 December 1971* (New Delhi: Indian Investment Center; 1972).

WBAR — World Bank—International Development Association *Annual Report.*

WBO — *World Bank Operations: Sectoral Programs and Policies* (Baltimore: Johns Hopkins University Press; 1972).

WBPO — *Policies and Operations: The World Bank, IDA and IFC* (Washington: the World Bank; June 1971).

WBPR — IBRD press release.

WBSP — *Annual Meetings of the Boards of Governors: Summary Proceedings* (Washington, World Bank).

WG — *The Widening Gap: Development in the 1970's,* ed. by Barbara Ward, J. B. Runnalls, and Lenore d'Anjou (New York and London: Columbia University Press; 1971).

Notes

Chapter One

1. *PR,* p. 30.

2. World Bank announcement on the June 1971 meeting of the India consortium. *WBPR,* June 18, 1971.

3. "International airlines in many developing countries are operated as a matter of national prestige; with some notable exceptions, they tend to lose substantial sums of money and often involve net foreign exchange losses as well." *WBO,* p. 175. "Since the capital costs of nuclear plants are higher by about a third than those of conventional steam installations, they are economic only where fossil fuels are unusually expensive. Even there, the minimum economic capacity of a nuclear plant is unlikely to be much less than 500–600 MW . . . . That would limit the use of nuclear facilities to systems of 3,000 MW or more. On this basis, only about 10 developing countries could reasonably plan to acquire nuclear facilities by 1975." *WBO,* p. 230.

4. Max Millikan wrote in 1968 that the action of the United States in supplying India with surplus grain under P.L. 480 "made available partly to dispose of embarrassing surpluses and partly out of a laudable impulse to help feed the hungry, may well have had the long-run effect of delaying serious Indian attention to the mounting problems of agricultural productivity." "India in Transition: Economic Development: Performance and Prospects," in *Foreign Affairs* (April 1968), p. 538.

5. I.G. Patel, "Aid Relationship in the Seventies," in *WG,* p. 302.

6. Bela Kadar, *Implementation Problems in Developing Countries, in Connection with More Efficient Utilization of External Resources* (Budapest: Center for Afro-Asian Research of the Hungarian Academy of Sciences; 1970), p. 3.

7. Hollis Chenery (now principal adviser on development policy to the president of the World Bank and in 1965 professor at the Center for International Affairs at Harvard University), "Effectiveness of foreign Assistance," in *Developing the Third World: the Experience of the 1960's,* ed. by Ronald Robinson (Cambridge: University Press; 1971), p. 207.

8. *The Growth of Output, 1960–1980: Retrospect, Prospect and Problems of Policy* (Paris: OECD; December 1970), p. 173. The OECD countries are Australia, Austria, Belgium, Canada, Denmark, France, Germany, Italy, Japan, Netherlands, Norway, Portugal, Sweden, Switzerland, United Kingdom, United States.

9. According to the report of the Development Assistance Committee for 1971, the net flow of official development assistance (disbursements less amortization payments) from DAC countries to less-developed countries and multilateral agencies amounted in 1970 to $6,808 million, and the interest payments that year on official development assistance were $448 million. The net transfer (net flow less interest) was therefore $6,360 million. But the net flow figures included $29 million from Portugal, which is not a rich country, and flows to Israel, Libya, and Kuwait, which are rich countries. The average annual flow to Israel in the period 1968 to 1970 was $63 million; in this same period there was a reverse flow of about $7 million a year from Libya and Kuwait. The DAC net transfer figures did not include official development assistance from the following rich non-Communist countries, since they are not members of DAC: Israel,

Kuwait, Libya, and New Zealand. Therefore, the net transfer in 1970 of official development assistance from rich non-Communist countries was probably about $6,500 million. (See *DACR* 1971, pp. 165, 172–3, and 187.) But this net transfer was not worth $6,500 million to the recipients. Insofar as the bilateral portion of this aid was tied to purchases in the aid-giving country, the value of that part of the aid may have been reduced on the average by 20 per cent. Moreover, since the DAC figures are produced by a body which represents only aid-givers, they presumably exaggerate the volume of aid the aid-givers supply; an indication of this is that DAC in its report in 1972 showed Portugal as first in all four rankings of the aid-giving performance of the sixteen DAC countries in 1971. It would therefore be safe to conclude that the net transfer of official development assistance in 1970 from rich non-Communist countries to developing countries was less than $6,000 million.

10. *WG.* The text of the declaration is given on pages 10-13.

11. John White, *Pledged to Development* (London: Overseas Development Institute; 1967), p. 184.

12. *JJ.*

13. *WG.*, p. 308.

14. Mahbub ul Haq, "A New Perspective on Development," *JJ*, p. 66.

15. John Kenneth Galbraith, "The Proper Purpose of Economic Development," in *Economics, Peace and Laughter* (New York: New American Library; 1972), pp. 165-6. Reprint of article first published in 1964.

Chapter Two

1. The following table, based on statistics provided me by the World Bank, shows how much of the financial resources of the Bank and IDA on December 31, 1972, came from the six principal rich member countries (Britain, Canada, France, Germany, Japan, and the United States). Two-thirds of the paid-in subscriptions came from these countries. Two-thirds of the reserves and two-thirds of the transfer of Bank profits to IDA are therefore credited to these countries.

	($ million)	Six principal rich countries
Bank		
Usable paid-in subscriptions	2,200	1,490
Reserves	1,700	1,130
Sales on capital markets	5,000	3,940
Sales to central banks	2,400	1,700
Total	11,300	8,260 (73%)
IDA		
Usable subscriptions and supplementary contributions	5,555	4,555
Transfer from Bank profits	705	470
Total	6,260	5,025 (80%)
Total	17,560	13,285 (76%)

2. *WBO*, p. 208.

Chapter Three

1. See Edward S. Mason and Robert E. Asher, *The World Bank Since Bretton Woods* (Washington: The Brookings Institution; 1973).

2. John White, *Regional Development Banks* (London: Overseas Development Institute; 1970), p. 83.

3. *WBSP*, 1969, pp. 11-12.

4. The World Bank, "under its past President, Mr. George Woods, and its current President, Mr. Robert McNamara, has been aggressively converting itself from a conservative semi-commercial bank into a development assistance agency."—Harry G. Johnson, *"The Crisis of Aid" and the Pearson Report* (Edinburgh: University Press; 1970), p. 9.

5. *SWP*, pp. 108-9.

6. *HK*, p. 631.

7. Articles of Agreement III (2).

Chapter Four

1. *CDP*, par. 50.

2. This is derived as follows from Table 3:

Middle-income countries	
Loans 1969-72 (average)	$509 million
Popn.	236 million
Loans per cap.	$2.16
Poor countries	
Loans 1969-72 (average)	$1,041 million
Popn.	502 million
Loans per cap.	$2.07
Very poor countries	
Loans 1969-72 (average)	$770 million
Popn.	1,076 million
Loans per cap.	$0.72
Total for developing countries	
Loans 1969-72 (average)	$2,321 million
Popn.	1,814 million
Loans per cap.	$1.28

3. A/Res/2768 (XXVI), November 18, 1971.

4. In my essay on the World Bank, published by the World Bank in September 1965, I divided the countries of the world into these same four groups of rich, middle-income, poor, and very poor, based on GNP per capita and population in 1963 or 1964. The main differences between the membership of the categories in the 1965 essay and in this book are: (1) China was in the category of poor countries in 1965 and is in the category of very poor countries in this book; (2) Japan and Hungary were in the category of middle-income countries in 1965 and are in the category of rich countries in this book; (3) Poland was in the category of rich countries in 1965 and is in the category of middle-income countries in this book. See "The Future of the World Bank: An Essay by Escott Reid" (Washington: World Bank; September 1965). Statistical tables pp. 60-71. The statistics in the annual *World Bank Atlas* "carry on" the statistics presented in this essay. See the foreword to the first edition of the *Atlas* in 1966.

5. *DACR*, 1970, p. 155.

6. McN, April 14, 1972, p. 17.

7. Norman Macrae's special article in the London *Economist* for January 22, 1972, page xvii, contained the following table, dividing the countries of the world into four categories: the United States, the other rich countries, the middle-class countries, and the poor countries:

	Popn. (million)	Total GNP's (£ billion)	GNP per head £	Recent % per ann. growth in real GNP	% per ann. popn. growth
United States	200	400	2,000	4½ until recent recession	1
"Other rich" (west Europe, "old" dominions, Japan)	500	500	1,000	From under 2 (Britain) to over 10 (Japan)	1
"Middle class" (Communist Europe, Mediterranean, some Pacific Asia, some Latin America)	600	450	750	5 to 10	Over 1
Poor countries	2,300	200	85	Generally around 5	2½
Total	3,600	1,550	430	Around 5	2

The main difference between this table and mine is that Macrae puts the U.S.S.R., East Germany, Czechoslavakia, and Hungary, with a total population of 285 million, in the category of "middle-class," not "rich," countries, and that he does not divide his category of poor countries into poor and very poor. His estimate of £430 for GNP per head in the world is about 25 percent above the figure of $876 in my table, and his estimate of "recent" per annum growth in real GNP for the world is 5 per cent, as against my estimate of 6 per cent for the period 1960-70.

8. The core of the problem of extreme poverty within the membership of the World Bank is the extreme poverty of five very populous countries: India, Indonesia, Bangladesh, Pakistan, and Nigeria. They contain almost 80 per cent of the people of the very poor Bank countries (840 million out of 1,075 million). All but 30 million of those 1,075 million live in three areas: mainland Asia south of China and east of Iran, where 745 million live; Africa south of the Arab states and north of Angola, Zambia, and Mozambique, where 190 million live; and Indonesia, with a population of 115 million.

The core of the problem of poverty within the membership of the World Bank, meaning by poverty the levels of living in the low-income countries (the very poor countries plus the poor countries), lies in Asia, Africa, and Indonesia. Here live almost nine out of ten of the peoples of the low-income member countries of the Bank Group (1,390 million out of 1,580 million). One hundred and fifty million live in the low-income countries of the Americas, which lie south of Mexico and north of Argentina, Uruguay, and Chile. Elsewhere there are only two low-income countries which are members of the Bank: Turkey, and Papua and New Guinea.

Chapter Five

1. *WBSP,* 1968, p. 10.
2. *WBSP,* 1969, p. 18.
3. *WBSP,* 1971, p. 28.
4. McN, April 14, 1972, pp. 5, 6, 7, 17.
5. McN, October 18, 1872, p. 11.
6. McN, September 25, 1972, p. 20.
7. Mahbub ul Haq, "A New Perspective on Development," in *JJ,* p. 63.
8. *WBSP,* 1972, p. 26.
9. McN, April 14, 1972, p. 17.
10. *WBSP,* 1971, p. 29.
11. International Development Research Centre, Ottawa, mimeo., p. 12.
12. *SCO,* p. 283.
13. *JJ.*

Chapter Six

1. *WBSP,* 1971, pp. 21, 24-25.
2. *DACR,* 1970, pp. 116, 121-2.
3. *DACR,* 1971, p. 22.
4. *SCO,* p. 1.
5. *DACR,* 1971, p. 105.
6. Local costs of projects are estimates, contained in appraisal reports, of where ultimate procurement will take place following international competitive bidding. The figures for local procurement are intended to be net of the import component of locally purchased goods. The estimates depend on a large number of assumptions and are subject to wide margins of error.

Chapter Seven

1. Ernest Stern, "Foreign Assistance and Unemployment," in *JJ,* p. 21.
2. Barend A. de Vries, "Unemployment and Poverty—What Remedies Are Available?" in *FD,* No. 1, 1972, p. 12.
3. Mahbub ul Haq, "A New Perspective on Development," in *JJ,* p. 61.
4. *DACR,* 1970, pp. 124-5.

5. In the 1970 IDA credit for small industries in East Pakistan, a small industry was defined as an industry which was not a cottage industry and which had fixed assets, excluding land, of not more than the equivalent of about $200,-000. A cottage industry was defined as a small family enterprise without motive power which does not have the potential to be operated along sound industrial lines. Cottage industries usually produce traditional items by traditional methods. Small-scale industry in India is defined by the Indian authorities to include units with up to 750,000 rupees ($100,000) of equipment, or one million rupees ($133,-000) in the case of ancillary industries.

6. WBO, pp. 107, 123, 129, 133. Enterprises with less than 20 employees received 4 per cent of the $918 million lent through development finance companies, or $37 million. Enterprises with less than 100 employees received 21 per cent of the $918 million, or $193 million, as well as 3 per cent, or $9 million, of the $305 million lent by IFC.

7. *WBO*, pp. 91, 122-3.

8. *SCE*, p. 184.

9. See Arun Shourie, "Growth, Poverty and Inequalities," in *Foreign Affairs* (January 1973), especially pp. 345, 350, 351.

10. Department of External Affairs, Ottawa. Statements and Speeches.

Chapter Eight

1. *DACR*, 1970, p. 155.

2. *WBO*, p. 95.

3. *WBPO*, p. 61.

4. *IFCAR*, 1971, p. 11.

5. William S. Gaud, "Private Foreign Investment in the '70's." Address of October 31, 1972 (Washington, IFC.), p. 9.

6. *WBPO*, p. 31.

7. See Andrew M. Kamarck, "The Allocation of Aid by the World Bank Group," in *FD* (September 1972), p. 24.

8. Approach of the World Bank to the problems of aid coordination for individual developing countries (Washington: World Bank, Development Services Department; June 1971), mimeo., p. 6.

9. IBRD Articles of Agreement. Article IV, section 4 (c).

Chapter Nine

1. *WBO*, Tourism, pp. 375-403.

2. The term "permanent tourist" is used by D. A. Ball in his article "Permanent Tourism: A New Export Diversification for Less-Developed Countries," in *International Development Review* (1971/4).

3. Ball, pp. 20-3.

4. Norman Macrae, "The Future of International Business," in the London *Economist* (January 22, 1972), p. xvii.

Chapter Ten

1. *WBO*, p. 274.

2. Savak S. Tarapore, "Transmission of Technology to Developing Countries," in *FD* (June 1972), p. 20.

3. *DACR*, 1971, p. 113.

4. *WBO*, p. 274.

5. *WBO*, p. 179.

6. *WBO*, p. 168.

7. *SWP*, p. 32.

8. *SCO*, pp. 340-2.

9. *PR*, p. 111, cited in *SCO*, p. 342.

10. *WBO*, p. 459.

11. *SCE*, pp. 76, 81.

12. Ernest Stern, "Foreign Assistance and Unemployment," in *JJ*, pp. 21-2.

13. *PS*, pp. 26-7.

14. *WBAR*, 1972, p. 19.

15. *SWP*, p. 110.

Chapter Eleven

1. *WBSP*, 1971, p. 29.

2. *PS*, p. 21.

3. Mahbub ul Haq, "Employment in the 1970's: a New Perspective," in *JJ*, p. 66.

4. *PS*, p. 10.

5. This is an adaptation of C. E. Lindblom's classic statement of his conception of the proper relationship between an aid-giving country and India in his "Has India an Economic Future?" *Foreign Affairs* (January 1966), pp. 250*ff.* In his article he said:

> Although the United States and other lenders would be mistaken if they tried to buy the policies they like in India by making aid contingent on India's accepting their advice, at the same time they will do well to make clear that the attractiveness of lending to India—the prospect that it will pay off either to India or to the lender—depends on Indian policy. India can be expected to understand that no prudent lender ignores the size of the pay-off in calculating what it is willing to put into the growth process. Even on extreme assumptions about altruism in foreign lending, governments—especially democratic governments—cannot lend and give without tailoring what they do to fit their estimates of the contribution it will make to Indian growth. The distinction between trying to buy, with aid, the policies we like and coming more generously to the assistance of policies that promise growth is a fine one; but it is a genuine one. Trying to buy desired policies opens up a range of possibilities for negotiation in which a foreign lender might, as a tactic for forcing India to knuckle under, offer more aid than the country's economic prospects warrant. Conversely, a foreign lender might, for a good enough bargain in the adjustment of Indian policies, offer more aid, or more aid of a particular kind than is required in the light of prospects for growth. By contrast, supporting India less strongly when prospects for using aid effectively are poor, and more strongly when they are more promising, is a method of using foreign resources in a systematic way for encouraging Indian growth. This method challenges Indian sovereignty no more than does any significant mutual accommodation among powers.

6. Max Millikan wrote in 1968 that India's devaluation of the rupee in 1966, accompanied by some liberalization of import controls, "were undertaken at the strong urging of the International Bank and the U.S. Government." He went on to say that "there was a widespread view in India that these measures could be effective only if they were combined with a substantial increase in the availability of foreign exchange through foreign aid. There were at least implicit promises from the United States and other sources that, if these measures were in fact adopted, a higher level of aid would be forthcoming. In fact the aid flow was first interrupted and then, apart from food, resumed at a significantly lower

level."—"India in Transition: Economic Development. Performance and Prospects". *Foreign Affairs* (April 1968), p. 543.

7. "Leaning Against Open Doors?" by L. K. Jha, in *The World Bank Group, Multilateral Aid, and the 1970's*, ed. by John P. Lewis and Ishan Kapur (In press: to be published by Lexington Books).

8. *Ibid.*

9. Gunnar Myrdal, *The Challenge of World Poverty* (Penguin; 1970), p. 315.

10. *PR*, p. 130.

11. *The Challenge of Growth and Change.* Economic Council of Canada. Fifth Annual Review, September 1968. (Ottawa: Queen's Printer; 1968), p. 128.

Chapter Twelve

1. See note 9 on Chapter One.

2. Harry G. Johnson estimated in 1966 on the basis of 1959 statistics that free trade in sugar would increase the export earnings of "the less-developed countries that have a comparative advantage in sugar production" from seven major rich western countries by about $750 million—Harry G. Johnson, *Economic Policies towards Less-Developed Countries* (Washington: The Brookings Institution; 1967), p. 266.

3. The following table on the effect of raising the prices of tea, coffee, and cocoa is based on two assumptions. The first is that an increase in price in real terms of 3 per cent a year in the period 1971-80 would not result in a decline in volume. The second is that the volume of exports would increase in the period 1971-80 at the rate achieved in the past: the rate for coffee from 1959-61 to 1967-69 was 2.8 per cent a year; for cocoa from 1946 to 1970, 3 per cent a year; for tea from 1955-57 to 1967-69, 2 per cent a year.

See table on page 274

4. *CDP*, par. 50.

Chapter Thirteen

1. Hollis B. Chenery, "Targets for Development," in *WG*, p. 45.

2. Chenery, p. 47.

3. Chenery's category of countries in the income range of $100 to $300 GNP per capita includes the poor countries less those that had a per capita GNP of more than $300 plus the very poor countries with at least $100 GNP per capita.

	GNP per cap. ($) 1970	Popn. (million) 1970	Average annual loans 1969-72 ($ million)
Poor	160-430	502	1,041
Less	310-430	245	701
Sub-total	160-300	257	340
Plus			
India	110	538	294
Others	100-150	209	291
Total	100-300	1,004	631
Per cap. ($)	100-300		$.63 (cents)

EXPORT VALUES CALCULATED AT PRICES RISING AT 3 PER CENT P.A.

	Actual 1970	1971	1972	1973	1974	1975	1976	1977	1978	1979	1980
Coffee price ¢/lb./a	54¢	56.2	57.9	59.6	61.4	63.2	65.1	67.0	69.0	71.0	73.1
World export value	mln $2,813	2976.1	3148.7	3331.3	3524.5	3728.9	3945.2	4174.0	4416.1	4672.2	4943.2
Cocoa price ¢/lb./b	34.2¢	35.2	36.3	37.4	38.5	39.6	40.8	42.0	43.3	44.6	45.9
World export value	mln $ 841	891.4	944.9	1001.6	1061.7	1125.4	1192.9	1264.5	1340.3	1420.7	1505.9
Tea price ¢/lb./c	49.7¢	51.2	52.7	54.3	55.9	57.6	59.3	61.1	62.9	64.8	66.7
World export value	mln $ 573	601.7	631.7	663.3	696.5	731.3	767.9	806.3	846.6	888.9	933.3
World total export value	$4,227	4469.2	4725.3	4996.2	5282.7	5585.6	5906.0	6244.8	6603.0	6981.8	7382.4

/a Santos 4, Spot N.Y.
/b Beans, Accra, Spot N.Y.
/c London Anchor, avg sale all teas

EXPORT VALUES CALCULATED AT CONSTANT 1970 PRICES
(Coffee—2.8%, Cocoa—3%, Tea—2%)

	Actual 1970	1971	1972	1973	1974	1975	1976	1977	1978	1979	1980
World coffee—export value	mln $2,813	2891.8	2972.7	3055.9	3141.5	3329.5	3422.7	3518.5	3617.0	3718.3	3822.4
World cocoa—export value	mln $ 841	866.2	892.2	919.0	946.5	974.9	1004.2	1034.3	1065.3	1097.3	1130.2
World tea—export value	mln $ 573	584.5	596.2	608.1	620.2	632.6	645.3	658.2	671.4	684.8	698.5
World total—export value	$4,227	4342.5	4461.1	4583.0	4708.2	4937.0	5072.2	5211.0	5353.4	5500.4	5651.1

4. The population estimate for 1983 is derived as follows from the population estimate for 1985 given in Table 3:

	1983 (million)	1985 (million)
Middle-income countries	310	325
Poor countries	710	745
Very poor countries other than India	745	780
India	710	740
Total	2,475	2,590

5. If Bank loans had gradually been moving up to a level of $3,350 million a year by 1983, disbursements on Bank loans should have reached about this level by 1985. The return flow of amortization payments and interest and other loan charges might be running at about 70 per cent of this. The net transfer resulting from Bank loans would then be 30 per cent, or about $1,000 million. Disbursements on IDA loans of $2,750 million a year by 1983 could not rise above $2,450 million a year by 1985, since $300 million would be transferred to the Bank to subsidize Bank loans. By 1985, IDA would be receiving about $50 million a year in amortization payments. The net transfer resulting from IDA loans would be about $2,400 million a year. The total net transfer from Bank and IDA loans would be about $3,400 million in 1985. To this might be added $150 million of net transfer resulting from IFC investments, making a grand total for the whole Bank Group of $3,550 million.

6. The estimate of 1.25 per cent is for undivided India from 1900 to 1947. *WG,* p. 49.

7. This judgement would appear to conflict with that of the Pearson Commission, but the Commission made an important qualification to its judgment. It said on page 11 of its report: "Can the majority of the developing countries achieve self-sustaining growth by the end of the century? For us the answer is clearly yes." But, on page 126, it said (underlining added): "By the year 2000 it [development aid] would largely have disappeared *unless sometime before that date the international community decided to support even faster rates of growth* [than 6 per cent per annum]." Rosenstein-Rodan's formula is (underlining added): "The purpose of international aid to developing countries is to accelerate their economic development to a point where a *satisfactory* rate of growth can be achieved on a self-sustaining basis."—(P. N. Rosenstein-Rodan, "Criteria for Evaluation of National Development Effort," in *Journal of Development Planning,* No. 1, p. 1.

Chapter Fourteen

1. *DACR,* 1971, pp. 92-3.
2. *WBPO,* pp. 30-1.

Chapter Fifteen

1. *PR,* pp. 123, 230.
2. "The French are always pressing us to slant IDA funds towards French Africa. Similarly, the Japanese whose interest is in Southeast Asia are persuading us to put more assistance into that area. And the United States, I need scarcely add, is always telling us that more funds should be channelled into Latin America." —Burke Knapp, the senior vice-president of the Bank, in his paper "Determination

of Priorities, and Allocation of Resources," Chap. Three of *The World Bank Group, Multilateral Aid, and the 1970's,* ed. by John P. Lewis and Ishan Kapur (In press: to be published by Lexington Books).

3. *PETR,* p. 21.

4. By mid-1974, IDA will have lent about $5,500 million. By 1990, the amortization payments on these loans will be about $100 million a year (3 per cent on $2,170 and 1 per cent on $3,300). For every $1,000 million a year which IDA had lent in the five years after mid-1974 on the present IDA terms, the amortization payments would go up by $50 million a year by 1990; if amortization payments were increased from the present 1 per cent a year in the second ten years to 2½ per cent, this figure would be $125 million a year.

5. McN, April 14, 1972, p. 16.

6. *Reform of the International Monetary System.* Report by the executive directors of the board of governors (Washington: International Monetary Fund; 1972), p. 51.

7. Harry G. Johnson, *The Crisis of Aid and the Pearson Report* (Edinburgh: University Press; 1970), pp. 21-2.

8. I. G. Patel, "Aid Relationship in the Seventies," in *WG,* p. 310.

9. Nixon, U.S.I.S. (Ottawa), pp. 3, 13; Speech by Mitchell Sharp, Secretary of State for External Affairs of Canada, March 29, 1971. (Statements and Speeches No. 71/10. Department of External Affairs, Ottawa.)

10. The information about magnesium nodules is taken from *Report on limits to Growth.* Study by a special task force of the World Bank (Washington: World Bank; September 1972), mimeo., pp. 7, 8, 23, 43, 44. A shorter version of this paper is contained in an article by Mahbub ul Haq, "The limits to Growth: a Critique," in *FD* (December 1972). The reference to magnesium nodules is on p. 5.

11. *CDP,* p. 24., paras. 67, 68, 69.

Chapter Sixteen

1. UN Charter: articles 55, 56, 58.

2. Hugh L. Keenleyside, "What's Wrong with the United Nations?" in *Saturday Review* (June 19, 1971), p. 30.

Chapter Seventeen

1. *WBO,* p. 124.

2. *The International Bank for Reconstruction and Development 1946-1953* (Baltimore: Johns Hopkins Press; 1954), p. 23.

3. *JR,* Vol. 1, pp. 47-8.

4. McN, November 13, 1970.

5. The Bank's press release of July 24, 1970, on the meeting of the Pakistan consortium, said: "The members noted the Pakistan Government's request for external assistance in the current fiscal year of $570 million and accepted that Pakistan could effectively use aid in this amount. Several members were already in a position to indicate what assistance they expected to be able to provide, others undertook to do so as soon as possible." The Bank's press release of June 14, 1972, on the meeting of the Indian consortium, said: "It was noted that India needs substantial new commitments of aid in support of the Government's efforts to increase the pace of economic progress. Members agreed that, for the year that began on April 1, 1972, commitments of non-project assistance of about $700 million including debt relief and of project assistance of about $550 million would be necessary to prevent a sharp decline in the transfer of resources to

India. Most members indicated the contribution they woud be able to make, subject to necessary approval, toward these goals. Other members expected to be able to do so later in the year and gave their support to the over-all program." Press releases on meetings of consultative groups do not contain references like these to the contributions governments might make, though they do normally give a blessing to a target for assistance. Thus the press release of January 17, 1973, on the consultative group dealing with Tanzania said that the group "recognized that external aid flows would have to increase substantially and that most if not all capital assistance would have to be made available on soft terms in order to avoid an excessive debt servicing burden in the future." It went on to note "that projected disbursement requirements over the next five years were estimated by the World Bank at around $400 million [and that] in order to achieve such a disbursement target new commitments would have to amount to about $500-550 million during that same period." The consultative group on Tunisia had gone a little further in its press release of October 20, 1972. It said that it "felt that the amount of external resources required for the implementation of the Development Plan was realistic, and, in particular, that it was consistent with the amounts of financing likely to be made available by potential lenders for priority objectives."

6. *WBO,* p. 269.

7. McN, October 18, 1972, p. 5.

8. McN, November 13, 1970, p. 8.

9. Table 5, p. 000.

10. John White, *Regional Development Banks* (London: Overseas Development Institute; 1970), p. 194.

11. *PETR,* p. 25.

12. Resolution on "The Capacity of the United Nations Development System," adopted on January 20, 1971. A/Res/2688 (XXV).

13. McN, November 13, 1970, p. 9.

14. Resolution on "International Development Strategy for the Second United Nations Development Decade," adopted on November 11, 1970. A/Res/2626 (XXV).

15. *PETR,* p. 35.

Chapter Eighteen

1. *WBAR,* 1970, p. 23.

2. *Approach by the World Bank to the problems of aid coordination for individual developing countries* (Washington: World Bank Development Services Department; June 1971), mimeo., p. 6.

3. "In joint financing, bilateral lenders agree to provide finance, usually within some speciifed limit, for supply contracts awarded to their nationals as a result of international competitive bidding.... In parallel financing, equipment or services for different portions of a project are financed separately by the Bank and bilateral lenders, with international competitive bidding applied to the Bank's portion."—WBO, p. 222.

Chapter Nineteen

1. Article IV, section 10 of the Bank's articles of agreement provides that: "The Bank and its officers shall not interfere in the political affairs of any member; nor shall they be influenced in their decisions by the political character of the member or members concerned. Only economic considerations shall be relevant to their decisions, and these decisions shall be weighed impartially in

order to achieve the purposes stated in Article 1." Article V, section 6 of IDA's articles of agreement and Article III, Section 9 of IFC's articles of agreement contain similar provisions.

2. Article 2.7 states that the "application of enforcement measures under Chapter VII" (of the Charter) is not prejudiced by the prohibition against the United Nations intervening "in matters which are essentially within the domestic jurisdiction of any state." Chapter VII is the chapter on "action with respect to threats to the peace, breaches of the peace and acts of aggression." The "enforcement measures" are the economic sanctions provided for in Article 41 and the military sanctions provided for in Article 42, which the Security Council "decides" under Article 39 shall be taken "to maintain or restore international peace and security."

3. Under the standard conditions of loans, the Bank has the right to premature a loan (that is, to cease disbursements and to call for immediate repayment for past disbursements) if the borrower fails to carry out the conditions of the loan. The situation in East Pakistan in 1971 made it impossible for Pakistan, not only to carry out the conditions of loans for projects in East Pakistan, but also, owing to its lack of domestic resources resuling from the situation in East Pakistan, to provide the rupee funds it had contracted to provide, as a condition of the loan, for most of the loans from the Bank Group for projects in West Pakistan. The other argument for ceasing disbursements was that this would cut the Bank Group's possible losses on its loans from $960 million, the total of outstanding loans, to about $645 million, the disbursements aready made on outstanding loans.

4. On June 30, 1971, the outstanding Bank and IDA loans to Pakistan, including loans signed but not yet effective, totaled $960 million, of which $315 million had not been disbursed.

5. On June 30, 1971, the outstanding Bank and IDA loans to India, including loans signed but not yet effective, totaled $2,084 million, of which $360 million had not been disbursed.

Chapter Twenty

1. *HK*, p. 580.

2. In 1983 the population of China is likely to be about 1,050 million, almost 50 per cent more than that of India, which is likely to have a population of 710 million. During the sixties, GNP per capita increased in China at a rate of 2.1 per cent a year and in India at a rate of 1.2 per cent. In 1970, China's GNP per capita was $150, India's $110. It is therefore possible that by 1983, China's GNP per capita will be 50 per cent bigger than India's. India's lower GNP per capita could justify IDA's granting India $1.55 a year per head of population ($1,100 million a year) and China 95 cents (1,000 million a year). If China and the Bank Group agreed that $150 million of the IDA money allocated to China be used to pay the interest for ten years on Bank loans to China, China's borrowings from the Bank might go up from $200 million a year to $500 million.

3. Mahbub ul Haq, "Employment in the 1970's: a New Perspective," in *JJ*, pp. 67-8.

Chapter Twenty-one

1. The London *Economist* (October 12, 1968), p. 63.

2. Neville Maxwell, *India's China War* (London: Jonathan Cape; 1970), p. 113.

3. The secret memoranda of the discussions at the meetings December 3, 4, and 6, 1971, of the Washington Special Action Group of the National Security Council were published in *The New York Times* for January 6, 1972, page 16.

4. Gordon Robertson, "The Changing Role of the Privy Council Office," in *Canadian Journal of Public Administration,* XIV, 4 (winter 1971), pp. 487-508.

5. The officers listed in the annual report of the Bank for 1962 were Black,* Iliff, Knapp,* Aldewereld, Broches, Cargill, Cavanaugh,* Cope, Demuth,* Graves,* Hoffman,* Howell,* Martin,* Mendels, Miller, Moussa, Rist, Schmidt,* de Wilde,* Wilson, and Adler.* Those whose names are asterisked were citizens of the United States,

6. BN, April 1973.

Chapter Twenty-two

1. The votes cast by Belgium, Canada, and the Netherlands include the votes of all the countries which elected them. The total votes of the eight countries in the Bank are 168,518 and in IDA, 517,118.

2. PS, pages 8-9. The statement by I. G. Patel from which these quotations come does not relate specifically to the directors of the Bank Group; it relates to the whole group of people in aid-giving countries who are concerned with aid-giving.

3. "There has been no appreciable improvement over the past four years in the role of aid agencies on donor delegations to UNCTAD, ECOSOC, IBRD, etc., meetings. Trade and Finance Ministries dominate the scene with their largely domestic constituencies to defend, with Foreign Ministries occasionally taking over. Seldom does the choice go to the head of the aid agency, though he has most knowledge of the needs of the developing countries and most at stake in success or failure .... Neither party to the development partnership is well served in this situation." (*DACR,* 1972, p. 17.)

Chapter Twenty-three

1. *SWP,* inaugural speech by Y. B. Chavan, pp. 107-11.

2. The Soviet Union might be given a subscription to the Bank about halfway between those of the United States and Britain. This would give it about 50,000 votes under the proposed amendment to the articles of agreement of the Bank. Czechoslovakia and East Germany might each be given subscriptions about twice the size of Austria's; this would give each of them about 5,500 votes. If Bulgaria were given the same subscription as Greece, Hungary the same as Venezuela, and Poland the same as Spain, they would have about 1,200, 2,500, and 4,000 votes respectively. Since China has about 300 million more people than India, a China represented by Peking would probably have, under the proposed amendment to the articles of agreement giving each country thirty additional votes for every million population, a vote of about 34,000 compared with the Indian 25,000. The votes would then be something like this:

		Percentage
Rich countries		
United States	70,000	15
Others	190,000	42
Total	260,000	57
Middle-income countries	45,000	10
Low-income countries	150,000	33
Total	455,000	100

Chapter Twenty-four

1. *PS*, p. 9.

2. *The Colombo Plan for Cooperative Economic Development in South and South-east Asia.* Report by the Commonwealth Consultative Committee London, September-October 1950. (London: H.M. Stationery Office), p. 63. This passage in the report was written by Douglas LePan—then a member of the Canadian Department of External Affairs—poet, novelist, economist, and scholar.

Index

Design by Leslie Siemens
Phototypography by TypeWright
Other typography by Dayton Typographic Service
Printing on the Banta Belt Press by the George Banta Company